CLOSED FOR RENOVATION
ON THE ROAD TO EMMAUS

A spiritual guide of the Holy Land
towards a permanent pilgrimage

CLOSED FOR RENOVATION
ON THE ROAD TO EMMAUS

A spiritual guide of the Holy Land towards a permanent pilgrimage

Copyright (c) 2015 by Peter E. Sabella
First published in Jerusalem in 2015.

All scripture quotes are from the Oremus Bible Browser, NRSV and NRSV anglicized, at www.bible.oremus.org, unless otherwise indicated.

All photos in this book, unless otherwise indicated, are by Peter E. Sabella or from the public domain.

The Via Dolorosa representations in this book were designed and produced by Emerezian Printing and Publishing Establishment using images of Father Andrea Martini's 'The Stations of the Cross' on display in the Franciscan Chapel of the Blessed Sacrament at the Church of the Holy Sepulchre in Jerusalem.

First USA Edition by Waterfall Books L.L.C. in September 2022.

The Library of Congress has catalogued
this book under Control Number: 2022913731

ISBN (Color version): 979-8-9866581-2-4 (paperback)
ISBN (Color version) 979-8-9866581-5-5 (paperback)
ISBN (Black & White version): 979-8-9866581-6-2 (paperback)
ISBN: 979-8-9866581-1-7 (kindle)

Published by Waterfall Books L.LC.
www.waterfall-books.com
Email: waterfall-books@outlook.com

CLOSED FOR RENOVATION

ON THE ROAD TO EMMAUS

A spiritual guide of the Holy Land towards a permanent pilgrimage

PETER E. SABELLA

Waterfall
BOOKS

CLOSED FOR RENOVATION
ON THE ROAD TO EMMAUS

Owner of this book:

_____

Address:

_____

_____

_____

In the beginning was the Word.

John 1:1

In cruel times,
in moments of trial and temptation,
when things seem out of sorts,
for a better understanding of the past and the future,
for a personal relationship with God,
for a stronger faith,

Jesus asks you,
"Who do you say that I am?
Who am I to you?"

*Every Christian
should walk the road to Emmaus.*

The sooner, the better.

To all priests and pastors, to all pilgrims
that walk in the footsteps of the Lord.
I pray that this book will help you
in your journey of faith.

Thank you.

To Caroline Lucy Smith,
your faith and deep love for the Lord
was a guideline and an inspiring spirit
through every step of writing this book.
You have been my walking partner on
my road to Emmaus.

Thank you.

ACKNOWLEDGMENTS

I express appreciation to Reverend Kate Peacock, rector, (Diocese of St. Albans) for her valuable input and first proofreading of this book.

I am grateful to my brother, Tony Sabella, for his comments and input.

I thank Christopher Mallory for his substantive edit and proofreading of the manuscript. I learned a lot from his work and am grateful to him for helping me turn this book into one that I am proud of.

FOREWORD

Before you start reading this book, a better understanding of Jesus' world and culture can help reshape and deepen our understanding of him. Context matters, and as much as we think we understand him, without understanding his society and the cultural and political environment he lived in, we will almost certainly be jumping to wrong conclusions and interpretations.

Even after we are equipped with such knowledge, we will never be able to fully comprehend Jesus' wisdom. As the Son of God, his holy wisdom will always supersede the wisdom of generations of scholars and biblical analysts combined.

In his wisdom, he understood and appreciated that even he had to go against the tide of scriptural interpretation at times.

With that in mind, some thoughts in this book will undoubtedly not be appeasing. They might be disturbing and upsetting, saddening and disillusioning. The disciples on the road to Emmaus had similar feelings. But they stood fast and kept walking, while listening to Jesus until they reached their destination.
I hope you do the same.

It is with sincere gratitude and deep humility that I wish to acknowledge several Christian leaders in the Holy Land and elsewhere who have expressed their support for this book. I invite you to read some of these endorsements on the following pages.

Peter E. Sabella

Why do Christians visit the Holy Land? Clearly, there are various reasons. Christians are aware that their faith has roots in a particular time and a particular place. This land has been touched by the reality that has made us alive and set us on fire. Pilgrims come here, partly, to reconnect with the events and mysteries that have brought us alive, which occurred here. Here they find the hope that life will be renewed. Pilgrims can consider themselves to be a "holy land", in which Christ wishes to be born, to be raised up and to give witness.

Fundamentally, something great occurred in the Holy Land, which has made a difference. Jesus established a new covenant, a new testament. It is this that has made a difference and has touched and changed us. He established a new way of life, Kingdom living. With the establishment of the New Covenant, physical descent was no longer a determining factor for entrance into the people of God. Only those who believed in the Messiah could enter or remain a part of the Israel of God. Now, all, Jew and Gentile, are invited to the Kingdom, to become the People of God. All are invited to visibly demonstrate the comprehensive rule of God over every area of life. In short, to do His Will. We want to make sure that we are really inhabiting that difference, understanding it, praying through it, getting our heads and our hearts around it more fully.

So Christians come to the Holy Land looking for a better understanding of that. Something has made new things possible on this spot in this way. How do we get our minds and our hearts around that? The present volume by Peter Sabella is a guidebook with a difference. The reader is confronted with the thought provoking and the deeply emotional challenges of the holy places, the history and the moving events associated with the life and sufferings of Jesus Christ. This is done by selected passages from the Word of God, thoughtful reflections and questions, instructions and prayers, all signposts as it were, aiding the pilgrim to enter a more intimate union with God and foster a deeper commitment to practice the Christian faith.

Thanks to Peter Sabella for producing this volume that serves as "a spiritual guide towards a permanent pilgrimage".

Fouad Twal
Latin Patriarch of Jerusalem (August 5, 2015)

+ Fouad Twal

To go on pilgrimage to the Holy land is never a neat straightforward experience. Even those of us who have been several times, and perhaps even led different groups over the years, know that every visit produces something different.

Those who have been brought up in the Christian faith often go with preconceived ideas from their familiarity with the scriptures. Often these ideas can be challenged by the physical appearance of the Holy Land today, or people can be disturbed by the political tension and turmoil.

For the pilgrim coming on a first visit or a repeat visit, there are then challenges, but also deep rewards.

Peter Sabella has been a wise guide to pilgrims over many years now. Any guide to the Holy land deals with a remarkable range of people. Most often these will be people who profess the Christian faith, but they will come from every conceivable denomination. Some of these will hold a very sincere but simple faith, others will come with research degrees in theology. There will of course also be the searchers and the skeptics. It takes great patience and care to be a wise guide to such a variety of people, but Peter Sabella manages this with a rare skill.

He comes of course with his own background of faith, but rather than pin him down by denomination, perhaps most important of all is that he is a Christian brought up in the Holy Land. As many will know that is a not an easy situation, and the Christian population has been reducing in recent years. Peter is tactful and patient, but his guiding is a vocation and his faith comes through in all that he says. What he most cares about is helping someone move from being a tourist to a true pilgrim.

Those who have benefited from his guiding will have heard parts of what is in this book. But here he has been able to provide both information, and his own faith and perspective. There are parts where he deliberately asks for a response, and for the reader to reflect and ponder on the questions he puts. He never imposes a viewpoint, but provides many possibilities. Not everyone will agree with every interpretation, but what cannot be in doubt is his desire to let Jesus speak to the pilgrim today.

The Holy Land shows both the possibilities for human flourishing in response to the call of Jesus to turn and follow him, and also the ways that humanity falls into conflict and separation. This is a book that speaks of resilience and hope in a fallen world. It is one that helps the pilgrim to hear afresh the call of Jesus to follow, which as Peter Sabella says, comes from letting the time of pilgrimage be one of "being closed for renovation" so that one can "re-open" to all the possibilities of service in Jesus' name.

Nigel Stock
Bishop at Lambeth Palace, London (August 28, 2015)

We would like to congratulate Peter Sabella on Closed for renovation on the road to Emmaus – A spiritual guide of the Holy Land towards a permanent pilgrimage.

The publishing of this guidebook is not only a great achievement for Mr. Sabella, as the culmination of a fifteen-year career as a Holy Land tour guide, but it will help countless pilgrims navigate this land with a unique and spiritual approach.

As the guardians of ancient Christian heritage, We know first-hand how important it is for pilgrims to have a comprehensive encounter of the Holy Land, and especially Jerusalem. Their experience here will last a lifetime, playing a key role in strengthening their faith through imagery and direct contact with the holy places.

It is in this land where heaven and earth meet, and where spiritual refreshment is found. For, "As the deer pants for flowing streams, so my soul pants for you, my God" (Psalm 42:1).

We pray that this book be used and shared by many, and that our pilgrimage in the Holy Land indeed inspires a blessed earthly pilgrimage, guiding us toward salvation. "For here we have no lasting city, but we seek the city that is to come" (Heb. 13:14).

With our Patriarchal blessings and best wishes,

Theophilos III
Greek Orthodox Patriarch of Jerusalem (September 7, 2015)

The road to Emmaus is an arduous one, even physically. Maybe it is just as arduous as it was in Jesus' time. Jesus had to walk along the dusty and stony footpaths of the Judean hills in order to reach Emmaus from Jerusalem. After the excellent tarmac of the Israeli roads, the bus moves slowly along what seem to be country lanes, full of potholes and dust, winding alongside the small terraced fields and olive groves. This must have been the same environment in which Jesus walked on Easter Sunday when he met the two disciples on their way to Emmaus and confirmed them in their wavering faith.

The title of this work evokes this sense of pilgrimage as a journey of faith. The author explains how a pilgrimage to the Holy Land entails an experience of spiritual inner renovation, which calls for a closure to all distractions, in order to open oneself to the powerful Word of God which echoes in this Land. Indeed, the experience of a pilgrimage to the Holy Land is all about a personal meeting with the historical Jesus of Nazareth. The Land and its peoples speak about Jesus. They are a sacrament of His presence. Once you get into contact with them you will never be the same as before.

That is why this book is a good instrument to help you accomplish a pilgrimage in the authentic sense. Its historical annotations, brief but helpful, the abundant texts of Holy Scripture, the reflections and prayers, are truly enriching and can be fruitful in a Christian pilgrimage to the Holy Land. Indeed, the ability to stop, read, reflect and pray in the very places where Jesus Christ was conceived, born, walked, lived, died and rose from death, is the key to a genuine conversion to the Gospel and to a radical change in our way of living the Christian life.

This is the aim of Peter E. Sabella in compiling this booklet and I am sure that it will bear good fruit in the hearts of many well-intentioned pilgrims. For this effort the author merits our special thanks. We who live in this Holy Land which has become our permanent home appreciate and encourage all initiatives aimed at bringing Jesus alive to all those who walk in His footsteps in this Land of contrasts and blessings, of hatred and love, in this Land where it all began that evening when the two disciples met the Risen Lord on the road to Emmaus.

Fr. Pierbattista Pizzaballa ofm
Custos of the Holy Land (September 25, 2015)

CONTENTS

PETER E. SABELLA

Peter E. Sabella is a Christian born and raised in Jerusalem. He tries to portray a universal Jesus and yet stresses the contextual dimension of Jesus' life in a land that has always been torn with conflict.

He holds a masters' degree in peace and development studies from the University of Gothenburg, Sweden.

He applies his knowledge and expertise to create awareness of the universal need of peacemaking and connect Jesus' message of peace, justice and love to current realities. Ultimately, he presents a guide book at the heart of actuality.

> In the first place it should be known that if a person is seeking God,
> His Beloved is seeking him much more.
>
> St. John of the Cross

INTRODUCTION

A GUIDE FOR CHRISTIAN PILGRIMS

If the purpose of your coming to the Holy Land is exclusively an interest in sightseeing, culture or history, then this book is not for you. There are hundreds of other books that can help you. However, if your intention is to seek a spiritual experience, even if you are not really sure what to expect, then this book can be of value to you. You are no longer a tourist, you are a pilgrim.

Many Christians are cafeteria Christians. Many go to church twice a year, at Christmas and Easter. Many have been brought up as Christians without really appreciating why or who they are as such. Many attend church services and masses regularly, but the flame of Christ has long been dimmed, even extinguished in them. Many have Christ's flame in them, but they still want a little more of him. They are hungry and want to fan the flame.

In the beginning. Perhaps, you found an announcement on the board of your local church that the pastor was putting together a pilgrimage to the Holy Land. Maybe, you got a telephone call from a friend announcing the trip. You might be on a personal exploration of your own, hoping that your visit to the Holy Land might bring a revelation; it might have some kind of spiritual impact in your search for God. It does not really matter how and why you heard of the trip. What matters is that having decided to sign up, you have made a choice to participate and to walk on the road to Emmaus with Christ.

A life changing experience. Whether you are conscious of it or not, your life is about to change – nothing will be the same again. Walking the land where Jesus walked, seeing the landscapes that he saw, feeling the breeze coming from the Sea of Galilee, the same breeze that ruffled his hair, are reasons that by themselves can nourish your heart for days.

You, the pilgrim. The travel agent has been busy for months finding a flight, accommodation and transportation. If you are travelling with an organized church group, your pastor must have been preparing homilies, prayers, hymns, services and masses. Your guide is ready to lead the way and walk with you a 2,000 year-old journey.

All these people are working for your convenience, doing their best to pave your way. Yet, remember one thing, it is your journey. You are a pilgrim.

Things may go wrong; you have arrived at the airport and there is nobody waiting for you. Do not be frustrated – you are a pilgrim.

You walk into your hotel room and there is no TV or hair dryer. Do not be upset; remember, you are a pilgrim.

Your tour managers have to modify the itinerary or cancel a visit somewhere. Do not get grumpy; remember, you are a pilgrim.

Your roommate is a babbling river. Deal with it, but remember – you are a pilgrim.

As a pilgrim, you have to remember that the Lord did not have all the conveniences that you enjoy today. Christ walked; you have air-conditioned transportation. You are sleeping in a nice room; he had to sleep in the open air, in a tent or in a shack somewhere.

Open up and use parts of your brain and heart that you might not have used before. Give up temporarily some of your daily habits and conveniences. Be ready for and open to new realities and truths that might disrupt perceptions you have considered sacred for years. Set aside your position long enough to open yourself with compassion and love, and listen earnestly to what God is saying to you.

As a pilgrim, being challenged is part of your sacred voyage and self-examination in which you may encounter God in many ways and different places. Accept the challenges and ponder over them. They will help you discover your real self, for the Lord works in mysterious ways.

As a pilgrim, do not be afraid to ask questions that might categorize you as a novice in the faith. We all are. The more we know, the more we discover how little we really do know. One thing to keep in mind, though – when God knocks on your door, make sure you open it. Allow your heart to be changed and let the place pass through you, not the other way around. In the words of Rev. Peter J. Miano, founder of the Society for Biblical Studies, "*Tourists pass through places, but pilgrims let places pass through them, allowing their hearts to be changed.*"[1]

ESSENCE OF PILGRIMAGE

Yes, brother, sister, you are on a pilgrimage and everything is different. A pilgrimage is a time to walk the road to Emmaus, carrying the loads of the past and the expectations of the future. It is a time to think of the hard questions of life, it is a time to dig deeper inside yourself to find out more.

A pilgrimage is a time for a renovation of heart and mind, both of which are profoundly intertwined – and with renovation comes restoration, then transformation. The heart pumps blood to the mind to survive, and the mind sustains the pumping of blood to the heart to function. Renovation of only the heart is incomplete without the mind. Yet of the two, the heart stands first. Once you have renovated the heart, the mind renovates itself and reconciles with the changes of the heart.

Old city, Jerusalem, photo by Marc Rock

Above all, a pilgrimage is a time to ponder on Jesus' question of all questions, *"Who do you say that I am! Who am I to you?"*

Peter the apostle dedicated his whole life to finding an answer. He left everything and undertook a permanent pilgrimage.

PROCESS OF RENOVATION

When a renovation is in progress, it requires time and effort. It is associated with a lot of chaos and muddle. But it is all worthwhile, since the outcome is a new refreshed design and look.

Peter the apostle had to go through the process of renovation. During his pilgrimage, he started as a narrow-minded fisherman, and became a universal shepherd of human hearts. That was his road to Emmaus. Paul the apostle had to go through the same process. He started his pilgrimage as a persecutor of Christians, but ended as a persecuted Christian. That was his road to Emmaus.

On your road to Emmaus, without knocking down inner walls and reaching out to your inner self, to the depth of your heart, and without engaging your brain in challenging thoughts, you cannot achieve genuine spiritual transformation. You will only reach half way on the road to Emmaus. The most you can hope for is spiritual revival.

If you are seeking spiritual transformation, there is one key thing that you have to do upon your arrival to the Holy Land. You must post a sign on your heart that reads "**Closed for renovation**" on one side and "**Open for renovation**" on the other.

You need to post the sign "Closed for renovation" because you need to transmit to the outer world, especially to your friends and family, whether they are with you on a pilgrimage or back home, that you are serious about what you are doing. They have to give you the necessary space and time to walk the road to Emmaus in the Holy Land. They have to become an active ingredient, an accelerator and supporter of your renovation process.

You need to post the sign "Closed for renovation" because you need to truly commit yourself to the choice you have made by participating in a pilgrimage. This might be your only time to visit the Holy Land as a pilgrim. You have to mentally and emotionally take leave from your work, family, daily habits and commitments. You need to be focused on one thing; your pilgrimage. You have to be totally present in the Holy Land in *body* and *soul*.

Having transmitted your seriousness and commitment to the pilgrimage, you can start working on the core with the other side of the sign. You are open for renovation because the primary anticipated outcome of your pilgrimage is a closer relationship with God. One of the best ways to get closer to God is to get to know yourself better. *"In order to find God, whom we can only find in and through the depths of our own soul, we must therefore first find ourselves. To use common figures of speech, we must 'return to ourselves,' we must 'come to ourselves.'"*[2]

Besides the fulfillment of scripture, God had to become fully human, passing through all stages of life to better know humanity. It is true that he created humankind; it is also true that he gave us a brain to think and a soul to feel. Between them, he planted the power of choice. He had to learn how humans use it in their lives. Humans have a choice between good and evil, they have a choice to live in the past or to fantasize in the future. In the Garden of Gethsemane, Jesus' humanity had a tough choice to make.

God became human to prove that the true power of choice lies in the here and now – and nowhere else. Living in the kingdom of God, living in eternal life is now, a moment in the present. For a better knowledge of God, you have to get to know yourself now. Mary, the mother of Jesus, had to make the choice in her *now* moment; only then was she able to walk her road to Emmaus and realize who God was to her and the role he was to play in her life. As a pilgrim, you are invited to share in a similar experience. But for that to happen, you need to abandon yourself *now* to God, and to be here in body and soul and repeat her words, *"let it be done to me according to thy word."* Every place you visit becomes your home, without distraction, closed for renovation from the outside and open for renovation from the inside; ready to walk your road to Emmaus.

During your renovation process, you have to accept the muddle of transition and anticipate the long-awaited new self. Rev. David Robertson, pastor of High River United Church in Canada, wrote, *"This is not a process for the faint-hearted. It is spiritually demanding and intentional work. Life during renovation can be quite lonely. A renovation of the heart can also include bouts of depression (which is often associated with grief and loss as well as restoration). It can also feel like things are out of sorts while our interior space re-orders itself. It's not easy. But imagine the new way of being that comes from the work. Imagine the new way of seeing the same thing!"*[3]

As you walk the land of Christ, this book is intended to help you dig deep inside your heart and create an internal mess within. There will be a time, your own special time, when it will hit you and the process of transformation will begin from within. *"The crucial turning point is when we start to look within, when we learn to reflect on our lives instead of just skating across the surface. This is when we can find out who we are, what we are about, what's important to us, what our core values are – the things that we would like to build our life on."*[4] Jesus said, *"No new wine can be poured into old wine skins."*[5] The hope is that you will become a new wine skin after covering a short distance on your road to Emmaus. With your sincerity, you will be able to see yourself and God through a different lens. This book is a guide to a transformative spiritual journey in the minor context of the Holy Land road to Emmaus. It is hoped that once you reach the desired distance, you will want to continue your road to Emmaus towards a permanent pilgrimage.

HISTORICITY OF THE BIBLE

The Holy Land is still undergoing extensive archaeological research. Since the early 19th century, archeologists, scholars and historians have strived to uncover secrets and treasures of ancient civilizations and cultures of the Middle East, especially in Israel and Palestine. However, their greatest challenge remains: whether to accept or refute different biblical accounts as historical facts. For example, when reviewing the Exodus account and the rise of the glorious kingdoms of David and

Solomon (around 1300 BC to 930 BC), scholars encounter a dark era, without any substantial evidence from non-biblical sources to verify biblical accounts. Their only source of information in their attempt to reconstruct the origins of Israel is the Bible, namely the books from Genesis to Joshua.

After studying and analyzing these books for years, scholars developed theories and conclusions. Israel Finkelstein, an archaeologist from the University of Tel Aviv said, *"Today more than 90% of scholars agree that there was no Exodus from Egypt, 80% feel that the Conquest of the Land did not take place as described in the Bible, and about 50% agree that there was no powerful United Monarchy."* Professor Magen Broshi, archaeologist at the Israeli Museum noted, *"the notion of the Conquest of the Land in the Book of Joshua is an epic, no more."*[6]

Yet, because what is at issue is the Bible, the source for the faith of millions, people are not comfortable with scholars' claims, and nobody can compel them to accept their conclusions. Naomi Shemer, a leading Israeli singer and song writer once noted, *"I am not competent in archaeology, but what does it matter if this issue exists or not? Let's say that the Bible never actually existed, but was a fable: but this fable has proved to be more alive than all the stones."*[7]

As a result, scholars in charge of archeological digs are undoubtedly affected by their previous conclusions. One of them might look at a piece of evidence and think that it supports a theory on a biblical account, while another scholar looking at the same evidence might hold a contrary view.

To better understand, take the books of Genesis through Joshua as an example. The more conservative scholars, Christian and Jewish, regard their accounts as true and accurate. This group chooses to disregard all the credibility problems and contradictions that are present in these narratives. Miller-Hayes in their history of ancient Israel and Judah wrote, *"if the historian who follows this option is prepared to take the biblical account fully 'as it stands,' the resulting historical survey will begin with the creation of the world approximately six thousand years ago, presuppose an early period during which human beings lived enormously long life spans, date the Israelite exodus from Egypt during the fifteenth century BCE, describe the Israelite taking of Canaan as a miraculous conquest, and so forth."*[8]

At the other end of the spectrum is a group with a totally opposite view. It claims that given all the credibility problems – apparent contradictions, lack of extra biblical information and poor connection of stories – these biblical books do not and cannot qualify as historical books. Consequently, this group regards the Bible more as a collection of legends and stories drawn from and influenced by earlier cultures and sources.

A third group of scholars holds a middle position: a compromise. It claims that despite the apparent contradictions and inconsistencies that exhibit serious credibility problems, there is still some historicity and some credibility to the biblical accounts. This group's main challenge is to try to interpret and extract true historical information from the narratives.[9] As a result, in this group there are many theories and interpretations. Though still mostly based on biblical information, this group does not necessarily follow the account literally. It all depends on the scholars approach, judgment, intuition and imagination. In addition, it depends on the scholar's ability to extract authentic information and verify its resourcefulness, the ability to relate pieces of information, reliance on up-to-date archaeological findings, previous convictions and the model that influences the conclusions.

David's Tower Museum, Jerusalem

Miller-Hayes identify two such models: one derived from an assumed Middle Eastern cultural pattern known as the nomadic model, and the other from the social sciences. According to them, the nomadic model assumes that the Arabian Desert had long been a constant source of nomads who infringed from time to time upon the surrounding cultivated areas, seeking territory and grazing lands for their flocks. Adherents to this school of thought believe that the ancestors of Israel and Judah entered Palestine as nomadic groups. They had managed gradually to settle in unoccupied areas and established relationships with the indigenous population.

The second model maintains that the number of exodus newcomers was in the thousands and that the main body of so-called Israelites was the result of socio-economic and political development that took place within the Palestine of the Late Bronze and Early Iron ages. Miller-Hayes refer to it as a "revolt of marginal and oppressed elements within the heterogeneous population of the land directed against the economical and political structures of the Canaanite city-states and their monarchical, feudalistic governments."[10] They add that, "The outcome, in short, was Israel, a new religio-political entity characterized by its covenant allegiance to the god Yahweh and its adherence to a classless and egalitarian social order."[11]

We will never know whether a certain story happened exactly the way it was narrated in the Bible. Every nation needs and creates its own history. Objective history is an impossibility. It is all subjective to the author's intentions. A defeated nation looks at its role in the making of its history from a totally different angle than the nation that subdued it. The historicity of the biblical narrative has to be viewed through the same lens. The Israelites wrote their history; it was much easier to pass on to future generations a glorious and dramatic history when God was always on their side – in spite of their sins, transgressions and disobedience – rather than a shameful history. Such socio-religious dynamism is part and parcel of any nation's narrative. In the case of Israel, its history has been so entwined with its religion and politics (see Annex 1). This dynamism was there during Jesus' incarnated presence on earth, and there is no doubt that it provoked some of his parables and radical teachings.

Predicament of the land

The predicament of the Holy Land is that its history has been entwined with its religions – like its religions with its politics – for thousands of years. It has been so much so to the point that, for the average person, they have become almost inseparable. Generally, a critique of one is portrayed as a critique of the other two. The fact remains: in the Holy Land of Israel and Palestine, religion, history and politics are three sides of the same coin. To shed more light on the connection of the three perspectives, consider the following questions.

When can one say that the history of a land is his history? Can a person sworn in as an American citizen only today claim the history of America as his? Can a convert to Judaism or a secular Russian Jew, making her *aliya* (return to Zion) and becoming an Israeli citizen, claim that Israel's history, or the biblical story, is hers just because she is a Jew? Can a Palestinian (Christian or Muslim), whose family has lived in historical Palestine for generations and who lives in modern-day Israel, claim the biblical history of Israel as his? And what about the Jewish citizen of an Arab country who has lived there for generations, is her history that of Israel or the Arab country of her birth? Can a Christian claim the history of Israel as his, simply because Jesus was a Jew?

Does the history of a land guarantee property rights of its people to the land? Who are its people, those who have been living on it for generations or those who have recently come to claim it, citing ancestral rights? Don't those who have lived on a land for generations have ancestral rights as well? Does the length of time a group of people resides on a land make a difference in the group's claim to own it? If somebody has an official title to a land that his family has held for generations, does he have to give it up because somebody else, with no official title, claims that his ancestors had been there before?

How do you think Jesus would have answered these questions?

_____

_____

_____

_____

_____

_____

_____

_____

_____

_____

_____

_____

_____

_____

_____

_____

The purpose of this guide is not to analyze books of the Bible. However, it is highly assumed that the Old Testament, in particular, is a compilation of historical as well as mythical stories. Some stories even amount to folk tales that were enhanced, dramatized and edited. Some have been attributed to one author, but most likely were written by more than one. The bottom line is that they were written with the intention to pass on important religious, social and political messages that developed over time by a group of people that called itself Israelite in a time when such creations were acceptable and possible.

Some of you may be infuriated with this approach to understanding the biblical story. Conventional wisdom would argue that this is the Bible, the holiest book for Christians, and such statements must not be made.

The Bible can withstand critical analysis. In spite of the volumes of books and articles, television broadcasts and thousands of online journals that have attempted to analyze the book, scrutinizing it to the point of total nullification of most of its contents, it still is the number one published book in the whole world. In addition, it has been around for some two and a half millennia. No other book has been translated into as many languages. This book can take it!

However, reading the Bible as a Christian, I have to read it with a focus on an outcome, which is why I am a Christian today. I am not called a Christian because I believe in Abraham, David or Moses. It is true that they all had a share in the story leading to my salvation. But they are not the center of why I am a Christian. I am called a Christian because I believe in Jesus

Christ as my Lord and Saviour. His walking on this earth and particularly in the land of historical Palestine made their story relevant to the plan of my salvation. Therefore, I have to read the Bible with an eye on the mystery of my salvation through Christ.

In addition, the Old Testament (the law and the prophets) had two functions. It was supposed to organize the relationship between God and his people, and between peoples. This has been reiterated in different places in the four gospels, such as the parable of the good Samaritan. The code by which Jesus viewed the scriptures until he came to this world was *"Love the Lord your God with all your heart, and with all your soul, and with all your strength, and with all your mind; and your neighbor as yourself."*[12] Once the Lawgiver had walked this earth his authority superseded all other authority, whether written or spoken. Jesus said, *"You search the scriptures because you think that in them you have eternal life; and it is they that testify on my behalf. Yet you refuse to come to me to have life. I do not accept glory from human beings. But I know that you do not have the love of God in you. I have come in my Father's name, and you do not accept me; if another comes in his own name, you will accept him. How can you believe when you accept glory from one another and do not seek the glory that comes from the one who alone is God? Do not think that I will accuse you before the Father; your accuser is Moses, on whom you have set your hope. If you believed Moses, you would believe me, for he wrote about me. But if you do not believe what he wrote, how will you believe what I say?"*[13]

With Jesus' authority in consideration, a third commandment has to be added to the other two to inherit eternal life. It is to believe in Jesus as bread of life (new law) and saviour. *"I am the bread of life. Whoever comes to me will never be hungry, and whoever believes in me will never be thirsty. But I said to you that you have seen me and yet do not believe. Everything that the Father gives me will come to me, and anyone who comes to me, I will never drive away; for I have come down from heaven, not to do my own will, but the will of him who sent me. And this is the will of him who sent me. That I should lose nothing of all that he has given me, but raise it up on the last day. This is indeed the will on my Father, that all who see the Son and believe in him may have eternal life; and I will raise them up on the last day."*[14]

I have had the honor to walk the land of Christ with world-class scholars of biblical archaeology and theology. I have learned that both schools can be treated as separate, and may often contradict each other, or can be treated together and often be contradictory, rather than complementary. It is imperative to understand that there is not one way of looking at any biblical text, archaeologically or theologically. If there was only one way, then all other scholars and theologians would have to pack up and leave. But if anyone claims to have the truth about any archaeological site or theological argument, then listener beware.

DEALING WITH THE ARCHAEO-THEOLOGICAL DILEMMA

Before attempting to address this issue, one point needs to be stressed. Archaeology teaches that a tradition needs a place. Over time, tradition and place become one and the same. Sometimes, for complex religious, social and political reasons, more traditions become pinned to the same location.

THE PILGRIM AND THE OLD TESTAMENT

What is significant for a pilgrim to treasure from the Old Testament is what the Lord said about it: *"The law and the prophets were in effect until John came; since then the good news of the kingdom of God is proclaimed, and everyone is strongly urged to enter it."*[15] As for the prophecies, most of them had been fulfilled in the Lord Jesus Christ. Some prophesies are yet to be fulfilled. These are made into a sensation on thousands of TV and satellite networks for thousands of churches around the world. They are also the subject of Sunday homilies and religio-political hermeneutics for priests and pastors.

When you truly have Christ in your heart, you need to trust that you possess in him *"the way, and the truth, and the life."*[16] One does not need to help God fulfill his prophesies because God is wise enough to choose his timing. God wants us to live and to concentrate on gaining virtues worthy of him in this life so that we become eligible for eternal life with him. If we want eternal life, then we need not worry, for Jesus said, *"I am the resurrection and the life. Those who believe in me, even though they die, will live, and everyone who lives and believes in me will never die."*[17]

The Holy One is God and only him, revealed in the person of the Holy Trinity.

The Holy Book became holy because it narrates the story of salvation from revelation to incarnation. In spite of that, it was still written and translated by sinners – like you and me.

The purpose of the Holy Bible as a whole is to tell the story of salvation. If it is not, then there is no reason to call it holy. At the same time, there is nothing wrong with interpretive ways of scripture as long as the message is to love God and love one another. The four evangelists who wrote their account of the life, death and resurrection of Jesus never deviated from the message of the ultimate love that Jesus had to offer. They wrote in different styles to different audiences, but they always kept God's ultimate agape (or divine love) for humanity at the forefront of their narration.

THROUGH THE PILGRIM'S SPECTACLES

As pilgrims, we have to learn to be spiritually attached to the sites, but at the same time physically detached from them. Tourists want to see the site and pass through it; therefore, their presence in any particular site is physical. As pilgrims we want to have the site see us and pass through us, and as a consequence our presence in a particular site is spiritual.

Many pilgrims' reaction to a visit of the Church of the Holy Sepulchre is often disappointment. They usually are eager to see Calvary and the Holy Tomb. But once they set foot there and see all the unholy actions taking place there, in addition to the divisions and the unusual Middle Eastern practices, adding to that the thousands of people pushing their way through, they lose heart. Suddenly, the Church stops being holy. This is the challenge that pilgrims face: they have to learn to look at things like tourists, but see them as pilgrims. They have to look at the rock of Calvary, but see Jesus' sacrifice. They have to look at the Holy Tomb, but see the Risen Lord. They have to learn to detach from the hustle and bustle and to be present, yet absent, both at the same time.

As pilgrims, another way is to look at sites from the perspective of the sites themselves. The Sea of Galilee and its landscapes saw the Lord and as a result they commemorate and honor his presence by passing through his earthly life. These sites can give pilgrims enough inspiration to help them see him and pass through his life as well.

As pilgrims and Christians, our faith is based on the Lord Jesus Christ. He is the cornerstone of both Old and New Testaments. In the words of St. Augustine, *"The Old Testament is the New Testament concealed, and the New Testament is the Old Testament revealed."*[18] As informative and enriching the Old Testament can be, the focus of this guide book is on the revealed, rather than the concealed. The law and the prophets had a purpose, and that purpose was fulfilled by the incarnation of the Lawgiver himself.

As pilgrims, most importantly, never forget that God humbled himself in total surrender out of divine love (agape) and put his life to save us, sinners, so that we may live and "have life, and have it abundantly." As pilgrims, when we read scripture and visit the sites, we need to keep our focus on our God of Love. Any reading of scripture that does not portray God's love needs to be given extra consideration and should not deflect our attention. God does not justify killing and conquest. He allowed himself to be killed so that we could be liberated from the yoke of slavery and conquest, both physical and spiritual.

HOLY LAND

Millions of pilgrims from the three monotheistic religions have been flocking to visit this land for thousands of years. Religious and political leaders have also invested huge sums of money and effort into the identification and preservation of holy sites. Temples, churches, mosques and shrines were built in certain places for some religious reason: a birthplace, a burial place, a visiting place, a miracle.

You are coming to the Holy Land. The truth is that there is nothing holy about this land. It is holy people who have walked this land and made it so holy. From a Christian point of view, if Jesus had not been here, the whole Bible would not make any sense. He made the land holy, and as a consequence many of the people mentioned in the Bible became not only holy, but saints as well. The Christian pilgrim would not be coming to see the cave of Elijah or the tomb of Abraham if it were not for Jesus.

At the same time, God is omnipresent. You encounter him at home, at your local church or anywhere. You can also read your Bible anytime, anywhere. So why come to the Holy Land?

Seeing is believing. Yes, we are supposed to believe without seeing! But, whether we admit it or not, there is a doubting Thomas in all of us. Peter the apostle had to see for himself that Christ's tomb was empty when Mary Magdalene announced it. Coming to the Holy Land and seeing for yourself will certainly help you understand some of the reasons and locations of scripture. It is a lifetime opportunity to better understand Jesus Christ, to encounter Christ in spirit, in the context of the geographical and socio-political environment he lived in. The landscapes, the settings, the trees, the birds, the people, the hustle and bustle can contribute to the reconstruction of a vivid picture of first-century Palestine. Many times, without any particular preparation, you are struck with an overwhelming feeling that gospel verses are coming to life.

Discover the roots of Christian faith. Jesus, Lord and Saviour, the mustard seed of our very presence as Christians was born, died and resurrected here. Fifty days after his resurrection, he sent us all a sacred gift, the Holy Spirit in tongues of fire. From then, the fire of his glorious love, transmitted and reaffirmed by the fire of his disciples' stimulating testimonies, spread out to the whole world. The Church of Jerusalem was rightly called the Mother of All Churches.

Encounter the land's peoples – its living stones. There is so much that you can learn from them – Christians, Muslims and Jews. As a Christian pilgrim, you have to meet your brothers and sisters of faith who can certainly give you a fresh and challenging perception on the understanding of scripture and life here. For their part, living stones undoubtedly appreciate your solidarity and faith.

Discover the current truth about the land. There is almost a daily mention of Israel and Palestine in the media. Yet, media time spans are barely enough to touch on the real subjects that matter. A visit to Israel and Palestine will certainly help you better understand the present realities.

The hope is that all these factors will

help your journey of faith and, with proper spiritual guidance, holiness will become an integral part of your life. It can always serve as a guiding beacon in your permanent pilgrimage, and someday it may inspire others to follow in your footsteps.

GRADES OF HOLINESS

When you come to the Holy Land, you might hear words such as, "This is the place where tradition holds that…", "This is the place where it is believed that…", "This is the place where he was…" You might ask, how do we really know the place of something that happened thousands of years ago? How do we know that the tradition of any holy site is accurate or not?

The answer is a mélange of archaeology, history, the Bible and local tradition. When you put together all of the archaeological information, historical references and local traditions of any particular site, you can get a very close assumption to a supposed location of an incident. Having said that, holy sites can be classified into three grades.

Grade 1. These are traditional sites that are the closest to being the most authentic. There is enough evidence, especially archaeological and historical, to verify the location of the tradition. There is not 100% proof, but there is more than enough.

Grade 2. These are sites that have a tradition based on fair grounds that are 50% authentic. There is some historical and archaeological evidence to verify the location of the tradition.

Grade 3. These sites are based more on local tradition, rather than historical or archaeological evidence.

There will always be somebody who contests these grades; it is human nature. Sometimes, when these classifications are made, people get absorbed by them. If this happens to you, remember, that they are made for your understanding and peace of mind about the sites' authenticity. Do not let grades overshadow the deeper messages of the sites you are experiencing.

HISTORICAL REFERENCES TO JESUS

Is there any extra biblical, historical or archaeological evidence that Jesus ever existed? Certainly, billions of people who believe in Jesus Christ cannot all be wrong.

There are many faith-related questions that theologians and religious experts can answer quite extensively. Similarly, there are also many questions that are hard to answer. Ultimately, you have to come to terms with your faith and be satisfied with the answers to your questions. A pilgrimage in the right settings and spirit can certainly offer a better understanding of faith.

Some questions of history can be answered. As compelling and rich the answers may prove to be, there will always be room for doubt. How do you know that what the historian in the first century was writing is true? How do you know that the text we have today was not filtered by ages of Christian control over the texts? How, why and where? The truth is that there is no 100% guarantee to anything.

Any piece of history will be subject to at least three opinions – one that supports, a second that rejects and a third that adopts some middle ground. This guide aims to take extra biblical historical evidence at face value; the mere mention of Jesus and Christians soon after his death is evidence enough that he existed and was not a myth.

Three extra biblical non-Christian sources referring to Jesus and Christians date to the first and early second centuries, proving that he was indeed a historical figure. Most scholars consider the testimony of these sources to be genuine and of historical value.

Josephus Flavius

Josephus made three references important to Christian history. The first one has to do with the stoning of James (probably, James the Just, first Bishop of Jerusalem), brother of Jesus who was called the Christ. The second speaks of the killing of John the Baptist. The third refers to Jesus Christ crucified by Pilate. Of the three references the latter had been the most scholarly debated, and there have been many opinions on its historicity. Nevertheless, the whole debate is not whether Josephus mentioned Jesus or not. It is generally accepted that he mentioned him, but the debate is more about the content of the description he gave of Jesus that might have been modified by Christian apologetics.

The stoning of James. *"And now Caesar, upon hearing the death of Festus, sent Albinus into Judea, as procurator. But the king deprived Joseph of the high priesthood, and bestowed the succession to that dignity on the son of Ananus, who was also himself called Ananus [...] Festus was now dead, and Albinus was but upon the road; so he assembled the Sanhedrin of judges, and brought before them the brother of Jesus, who was called Christ, whose name was James, and some others; and when he had formed an accusation against them as breakers of the law, he delivered them to be stoned."* (Anon., n.d.)

The killing of John the Baptist. *"Now some of the Jews thought that the destruction of Herod's army came from God, and that very justly, as a punishment of what he did against John, that was called the Baptist: for Herod slew him, who was a good man [...] Herod, who feared lest the great influence John had over the people might put it into his power and inclination to raise a rebellion [...] Accordingly he was sent a prisoner, out of Herod's suspicious temper, to Macherus, the castle I before mentioned, and was there put to death."* (Anon., n.d.)

The crucifixion of Jesus. *"Now there was about this time Jesus, a wise man, if it be lawful to call him a man; for he was a doer of wonderful works, a teacher of such men as receive the truth with pleasure. He drew over to him both many of the Jews and many of the Gentiles. He was [the] Christ. And when Pilate, at the suggestion of the principal men amongst us, had condemned him to the cross, those that loved him at the first did not forsake him; for he appeared to them alive again the third day; as the divine prophets had foretold these and ten thousand other wonderful things concerning him. And the tribe of Christians, so named from him, are not extinct at this day."* (Anon., n.d.)

Pliny the Younger

Pliny, Roman governor around AD 111, wrote to his Emperor Trajan about his personal actions in the questioning and torture of Christians to force them to curse Christ: *"They were accustomed to meet on a fixed day before dawn and sing responsively a hymn to Christ as to a god, and bound themselves to a solemn oath, not to any wicked deeds, but never to commit any fraud, theft, adultery, never to falsify their word, not to deny a trust when they should be called upon to deliver it up. When this was over, it was their custom to depart and to assemble again to partake of a meal – but ordinary and innocent food."* (Anon., n.d.)

This reference reveals several key things:

- Jesus was worshipped as a god.
- Christians met on a fixed day of the week.
- The meeting occurred before sunrise.
- They sang songs to Christ.
- Christians were committed to holy behavior.

Tacitus

Tacitus, a Roman senator and historian around AD 115, reported in his Annals on the historical period of Emperor Nero and the great fire of Rome around AD 64, Tacitus made reference to Christ and his execution by Pontius Pilate. In addition, he wrote about his followers, Christians, living in Rome as well as in Judea from where Christ's message originated. *"Consequently, to get rid of the report, Nero fastened the guilt and inflicted the most exquisite tortures on a class hated for their abominations, called Christians by the populace. Christus, from whom the name had its origin, suffered the extreme penalty during the reign of Tiberius at the hands of one of our procurators, Pontius Pilatus, and a most mischievous superstition, thus checked for the moment, again broke out not only in Judaea, the first source of the evil, but even in Rome, where all things hideous and shameful from every part of the world find their centre and become popular."*[19]

Notes
1. http://www.seetheholyland.net/a-pilgrim-is-not-a-tourist/.
2. Thomas Merton, The New Man, Farrar, Straus & Giroux (Reissue Edition November 29, 1999) New York p. 63.
3. Pastor David Robertson, article for Advent written in 2010 entitled, "The Human Heart Under Renovation: Redefining Hope in a Conflicted World," Canada.
4. Dave Tomlinson, *How to be a bad Christian and a better human being*, Hodder and Stoughton, 2012.
5. Luke 5:37.
6. http://individual.utoronto.ca/mfkolarcik/jesuit/IsraelFinkelstein.html.
7. http://individual.utoronto.ca/mfkolarcik/jesuit/IsraelFinkelstein.html.
8. J. Maxwell Miller-John H. Hayes, *A History of Ancient Israel and Judah*, Westminster Press, 1986, p. 74.
9. For more information, review J. Maxwell Miller-John H. Hayes, ibid. pp. 74-77.
10. J. Maxwell Miller, ibid. p. 77.
11. J. Maxwell Miller, ibid. p. 77.
12. Luke 10:27.
13. John 5:39-47.
14. John 6:35-40.
15. Luke 16:16.
16. John 14:6.
17. John 11:25-26.
18. https://mdivbound.wordpress.com/concealed-revealed quoting St. Augustine.
19. Re-quoted in Lee Strobel, *The Case for Christ*, 1998 p. 82.

Ceramic tile

Vic Lepejian -
M.A. Applied Art,
Designer Ceramist,
Armenian Quarter,
Old City- Jerusalem

Photo by
Karen Baumann

Pilgrim's prayer

O Lord Jesus Christ, you simply said two words to the apostle Peter, and he left everything behind him and followed you. From the very beginning he was open to the possibility of having his identity and faith challenged.

I too, O Lord, want to follow you. I am also open to the possibility of having my identity and faith perceptions challenged. I have come to seek you. I want to walk with you, see you and hear your voice, like the other disciples did. I surrender myself to you.

Write your gospel in my heart, open my mind to receive your grace. Help me gain a new insight into my true self. Help me relieve my anxieties and frustrations when things do not seem to go my way. Help me become a permanent pilgrim, instead of a passing tourist.

Teach me the way to embrace with love my brothers and sisters on this pilgrimage and in this land, as you embraced those you met and ultimately your cross.

Lord, I have left family and friends behind. I ask you to keep them in your care and grace. Grant them patience and peace of heart, knowing that I am seeking a transformed spiritual relationship with you.

I am following in your footsteps, O Lord, hoping that when I return home, I will be a better person than the one who set out. Amen.

> Evangelization aims at a process of growth which entails taking seriously each person and God's plan for his or her life. All of us need to grow in Christ.
>
> Pope Francis

SHARING GOOD NEWS IN A DIFFERENT WAY

Jesus used parables, short stories, to pass on his message. Similarly, the gospel tells us the story of Jesus Christ according to four different evangelists, which can be summarized in one paragraph.

Through God's grace, a baby is mysteriously conceived in the womb of a virgin named Mary. After nine months he is born in Bethlehem and named Jesus, visited by outcast shepherds and venerated by outsiders. His family flees from King Herod who wants to kill the newborn child. Jesus lives unnoticed in an obscure town called Nazareth most of his life. From the age of 30, he teaches and preaches for three years around the Sea of Galilee, then heads to Jerusalem, where he confronts the Jewish leadership and is crucified by the Romans. Then he is resurrected, appears before his friends and is declared the saviour of the world.

The word gospel means the good news. The church stresses that there is only one gospel narrated according to four evangelists. Mark tells us the story in 16 chapters. Matthew passed it on in 28 chapters, while Luke in 24 and John in 21. The point is that each evangelist told the same story using a different approach that he thought would be fitting, given the resources he had available, the time frame, the social and political circumstances at the time of his writing and his audience.

The 21st century with its technological developments, freedom and commotion, consumerism, advertisements, sexual liberties, anxieties and all sorts of distractions has proved to be a major disturbance to religious practices around the world. To counterbalance that effect requires a different kind of religious leadership and a different reading of the gospel. Different does not mean deviating from the context or the doctrine, but using a more dynamic way that can adapt quickly to such disturbances and bring back the flock (read 1 Peter 5), especially its young, to the proper house. When one goes to church on Sunday, the pastor has a lot to do with the number of participants in the service. A pastor with charisma and ability to bring the scriptures to life brings in more people to church. A service with music or a choir complements and supports that effort and helps attract participants, rather than spectators.

It is the same with the gospel. The text was written almost 2,000 years ago for people living in the first century AD. The style of narration and compilation was probably fit for that time frame. However, now the text seems alien at times to our modern ears. That is what the skilled pastor does; he can bring the text to life and relate that old material to a modern world.

People are very creative in spreading any good news. Some people are straight forward and they just cannot wait to spread the word as soon as they know of it. Others try to devise all sorts of ingenious ways to pass on good news, from writing a note, to singing a song, buying flowers and gifts, writing in the sand, hiring a small plane with a good-news banner attached to it – the list is endless. Good news is supposed to be shared because it brings joy and happiness to the one who shares it and, hopefully, to the one who receives it.

With that in mind, the purpose of the next section and others in this guide, is to share parts of the gospel in a slightly different way than we are accustomed to, substituting some of its dryness with vivid pictures. Doing so may deviate from the original text at times, while trying to give life to places and characters with feelings and expressions. The text is not written to be taken as truth; the intention is to harmonize different texts, recent archaeological discoveries, a deeper knowledge of original scripture as well as cultural and political circumstances of biblical times.

Take time to pause, see and feel the event. Use your imagination and creative spirit to live the moment. The people mentioned in the gospel were real people like you and me. Remember the joy you feel when you witness the birth of a child; how you react if you lose a child in the crowd; the joy when you find him; remember your child growing up, going to school and to church, and those special moments in your lives – all these events applied to Jesus' family too. Jesus took our humanity in its fullness with all that it entails; its joys and sorrows.

As you read these lines and visualize them (scripture and other extra biblical text are italicized), walk with Jesus as he matures. Allow yourself to mature with him, learn what he is learning and live what he is living. Try to understand his day. The moment will come when he will knock at your door and connect with you, and the Holy Spirit will come upon you. Do not be afraid to let him in. Be honest and sincere. Allow the mustard seed to grow and bear fruit.

Fra Angelico, *Annunciation*, Museo Diocesano, Cortona

JESUS' EARTHLY LIFE

ANNUNCIATION

A righteous widower named Joseph of Bethlehem, city of David, was engaged to Mary from a small town in Galilee called Nazareth. Officially engaged by the high priest in Jerusalem, Joseph returned to his hometown to make the necessary arrangements for his new wife and to prepare for their wedding ceremony. Mary returned to Nazareth to prepare with her family the customary requirements for the wedding.

One morning, while Mary was filling her water jar[1] from the spring near her home, an angel of the Lord appeared and said to her, "Greetings, favored one, the Lord is with you." Mary, perplexed and frightened, immediately ran home. Her parents were not there. She jumped on the stack of mattresses arranged on the side of the living room and hid her head under a blanket. She prayed, "Oh, dear God, please strengthen me, what can this be?"

Suddenly, the angel appeared again. She could not see him, but she knew that he was there. She pulled the whole blanket and covered all her body, shivering. "Dear God, strengthen me!" she kept saying. Then the angel said again, "Greetings, favored one, the Lord is with you." Mary listened to the words and thought "His voice is very peaceful, and the greeting is certainly encouraging." There was a brief silence. To her, it felt like the angel was trying to give her a chance to think.

Though still frightened, she pulled her courage together and peeked from under the blanket in the direction of the voice. She could see the angel's feet beside her. She raised her eyes until they caught his. He smiled soothingly and said, "Do not be afraid Mary, for you have found favor with God."

"You are an angel; is that how you know my name?" she asked.

"I am Gabriel, do not be afraid, Mary, for you have found favor with God. Look at me and do not be afraid," he answered.

Mary sat up, holding the blanket tightly against her. Still shaking, she looked at him, then the angel continued, "*And now, you will conceive in your womb and have a son, and you will name him Jesus.*" Mary, shocked by the news, said in a trembling voice, "*How can this be since I am a virgin?*" The angel answered her, "*The Holy Spirit will come upon you, and the power of the Most High will overshadow you; and the child to be born will be called the Son of God.*

41

And now, your relative Elizabeth in her old age has also conceived a son; and this is the sixth month for her who was said to be barren. For nothing will be impossible with God."

Gabriel came closer to Mary and slowly reached out for her hands. After some hesitation, Mary let go of the blanket reached out to him. She had the strangest feeling as the angel kneeled gently, holding her hands. She knew that he was praying for her. The world stood still. He waited for her to respond. She bowed her head, closed her eyes and prayed silently. Then, she lifted her head, opened her eyes and looked straight at the angel.

With a confident voice she said, "*Here am I, the servant of the Lord; let it be with me according to your word.*" Then the angel departed from her.

VISITATION

Mary sat wrapped in her blanket, pondering the mystery she had just experienced, when her parents returned home. They found their daughter bewildered and silent. Mary told them about the revelation she had just witnessed. Her parents were amazed, but nevertheless believed her words. They remembered the days when they experienced such revelations and Mary was born to them as a result. "Precious daughter, you will have the son of the Most High. Praise the Lord. You must visit Elizabeth and see what she has to say. She must be very excited also. The Lord is so good to us. Elizabeth is now pregnant after all those years. He has blessed our family here and there. You must go and see her."

Mary looked at her father who was nodding his head in consent saying, "We are too old to travel anymore." The day after, *Mary set out and went with haste to a Judean town in the hill country, where she entered the house of Zechariah. When Elizabeth heard Mary's greeting, the child leapt in her womb. And Elizabeth was filled with the Holy Spirit and exclaimed with a loud cry, "Blessed are you among women, and blessed is the fruit of your womb. And why has this happened to me, that the mother of my Lord comes to me? For as soon as I heard the sound of your greeting, the child in my womb leapt for joy. And blessed is she who believed that there would be a fulfillment of what was spoken to her by the Lord.*"

And Mary said, "My soul magnifies the Lord, and my spirit rejoices in God my Saviour, for he has looked with favour on the lowliness of his servant. Surely, from now on all generations will call me blessed; for the Mighty One has done great things for me, and holy is his name. His mercy is for those who fear him from generation to generation. He has shown strength with his arm; he has scattered the proud in the thoughts of their hearts. He has brought down the powerful from their thrones, and lifted up the lowly; he has filled the hungry with good things, and sent the rich away empty. He has helped his servant Israel, in remembrance of his mercy, according to the promise he made to our ancestors, to Abraham and to his descendants forever."

And Mary remained with her for about three months and then returned to her home. Mary certainly needed all the support she could get from her parents to explain her abnormal situation to Joseph her husband when he returned to take her.

Mariotto Albertinelli, *Visitation*, Galleria degli Uffizi, Florence

JOSEPH'S PREDICAMENT[2]

A month later, Joseph arrived in Nazareth to take his wife home. Mary told him everything that had happened. Listening attentively, Joseph felt she was telling the truth. Mary's parents reassured him, but he was in shock. The socio-religious controversies he had to confront were too much to handle. "I will pray about this, and hope that God will get me through this predicament." He left the house and stayed at an inn in a nearby village.

That night, Joseph kept thinking about what to do with Mary and her unborn child. He said to himself, "*If I try to cover up her sin, I'll end up going against the law of the Lord. And if I disclose her condition to the people of Israel, I'm afraid that the child inside her might be heaven-sent and I'll end up handing innocent blood over to a death sentence. So what should I do with her? I'll divorce her quietly.*"[3] Joseph prayed that his decision was the right one and closed his eyes to sleep. He dreamt of an angel of the Lord saying to him, "*Joseph, do not be afraid to take Mary as your wife, for the child conceived in her is from the Holy Spirit. You shall name him Jesus, for he will save his people from their sins.*"[4]

The next morning, Joseph set out with haste to tell Mary about his dream. He was glad that such honor was bestowed on him. He took Mary as his wife, but to curtail social controversy over their relationship and the child in her womb, he decided not to return to Bethlehem until an opportune time, and moved his livelihood to Nazareth. Joachim, Mary's father helped him find a small cave near his home. Joseph, a builder by profession, divided the cave into two rooms, one to live and the other to work. "*Joseph had no marital relations with her until she had borne a son.*"[5]

BIRTH

One afternoon while Joseph was working in Sepphoris, a Roman city five miles away from Nazareth, a Roman soldier arrived in the city center to read aloud an imperial decree from Augustus Caesar. He announced a census of all subjects to begin in a month's time and ordered all to return to their hometown. Joseph arrived in Nazareth that evening to tell Mary what he had heard. "Mary, these are imperial orders and we cannot disregard them. We have to return to my hometown of Bethlehem in Judea."

"But I am in my ninth month," said Mary, "and it is a long distance to walk."

Joseph answered, "The good Lord will watch over us. I know it is far, so I will find a donkey to carry you all the way. We will stop and rest whenever you need. The census will start in a month. Who knows when the Romans will reach Bethlehem? If we are not there in time, we will be in trouble. You will meet my family. They will help us."

Mary consented. After dinner, they prayed together then went to sleep.

Two days later, they set out from Nazareth to Bethlehem. Joseph decided that it was better to take the road through the Jordan Valley because there were more villages on the way in case Mary needed help. Mary worried about her baby, about where they would stay in Bethlehem. Joseph tried to calm her anxious heart. He answered with a smile, "My cousin Absalom is in charge of the whole town. He is like a mayor. He will take care of us. Do not worry, dear."

Both talked endlessly about the child to be born. "I wonder what he will look like, the son of the Most High. Will he have black or brown hair? What will be the color of his eyes? Dark or light brown? Oh, I can't wait until he is born," said Mary cheerfully. "Whatever the color of his eyes, it is God's choice for him. But more important, what did the angel mean that Jesus will save his people from sin? How will he do that? Will he fight the Romans when he grows up? Will he inspire them into a new way of thought? Will he fight the corruption among the elders of Israel and restore our religion on the right path with the Most High?" Every day, they had a different idea of what it meant. Such thoughts kept them going and nourished them. Every day, they walked between 8 and 12 miles, depending on Mary's strength. After two weeks, they reached the outskirts of Jerusalem. They stopped to drink some water when Mary felt a lot of movement in her womb. "Jesus is really kicking in my womb. He must be feeling that we are near Jerusalem," she said.

"Of course he must be, since it is here where the Most High resides," answered Joseph. They decided to spend the night in Jerusalem.

The next morning, after a good breakfast, they set out to Bethlehem. They finally arrived in the early afternoon. They went through the village until they reached a large house at the edge of the town. Joseph helped Mary off the donkey. While she took a sip of water, she looked at the front of the house. It looked much like her own in Nazareth, a large cave dug in the bedrock. Limestone bricks stacked with mortar in rows covered the main entrance. There was a small window on the upper-right side. The large main door on the left was out of wood with a metal door knob and a round knocking handle on its upper end.

"Did you build this house as well?" Mary asked her husband. "I see Joseph written all over it."

"I designed it and helped build it too, dear," he answered.

He tied the donkey in front of the house with the other animals – two sheep, a goat and a young bull. He held Mary tenderly from the arm and helped her walk towards the door. He held the round handle and knocked twice. The door opened. Absalom, an old man with a serious white beard, was overtaken with joy when he saw his cousin, Joseph. They embraced warmly and entered the house where a young man was cleaning the stable under the living room.

Like any simple house of the time, the living room, also known as the upper room, served as the bedroom at night. Usually, if there was no need for the sleeping mattresses, they were stacked and placed in a corner of the room in the daytime. Joseph still held Mary firmly as she went up the steps to the living room. It was full of people; men on one side and women on the other. They were all talking cheerfully, while having a cup of hot herbal mix. "Luckily, we have those Romans, who ordered the census. Nowadays, it is the only way to see each other," joked one of them.

Joseph laughed and replied, "I think I know who is saying this nonsense – Abraham!"

The women, who saw pregnant Mary, rearranged the cushions for her to sit comfortably among the other women. Once everybody was settled, Absalom asked Joseph, "Where have you been all this time? We were worried,

House of Parables, showing an upper room and stable underneath, Taybeh, West Bank

you have been away for months."

Joseph answered, "I have moved my livelihood to Nazareth, the hometown of my wife, Mary. I know it is not customary for a man to do so, but I felt called by the good Lord and he has been very generous with me. I built us a small house near her parent's house and I have found a lot of building and carpentry work in Sepphoris, the new city in Galilee, not far away from there." He continued, "Mary had a very long ride; she is in her ninth month and I think the child is almost ready to be born!"

The woman cheered with joy and excitement. "May the good Lord bless you and the child in your womb," said one of them. Mary answered, "Thank you so much, may the good Lord bless you all as well!" Joseph asked about those present he did not recognize. "They are distant relatives," said Absalom, "who are back in Bethlehem for the census, like you. All 500 of us in this small town are related somehow. I have made arrangements for the travelers to stay either here with us or with other relatives. As for you and Mary, you are my guests for as long as you want."

Mary felt greater movement in her womb. Everybody noticed Mary's sudden excitement. Absalom's wife Leah told Sarah to take one of the mattresses down to the stable where Joseph led her. Joseph went back up and waited with Absalom in the upper room, the rest of the men went outside in the yard. Leah helped Mary lie on the mattress and checked her, "You are almost ready to deliver," she said, "It is soon." Sarah ran out to fetch a neighbor who was a midwife. Leah announced the good news to the men upstairs. So as not to disturb the women later, Absalom led

the animals into the stable while Joseph went down to fill the two mangers with hay stacked in the corner. As he filled the second manger, he felt Mary's presence. He looked and suddenly his eyes caught hers. She was trying to turn, but her round belly made it hard for her to move. She said tenderly, "Fill it up well, dear, make it very comfortable for the baby."

"I had the same idea," replied Joseph affectionately. "Please relax, don't get up and I will take care of it."

A few minutes later, Sarah returned with the midwife, who asked for hot water and some clean cloth. Leah provided everything she needed. In the early hours of the night, the birth was very smooth, almost without pain. The midwife held the baby, slapped his behind gently, as was the custom, and made him cry. Joseph's heart jumped with joy when he heard the baby. The midwife washed the baby with warm water, wrapped him in swaddling clothes and gave him to his mother. Mary could not believe it herself. She was finally a mother and deep inside her heart, she pondered how special she was in God's sight. She remembered the angel's words, "Greetings favored one." When she held baby Jesus in her arms wrapped in swaddling clothes, she understood what he had meant. Joseph went down to greet his wife and took the child in his arms, praising God. He placed the baby in the manger he had filled earlier with hay. It was warm and cozy, just like a crib. At that moment, the bull and the donkey sat beside the manger as if paying homage to the newborn. The sheep and the goat also came closer to rest at the foot of the manger.

VISIT OF THE SHEPHERDS

Later that night, while the women prepared a herbal drink, there was an unexpected knock at the door. "That is strange, who would come at this late hour!" said Absalom. Joseph was closest to the door and he opened it slightly to see who it was. He saw five men wearing shabby clothes, two of them holding staffs in their hands. Joseph's first impression was that they were shepherds.

"Good evening, sir," they said.

"Good evening, how can I help you?" answered Joseph.

"Well, we have something strange to tell you, but before we do, was a child born here today? We are shepherds who just came from the fields to ask around. Some men pointed us to this house and said that a child was born here today."

"That is true, but who are you and what do you want?" answered Joseph.

"Can we please see the child, only a glimpse, and then we will tell you everything we know."

Joseph was confused. He spoke to Absalom, then said to them, "Only one of you can come in, and just for a minute, holding a staff in his hand." The eldest of them went into the stable where he saw Mary and the baby. "It is true," he shouted with joy, "It is exactly as we were told, praise be to God."

"What are you talking about?" asked Joseph.

The shepherd answered, "As night fell, while we were keeping watch over our flock, an angel of the Lord stood before us. Everything around us felt glorious with the Lord's presence. We were terrified. But the angel said to us, *'Do not be afraid; for see – I am bringing you good news of great joy for all the people; to you is born this day in the city of David a Saviour, who is the Messiah, the Lord. This will be a sign for you: you will find a child wrapped in bands of cloths and lying in a manger.'*

He continued, "Then there were many more angels singing, *'Glory to God in the highest heaven, and on earth peace among those whom he favors!'*[6] We left two of us to guard our flock and came looking for the child. When I saw him lying in the manger, my spirit was overjoyed from this glorious occasion. Praise be to God. Can I please call my friends?"

Joseph and Absalom let them in. The women were marveled at the news. Just then, other relatives arrived and saw all these men at the door. The shepherds were still overwhelmed by the occasion and told everyone who too were in awe. All said, *"Glory to God in the highest heaven, and on earth peace among those whom he favors!"* *"But Mary treasured all these things and pondered them in her heart. Then the shepherds left and returned to the fields and their flocks."*[7]

CIRCUMCISION AND NAMING OF JESUS

On the eighth day after the birth, the child was circumcised into the covenant as Jesus. Nobody asked the parents why they chose the name, rather than that of the father, since they all respected Joseph very much.

His age, stubbornness, independence, righteousness, and above all, the joy he displayed every time he held the child in his arms were enough that no one would be able to change his mind.

A month passed, and Romans in charge of the census had still not passed through Bethlehem. However, there was news of official registrations in other towns, so Absalom let his guests stay longer in his overcrowded household to wait their turn patiently. There was so much love in that simple house. The occupants still marveled at what they had been told about the child by the shepherds. Of course, neither Joseph nor Mary wanted to disclose much of their own secret. All they said was that they had a feeling that their son was special.

PRESENTATION IN THE TEMPLE

After 40 days, as custom required, Joseph took Mary and her child to the temple in Jerusalem to fulfill the law requirements. While Mary went to the women's ritual bath, Joseph went to the money changers in the Tyropeon Valley street, just outside the western wall of the temple. He changed some money from Roman to Jewish coins to buy the sacrifice he had to offer on behalf of the child Jesus. He then went to the men's ritual bath before meeting with Mary. They walked in the street up and down looking and asking the prices of lambs, pigeons and doves. Joseph did not have enough money to buy a lamb. So he bought the minimum required of him by the law of Moses, a couple of turtle doves. The shopkeeper took out two doves, inspected them carefully under the watchful eyes of Joseph and tied their legs, making sure they were not injured or diseased. Joseph carried them along the street, while Mary held baby Jesus affectionately close to her heart. They finally reached the steps that led to the temple; both of them were very excited to be there again, reliving nostalgic memories of their previous visits. The majestic building revealed itself with every step they took. They reached the top and were about to enter the Court of the Gentiles, when Mary noticed an old man wearing a grey robe and a red outer garment coming towards them. "Look Joseph. Jesus must be as excited as we are to be here!" she said.

Joseph turned to look at Jesus when he noticed an old man wearing a white robe and a brown outer garment coming towards them. He had a very long beard that bore witness to the many years he had lived. He greeted them, and introduced himself as Old Simeon. Joseph seemed to remember the name. He remembered hearing about an old righteous and a devout Simeon, who was respected by everybody living in Jerusalem. Simeon who had overheard Mary saying that the face of Jesus was radiating, asked if he could hold the child. Mary obliged and Jesus' face became even more radiant. He reached out with his tiny hand and pulled the beard of Old Simeon, whose face, in spite of wrinkles, seemed to have received a spell of youthful hope and consolation.

He said praising God, "*Master, now you are dismissing your servant in peace, according to your word; for my eyes have seen your salvation, which you have prepared in the presence of all peoples, a light for revelation to the Gentiles and for glory to your people Israel.*"[8] Then he looked at Mary and said, "*This child is destined for the falling and the rising of many in Israel, and to be a sign that will be opposed so that the inner thoughts of many will be revealed – and a sword will pierce your own soul too.*"[9] He handed the child back to Mary, shook the hand of Joseph and went his

Philippe de Champaigne, *Presentation in the Temple*,
Musées royaux des Beaux-Arts de Belgique, Brussels

way. They were amazed about what he said about the child.

As they went further, another man stopped Joseph and told him, "What did the strange old man say to you?" Joseph didn't reply. "He has always been looking for the consolation of Israel," continued the stranger. He actually told me once that he had a revelation that he would not die until he saw God's Messiah. "What did he tell you? Does he think your child is the Messiah?" asked the man persistently. Joseph and Mary were suspicious of the inquisitive questions of that man and they kept going.

With the feeling of being followed, they

went into the second court of the temple. There seemed to be a lot of activity at one corner. Many people gathered around an old lady whom Mary knew. *"Her name is Anna. She is a prophet of great age. She had lived with her husband seven years after her marriage. Then she lost her husband and has been a widow ever since. She must be about eighty four years old now. She has never left the temple. She is worshipping here with fasting and prayer day and night. She has amazing dedication."*[10] While Mary was still speaking, the old lady suddenly stopped talking. It was as if she had heard Mary talking about her. She asked the people to open the way as she stood up hastily. She came straight to Mary and looked at her face, as if asking permission to hold the child, took the baby in her arms and raised him high up saying, "God, I give you praise, I give you thanks for this child; your wisdom is beyond our grasping, and this child at your word will be the redemption of all Jerusalem!"[11]

Joseph and Mary felt a strange trembling in their hearts. Ever since the annunciation, Mary tried to control her feelings, but could not hold back anymore. She was overwhelmed and caught in thought. The fullness of the message that the angel carried to her had finally been transformed into a child that she was holding in her own arms. She was thinking, "I am the one. I really am the favored one. I am the mother of the Messiah that everybody is waiting for. I cannot believe it. I am the mother of the salvation of Jerusalem. All these people, they are all waiting for him, my son, my most precious son."

Joseph noticed that Mary's features were changing. He could easily see that she was blushing; her dark black hair and white skin revealed that easily. She had an exceptional calm beauty. Joseph looked at her sweet eyes, and felt a part of her spirit reaching out to his heart. He seemed to have understood what Mary was thinking about. He touched her shoulder lovingly, she smiled, and both continued their walk in the direction of the inner court to offer the sacrifice. They stopped at the gate because beyond it was inaccessible to women. With the child and the doves, Joseph went straight in. He was greeted by one of the priests who sacrificed the doves to the glory of God, asking him to bless the child.

After an hour, Joseph came out, took Mary and headed down the steps to leave the temple. They noticed the man who had asked Joseph about Simeon still following them. Worried, they hurried down the steps and quickly mingled in the crowds to lose him. The family decided then to return to Bethlehem. The strange man who followed them in the temple reported to King Herod what he had heard from Simeon and Anna about the child. The king was furious, "I will not have another claimant to my throne."

VISIT OF THE WISE MEN

While King Herod was thinking of a way to find out who the child's parents were, Roman officials arrived to register all who were in Absalom's house. After the census, Joseph told his relatives who were so happy with the child that he had to return to Nazareth with his family. They kept them from leaving. Everybody in the house felt blessed; there was a compelling joy that was hard to let go. Eventually Joseph's small

Giotto di Bondone, *The Birth of Jesus*, Cappella degli Scrovegni, Padova

family stayed for a few months. Joseph and his relatives found work first in Herodium and then in Jerusalem.

During that time, Joseph and the other men were sitting outside the house one night. There was no moon and the skies were clear. They were talking about the beautiful stars of that night when they noticed one having a peculiar shine to it. They all saw it. It was moving for a few minutes, then stopped just above their heads.

"Isn't that strange!" said one of them.

"It is very strange!" answered Joseph.

"Look, its glow is increasing. I wonder what that is?" said another.

They all kept looking at it for about an hour when they saw some camels approaching from the distance. It was dark, but they could see that there were at least ten camels and a donkey with people on them. When the riders came closer, they stopped. They were wearing clothing that was not customary for Jews or Romans and were talking in a strange language that Joseph and the other men could not understand. The colorful clothing revealed they were wealthy. It was clear from their conversation that they were quite excited, talking about that mysterious star because they were pointing at it all the time.

The man riding on the donkey spoke to them, and a brief dialogue went on for a minute. He then turned to Joseph and the others, greeting them in their language of Aramaic. He explained that he was a local interpreter hired for a few days by the men he was accompanying. Pointing to them, he continued, "They are astrologers from the East and have something to say to the owner of the house. They have been studying the stars for many years. Based on their calculations, the apparition of that strange looking bright star and its movement is a manifestation of a great

king recently born. They followed the star until it led them to Jerusalem. They assumed that the child was born to the royal family and so they went to see King Herod asking him, "*Where is the child who has been born king of the Jews? For we have observed his star at its rising, and have come to pay him homage?*"[12] Herod invited them to stay with him in the palace. A few days later, after inquiring the chief priests and scribes about the Messiah, he called his guests and said that the king was to be born in Bethlehem. Herod told them, "*Go and search diligently for the child; and when you have found him, bring me word so that I may also go and pay him homage.*"[13]

Getting off the donkey and walking towards the house, he continued, "Gladdened by the news, they set out until they reached this place. They were saying that the star has stopped moving. They think it is over your house." Joseph's relatives listened and looked at each other. Then they turned to Joseph who tried to hide his joy at the news. "Please, come into the house," said Absalom. Joseph went in ahead of them and notified Mary of what was happening. The astrologers dismounted, and "*on entering the house, they saw the child with Mary, his mother; and they knelt down and paid him homage. Then opening their treasure chests, they offered him gifts of gold, frankincense and myrrh.*"[14] Mary was overjoyed. She kept pondering over those special moments and treasured them in her heart.

The wise men left the house and decided to set camp in the fields until the next morning. They planned to return to King Herod and tell him that they had found the newborn. That night though, their eldest had a strange dream. He was warned not to return to Herod for he intended to kill the child. In the morning, he told the other magi about his dream, and they all decided not to return to Jerusalem, but to seek an alternative route back to Persia.

Before their departure, they returned to Joseph and his relatives and told them of their dream. They all believed that Jesus' life was in danger. Joseph immediately remembered the inquisitive man who followed his family in the temple. "He must be Herod's spy!" he thought. He was especially concerned since he had heard that Herod had recently ordered the execution of two of his sons, Alexander and Aristobulus. All the country knew how paranoid the king was over questions of succession. "If he can kill his own sons, he can certainly kill Jesus. It is only a matter of time before he finds out where we are," he said to his relatives. That night an angel appeared to him in a dream and said, "*Get up, take the child and his mother, and flee to Egypt, and remain there until I tell you; for Herod is about to search for the child, to destroy him.*"[15] Joseph woke up Mary and his relatives to tell them about his disturbing dream. They all agreed that the young family should leave that same night. Joseph gave his hosts half of the gold that Jesus received from the wise men, took his wife and child and escaped to Egypt.

MASSACRE OF THE INNOCENTS

When the wise men had announced news of the rising star, Herod knew it was the child who his spy saw at the temple. Here was a golden opportunity to identify the newborn and get rid of him, but the magi never returned. Furious, Herod ordered his soldiers to seek and kill every male child aged two years or younger in Bethlehem and the vicinity. By this time, Joseph and his family were miles away under God's protection.

FIRST YEARS

Mary loved Jesus more than anything in the world. But like any other good mother, she had to go through tough days until her baby started sleeping the whole night. The days went by and Jesus was growing and becoming stronger. After a few months, "*when Herod died, an angel of the Lord suddenly appeared in a dream to Joseph in Egypt and said, 20'Get up, take the child and his mother, and go to the land of Israel, for those who were seeking the child's life are dead.' 21Then Joseph got up, took the child and his mother, and went to the land of Israel. 22But when he heard that Archelaus was ruling over Judea in place of his father Herod, he was afraid to go there. And after being warned in a dream, he went away to the district of Galilee. There he made his home in a town called Nazareth.*[16]

Jesus continued to grow. When he produced some teeth, Mary started giving him some food to eat; the first time, Joseph was there with her. She put Jesus in her lap holding the clay bowl of lentil soup. As Joseph dipped the spoon in the bowl, Jesus made a sudden kick and the bowl slipped off his mother's hand and onto the floor. Neither Mary nor Joseph knew how to react. For a moment, they looked at each other with sad amusement and then at Jesus who was giggling; he surely seemed to be enjoying what he just did. They could not contain themselves and burst out into laughter. After cleaning the mess, they tried again; this time Joseph held the bowl and spoon a safe distance from Jesus. As the baby took a first sip, he started shaking his hands and feet with excitement. Both his parents understood and gave him more until he was full.

One day when Joseph returned home from his workshop, Jesus crawled up to him. Joseph held him up high, gave him many kisses and put him back down on the floor. Jesus was still holding his dad's hand. He pulled himself up. Joseph quickly called Mary in the kitchen. "Look," he exclaimed, "he is standing up, he is going to walk!" Mary quickly joined them. After a couple of falls, Jesus started walking on his own. Excited, both parents took turns holding Jesus and covered him with lots of kisses. There was so much joy in that little house.

IN THE TEMPLE

"*Now every year his parents went to Jerusalem for the festival of the Passover. [42]And when he was twelve years old, they went up as usual for the festival. [43]When the festival was ended and they started to return, the boy Jesus stayed behind in Jerusalem, but his parents did not know it. [44]Assuming that he was in the group of travelers, they went a day's journey. Then they started to look for him among their relatives and friends. [45]When they did not find him, they returned to Jerusalem to search for him.*"[17]

Jesus was not afraid to remain alone in the city. He was concerned that his parents would be worried about him, but he knew deep inside that he would be found. In Jerusalem, he felt at home while walking in the streets, looking around with tremendous interest. He noticed everybody and everything. It was as if he were keeping a record in his mind. He saw Roman soldiers patrolling the streets, while others took their food break. Some led a prisoner tied in shackles. Jesus noticed that the prisoner could barely walk, his face bruised with a sad look begging for mercy. Jesus approached him. The soldiers, seeing a shadow approaching them, reached for their swords only to relax when they realized it was just a little boy. Jesus asked the man, "Why are you in chains?" The man looked at him with broken pride and answered, "I stole a loaf of bread from the market and I was caught." They were taking him to the Antonia fortress to be flogged. Jesus reached into the small bag he was carrying on his shoulder and gave a piece of bread to the prisoner with a compassionate smile as he was dragged away.

Later, Jesus noticed an old blind man begging at a street corner. Jesus sat opposite him, watching as hundreds of people passed by. He noticed that many were very rich from their clothing and the animals they were pulling to be sacrificed in the temple. Some Levites and priests with their traditional white vestments and white ephods also passed the blind man without paying much attention to him. After several hours, only four people noticed the beggar. Two of them gave him a coin, a Roman and a priest. Jesus felt very sad at what he witnessed.

It was getting late, and Jesus thought that the best place to be was at the temple. He hurried before it became too dark. As he got closer, a priest noticed him and said, "Young man, I saw you sitting in the street earlier today. Where are your parents?"

Jesus answered, "I am from Nazareth,

Giotto di Bondone, *Jesus Among the Scribes*, Cappella degli Scrovegni, Padova

and I got separated from my parents after the festival. But this is my father's house!" he said cheerfully pointing in the direction of the temple building.

"Your father's house? Come here, boy. Don't worry; you can stay with me until your parents find you. It is best that you stay in the temple. We will wait at the main entrance where lost children and parents usually get together. What is your name?"

"My name is Jesus. You are a good-hearted priest, I saw you give the beggar a coin, while many others were ignoring him."

"You are a smart boy. My name is Joseph. I am from Arimathea."

"Can you tell me more about the priests?" asked Jesus eagerly.

"I am a Levite priest. I am one of thousands of priests, descendants of the tribe of Levi. Under the law of Moses, we, as descendants of Aaron, are the ones who perform the rituals of Judaism. We are privileged to offer the sacrifices and incense to the Lord, and most importantly to give the Lord's blessing of peace and love to his people every day."

"Can you bless me?" asked Jesus.

The priest did not hesitate. He lifted his hands towards the heavens and uttered the words, "*The Lord bless you and keep you; 25the Lord make his face to shine upon you, and be gracious to you; 26the Lord lift up his countenance upon you, and give you peace.*"[18]

"Thank you. Please tell me, what is your day like?" asked Jesus.

"We wake up before dawn, immerse in a ritual bath to cleanse, meet with the other priests in the temple for the daily morning sacrifice. Then we cast lots for slaughtering the animals, cleaning the altar of sacrifices, burning the incense, changing the oil of the Menorah and other things."

"Yes, two days ago, my father Joseph and I came here and offered pigeons as our Passover sacrifice. My father told me that the sacrifice was supposed to help us get closer to God. To be honest with you, I did not really understand what he meant. Can you tell me more about sacrifices?"

There was something about Jesus that the priest could not fully comprehend; he felt that there was something in the boy's voice that compelled him to answer the question. "Our Lord is the God of Mercy and Love. He has created man in a physical body and a spirit. The body is the seat of the darker side of man, while the spirit is the place that houses the attributes of God. Man is in constant search of spiritual perfection. Once spiritual perfection is attained, a person feels much closer to his creator and tries to resemble his attributes of mercy and love. To that end, everything else God created is intended to help man accomplish this relationship with his creator. Man needs to keep that relationship revived and active all the time. Since man, whether intentionally or not, deviates from these actions of mercy and love, the sacrificial system can help him restore that relationship."

Jesus interrupted, "But how can the killing of an animal be an act of mercy and love?"

The priest said, "You see, my son, man rather than animal is the center of God's creation. The sacrifice is not an end in itself. It is part of a system that can only be accepted if accompanied by real intentions of the one in whose name it is being offered. Therefore, the offered sacrifice represents the death of the physical side of a man who is away from God."

Just then, a man pulling a large bull passed by. The priest continued, "That Pharisee with the sacrifice is trying to bring his entire being into the service of God by denying his own animal urges. He wishes to please his creator and hopes that the aroma of his sacrifice will be an accepted act of purification that will provide for a strengthening relationship with God and a revelation of one's true purpose."

Jesus said, "I saw that Pharisee today at the other end of the city, pulling his bull to the pool to be washed. He seemed to me more concerned with showing off the size of his sacrifice rather than offering a small coin to an old beggar whom he pushed aside."

"Son, do not take him as a good example. The world is full of good and bad. Such people need to offer a sacrifice in the hope that God will open their minds and hearts to his path of mercy and love," said the priest.

"So individuals can only be purified if they offer sacrifices. What about those who cannot afford to do so?" asked Jesus.

"Well, the law allows for a minimum sacrifice that would be accepted," answered Joseph.

"My parents told me that they had offered two turtle doves when I was presented as a baby to the temple," said Jesus.

"That is the minimum required from any Jew for his firstborn son," answered the priest.

"But don't pagans also offer sacrifices?" asked Jesus.

"Gentiles offer sacrifices to different gods and for different purposes. Jews offer their sacrifice to the one and only God, creator of all with the intention of getting closer to him. It is getting late, we'd better go home. We will come back early tomorrow morning," said the priest.

They went to his home in upper Jerusalem and spent the night. The next day they returned to the temple, but they kept going back to the gate where parents and lost children customarily waited.

Joseph the priest and Jesus had countless talks about God and life, Jews, Pharisees, Sadducees and Samaritans. They also talked about the Torah and the prophets. Joseph marveled at how smart Jesus was and how he was able to grasp some very deep religious arguments. He decided to introduce him to the elders and teachers. The second day passed, and still there was no sign of Mary and Joseph. The priest took Jesus again to his home for the night.

The next morning, they set out again to the temple. The priest took Jesus to the outer court where there was already an assembly of teachers. He introduced him saying, "This is Jesus. He is from Nazareth. After the festivals he lost his parents. He has been my guest for a couple of days. We have had lots of talks and he has demonstrated a wonderful grasp of the scriptures. I have some duties in the temple today, so I am going to leave him here with you until I return."

Joseph bid Jesus farewell in case he found his parents before the priest finished his duties. "I am sure you are going to become a great teacher one day. When you come back to Jerusalem, make sure you come and visit me," he said to Jesus.

"You are a good priest. I hope there are many like you, my friend. May my heavenly Father bless you and keep you. *[25]May he make his face to shine upon you, and be gracious to you; [26]May he lift up his countenance upon you, and give you peace,"* answered Jesus with a smile. The priest left with a mystified but satisfied look on his face.

The teachers welcomed Jesus in their midst. They conversed with him for hours. More and more of them were arriving. Just then, Mary and Joseph found Jesus sitting among the teachers, listening to them and asking them questions. *[47]And all who heard him were amazed at his understanding and his answers.* [48]*When his parents saw him they were astonished; and his mother said to him, "Child, why have you treated us like this? Look, your father and I have been searching for you in great anxiety."* [49]*He said to them, "Why were you searching for me? Did you not know that I must be in my Father's house?"* [50]*But they did not understand what he said to them.*[19]

Just then, Joseph of Arimathea returned. Jesus was so excited to see him. When Joseph thanked him wholeheartedly for taking care of their son, the priest invited them home for a meal. "There is something special about that boy," he admitted to his father. As much as Joseph wanted to share his secret about Jesus, he was committed to keeping it to himself for the sake of his son. Nevertheless, both Josephs became good friends and exchanged visits whenever they were in each other's towns. Their friendship continued for many years.

RETURN TO NAZARETH

Mary and Joseph took Jesus and started the return trip to Nazareth with friends who had come with them to look for the boy. Jesus was very enthusiastic about what he had heard and seen in Jerusalem. He kept repeating verses from scripture. Mary was amazed at his knowledge and conversed with him about some issues, but she could not keep up with his mature arguments. A few hours later, Jesus left his mother with other women and walked beside his father to ask all sorts of questions. Joseph did his best to answer, but after a while he got tired and said, "Son, when we return home, I will talk to Rabbi Moses about enrolling you in the synagogue school of Nazareth for a couple of years. I have done my share, teaching you to read and write, but I can tell by what I saw at the temple that you need somebody who is more literate than I am to help you grow in the faith. Rabbi Moses will teach you the scriptures and the psalms. He is an old wise man and you can learn a lot from him. You'd better behave and not disgrace me! Is that understood?"

"Yes sir," answered Jesus happily.

"You are also at an age when you have to learn your father's profession. So you will go to school in the morning and join me in the workshop in the afternoons," continued Joseph.

"When will I have time to play with my friends?" asked Jesus in a cheerless voice.

"You have been playing for 12 years, my son. It is time for you to behave like a man. I won't be around for long, and you need to take care of your mother after me."

Jesus' face brightened at the mention of his mother. He turned back and saw her walking between two women. Their eyes met. Joseph noticed this affection, and Jesus consented to his request.

GROWING UP IN NAZARETH

When they arrived in Nazareth, Jesus was enrolled in school only a few minutes away from home. He attended class with seven other children aged 12 to 14, five days a week from nine until noon. Though he enjoyed school very much, he was always eager to return home and jump into his mother's lap. Mary greeted him with much affection and he felt warmth and love as he hugged her. As he told her about the new things he had learned at school, Mary prepared the family lunch. He especially enjoyed the soup. He got used to his mother telling him, "Your father will be home soon; please help me bake the bread." He even started repeating it to himself before his mother said it. As Jesus placed the dough on the hot rocks of the oven and watched it rise, the smell of fresh bread always made him hungry.

Every day, when Joseph returned from his morning shift, the family had lunch together and then the men went to the workshop. Joseph spent hours teaching Jesus the secrets of his future profession. He taught him how to make wooden furniture, how to add finishing touches of intricate carving to make it into a piece of art. He taught him how to build houses made of stone or a combination of wood and stone using hammers, chisels and knives. After a few months, the boy excelled at what he was doing.

Years passed, then one day Jesus called his mother to the workshop, while Joseph was away delivering some furniture. "Look mother, I have made you an olive wood carving."

"Dear son, you don't have to do anything for me. You are my most precious gift."

"Oh dear lady, my Father in heaven has chosen you, and you have consented to his request. You are a blessing to me and I have made this for you. You will have to keep this a secret between us, for as you know in public, we have to abide by the law of the elders, at least for now."

Jesus took out a piece of carved wood wrapped in cloth, unfolded it and gave it to his mother. It was a small statue of an angel overshadowing his mother. Mary looked at it with amazement. "You made this for me. It is wonderful!" She caressed it, for it seemed so alive and was intricately carved.

Jesus replied, "The path to man's salvation from sin was set in motion following your consent to the announcement of the angel. You are the one I chose to become flesh in. You had the choice to refuse but you did not; I still remember your words, *'I am the handmaid of the Lord, let it be done to me according to thy word.'* Dear lady, harsh and cruel days are yet to come, your heart will be torn apart, and you will have doubts whether you made the right decision. I made this statue for you, as a reminder for you that you are a part of my Father's plan of salvation; the one who follows his will, has life eternal, and I dwell in him. When you have doubts, look at the statue, and remember that my Father's blessings have been bestowed on you ever since that moment." Jesus leaned over, and gave his mother a tender kiss on her forehead. Mary, moved by the moment, held on to her son sobbing.

On Fridays there was no school. So at dawn, Joseph would take Jesus to nearby villages and cities to look for work. Jesus enjoyed these journeys, especially visits to the largest city in the area, Sepphoris. During Joseph's negotiations with customers Jesus would sneak away to explore the streets and the theatre. He often lost himself in the rehearsals of comedies at the theater and music bands. Joseph rebuked Jesus a couple of times, because as a Jew he was not supposed to see the Roman theatre. But Jesus did not stop. As much as he wanted to obey his father, he could not resist. There was something in the music that kept calling him to return. Joseph eventually got used to Jesus' disappearance and stopped worrying since he knew where to find him. He even led activities of his own with Jesus and taught him about Roman life as well as Jewish customs.

Saturdays were assigned to the Lord. As there was no work, Joseph made sure that he and the boy took the ritual bath before going to the synagogue. Rabbi Moses usually asked Jesus to read from the scriptures in public, bragging in front of everybody that the boy was his outstanding student. Jesus read loudly and clearly. When he got older, he was also asked to comment on the text he read. Slowly but surely, Jesus became a very gifted scripture reader and an eloquent speaker.

DEATH OF JOSEPH

Jesus was growing up in human and divine favor. One Thursday morning, he was walking in Sepphoris with an aging Joseph who felt very tired; he said to Jesus, "Come and sit down here on the steps. My dear son, I am an old man and my time on this earth is almost done. But before I go, I feel I need to tell you how I see the things around us. You do not talk much about the work you are preparing to do for our people, but I want you to be aware of these things before you do. I love you and I love my people, but I know my people can be very vicious sometimes so you need to be careful. You see, my son, God has created us all – humans, Jews and Gentiles – in his own image, but for some unknown reason, he has chosen Jews and bequeathed us a duty above all other nations. God made us a holy people and a light to the world. The Gentiles worship many gods, but we worship the one and only creator of all the universe, blessed be his name. Our actions dictate what happens to the world. We keep sinning, and the whole world is punished as a result. After all, we are human. But God's mercy supersedes all. He gave us the temple and provided us with a system to atone for our sins. When that was not enough and we continued to deviate from his path, he sent us a prophet with a profound message urging us to return to the righteous path. Sometimes we returned, but most times, we have become too proud and too absorbed in our traditions and customs, that we have missed the point of our selection as a holy people. Maliciously, we have killed our prophets and unintentionally venerated our kings and the traditions of the elders more than our creator."

The death of Joseph, Church of St. Joseph, Nazareth

Joseph continued, "As a result, our people have been torn between the spirit and the truth; the spirit of the law and the sad truth of our abuse of it. Sadducees see themselves as an elite group; unfortunately they are too immersed in their religious practices in and around Jerusalem that they have become alienated from the people they are supposed to lead. The Pharisees are trapped in an endless debate of the law. The same law that was to liberate them from slavery has enslaved them: they don't know whether to eat the egg that the hen laid on a Sabbath day or not. The Samaritans have built themselves a temple and do things their way in total competition with our traditions. And now we have the zealots threatening to take up arms, the Essenes breaking away from the temple traditions, abandoning Jerusalem and its practices, calling everybody outside their community evil. The Holy Name only knows what will come next."

Jesus noticed that Joseph was overburdened with sorrow. As if consoling himself, he looked at Jesus caressing his shoulder and said, "My son, God has anointed you to change all that and unite us all again, your mother and I know that. May his name be blessed forever." Jesus looked back at the aging Joseph with a heartfelt gaze and warm smile, "You are a righteous old man. Thank you for all you have done for me. You have a special place in my Father's kingdom."

That night Joseph passed away. Mary and Jesus sat beside him as he took his last breath. Mary was sad to lose a husband, but her heart was satisfied to know that he was to be with God. Jesus bent over and gave his earthly father a kiss on his forehead saying, "You have given me your life. Truly I tell you, nothing you have done for me will go in vain."

The neighbors came over and took Mary to a nearby home, while they prepared Joseph's burial. Jesus watched with mystified eyes as psalms were recited. Joseph's body was washed then wrapped with white linen cloth and special bandages around the feet and hands. Finally a cloth covered his head and the prayers concluded.

At noon, a funeral procession in the whole town of Nazareth was held with Jesus and his cousins James, Joses, Simon and Judas carrying the body on a bier to the tomb. Mary and other women were walking in front with silent tears. A sad flute accompanying sung psalms conveyed a surreal feeling of joyful sadness. Everybody was sad to lose a righteous man, but joyful for him, knowing that he was going to meet his creator. As the body was brought to the antechamber, the women surrounded it with aromatic spices and perfumes. The men then pushed it into a shaft tomb that was sealed with stone.

As was customary, the family of the deceased was not to cook on the burial day, so Joseph's good friend, Rabbi Moses, invited everybody to his home for lunch. Many people from different towns heard of the death and came to express their condolences to Jesus and his family. They mourned for 30 days. Jesus continued his craft in the workshop and went to the synagogue on Sabbath days until he was 30 years old.

PARABLE OF THE SOWER[20]

After this introduction to Jesus' life, let us look at one of his popular stories that teaches us the truth about God and offers us purpose.

[5] *"A sower went out to sow his seed; and as he sowed, some fell on the path and was trampled on, and the birds of the air ate it up.* [6] *Some fell on the rock; and as it grew up, it withered for lack of moisture.* [7] *Some fell among thorns, and the thorns grew with it and choked it.* [8] *Some fell into good soil, and when it grew, it produced a hundredfold."* As he said this, he called out, *"Let anyone with ears to hear listen!"*

Jesus' explanation

[11] *Now the parable is this: The seed is the word of God.* [12] *The ones on the path are those who have heard; then the devil comes and takes away the word from their hearts, so that they may not believe and be saved.* [13] *The ones on the rock are those who, when they hear the word, receive it with joy. But these have no root; they believe only for a while and in a time of testing fall away.* [14] *As for what fell among the thorns, these are the ones who hear; but as they go on their way, they are choked by the cares and riches and pleasures of life, and their fruit does not mature.* [15] *But as for that in the good soil, these are the ones who, when they hear the word, hold it fast in an honest and good heart, and bear fruit with patient endurance.*

A pilgrim under renovation will naturally want to become good soil to receive the seed. You might have doubts and say, "I am not ready" or "This is for people holier than I am" or any other good reason. The good news is that Jesus did not come to save those who were holy, but sinners and doubters like you and me. You should not allow such preconceived ideas of who is in or out to trouble your mind; all you have to do is make the personal choice of accepting to be good soil for the word of God. Here is a clue that can help you now that you are UNDER RENOVATION – become a child, humble and more receptive.

MATTHEW 18:1-5

[18] *At that time the disciples came to Jesus and asked, "Who is the greatest in the kingdom of heaven?"* [2] *He called a child, whom he put among them,* [3] *and said, "Truly I tell you, unless you change and become like children, you will never enter the kingdom of heaven.* [4] *Whoever becomes humble like this child is the greatest in the kingdom of heaven.* [5] *Whoever welcomes one such child in my name welcomes me.*

LUKE 18:15-17

[15] *People were bringing even infants to him that he might touch them; and when the disciples saw it, they sternly ordered them not to do it.* [16] *But Jesus called for them and said, "Let the little children come to me, and do not stop them; for it is to such as these that the kingdom of God belongs.* [17] *Truly I tell you, whoever does not receive the kingdom of God as a little child will never enter it."*

Prayer

Heavenly Father, source of all things; you became a child to save the world. You have embraced my humanity in its fullness, so that I might have life and have it abundantly. You humbled yourself and came down from your throne in heaven to reconcile my humanity back to you. I surrender to your will.

Help me become rich soil where you plant a seed. When my seed grows into a tree and my leaves spread, help me stand fast against all sorts of winds. When my leaves sprout, help me spread their fruit to other seeds and other trees without boasting and self-indulgence.

With a humble heart I say, you are Lord of all. Amen.

Notes

1. The reference to Mary being at the spring is found in the apocryphal gospel of James (http://blog.cnaughton.com/mediafiles/pdfs/james.pdf, n.d.), Chapter 11.
2. Joseph's predicament consult (http://blog.cnaughton.com/mediafiles/pdfs/james.pdf, n.d.), Chapter 13.
3. http://blog.cnaughton.com/mediafiles/pdfs/james.pdf, n.d.), Chapter 14.
4. Matthew 1:21-22.
5. Matthew 1:25.
6. Luke 2:10-13.
7. Luke 2:19.
8. Luke 2:29-32.
9. Luke 2:34-35.
10. Luke 2:36-37.
11. Luke 2:38.
12. Matthew 2:2.
13. Matthew 2:8.
14. Matthew 2:11.
15. Matthew 2:13.
16. Matthew 2:19-23.
17. Luke 2:41-46.
18. Numbers 6:24-26.
19. Luke 2:48-50.
20. Luke 8:4-15.

Possible terrain mentioned in the parable of the sower, West Bank

> Blessed are you among women and blessed is the fruit of thy womb.
>
> Luke 1:42

EIN KAREM

Let us continue our pilgrimage by exploring sites of the Holy Land following the general chronology of Jesus' life.

We begin in the little town of Ein Karem west of Jerusalem, which according to tradition is the location of the house of Zechariah and his wife Elizabeth, the parents of John the Baptist. Two churches were built there in the 19th and 20th centuries on the ruins of previous churches from Byzantine and Crusader times.

CHURCH OF THE VISITATION

The Church of the Visitation honors Mary's visit to Elizabeth. It was built in 1954 by Italian architect Antonio Barluzzi and is maintained today by Franciscan friars. On the walls of the outside court is Mary's canticle of praise, known as the Magnificat, in many languages.

LUKE 1:39-56

39 In those days Mary set out and went with haste to a Judean town in the hill country, 40where she entered the house of Zechariah and greeted Elizabeth. 41When Elizabeth heard Mary's greeting, the child leaped in her womb. And Elizabeth was filled with the Holy Spirit 42and exclaimed with a loud cry, "Blessed are you among women, and blessed is the fruit of your womb. 43And why has this happened to me, that the mother of my Lord comes to me? 44For as soon as I heard the sound of your greeting, the child in my womb leaped for joy. 45And blessed is she who believed that there would be a fulfillment of what was spoken to her by the Lord."

46And Mary said, "My soul magnifies the Lord, 47and my spirit rejoices in God my Saviour, 48for he has looked with favor on the lowliness of his servant. Surely, from now on all generations will call me blessed; 49for the Mighty One has done great things for me, and holy is his name. 50His mercy is for those who fear him from generation to generation. 51He has shown strength with his arm; he has scattered the proud in the thoughts of their hearts. 52He has brought down the powerful from their thrones, and lifted up the lowly; 53he has filled the hungry with good things, and sent the rich away empty. 54He has helped his servant Israel, in remembrance of his mercy, 55according to the promise he made to our ancestors, to Abraham and to his descendants forever." 56And Mary remained with her about three months and then returned to her home.

Church of the Visitation, Ein Karem

Shrine, Church of the Visitation, Ein Karem

Reflection

Regardless of distance, good news travels quickly. It travels even quicker when people are excited. Mary received not only one, but two wonderful pieces of news: her own pregnancy of the son of God, and her cousin Elizabeth's pregnancy, she who was called barren. She was so thrilled and excited that she traveled 100 miles in haste.

Mary was the first missionary carrying the good news – the gospel in her womb. She exemplified the joy of mission she undertook, and her excitement caused baby Jesus, just a few days old, to react in her womb and reach out in his spirit to another baby in another womb. John, a few months older than Jesus, leapt with joy and his mother felt it. She too was filled with the joy of the Holy Spirit.

The joy of preaching the gospel is equivalent to the joy of receiving it. The word lives in its giving and receiving.

Prayer

Mary served as mediator, physically and consciously carrying the gospel, Jesus Christ, in her womb. She said, *"Surely, from now on, all generations will call me blessed; for the Mighty One has done great things for me, and holy is his name."* She humbled herself and received the greatest gift of all. She became Blessed Mother of the Word.

Lord, I humbly pray that I am also worthy of carrying your word in my heart and that I show a similar excitement as I proclaim it. Like Mary, I want to be called blessed now and forever. Amen.

Mary's canticle of praise (Magnificat),
Church of the Visitation, Ein Karem

Mary meets Elizabeth, Church
of the Visitation, Ein Karem

CHURCH OF ST. JOHN IN THE MOUNTAINS

The Church of St. John in the Mountains commemorates the place of John the Baptist's birth. Built with financial contributions from the people of Spain, the blue tiles and paintings enrich the biblical story with Spanish style. In the left aisle of the church, a cave crypt marks the birthplace of St. John.

LUKE 1:57-80

57Now the time came for Elizabeth to give birth, and she bore a son. 58Her neighbors and relatives heard that the Lord had shown his great mercy to her, and they rejoiced with her. 59On the eighth day they came to circumcise the child, and they were going to name him Zechariah after his father. 60But his mother said, "No; he is to be called John." 61They said to her, "None of your relatives has this name." 62Then they began motioning to his father to find out what name he wanted to give him. 63He asked for a writing tablet and wrote, "His name is John." And all of them were amazed. 64Immediately his mouth was opened and his tongue freed, and he began to speak, praising God. 65Fear came over all their neighbors, and all these things were talked about throughout the entire hill country of Judea. 66All who heard them pondered them and said, "What then will this child become?" For, indeed, the hand of the Lord was with him.

67Then his father Zechariah was filled with the Holy Spirit and spoke this prophecy: 68"Blessed be the Lord God of Israel, for he has looked favorably on his people and redeemed them. 69He has raised up a mighty saviour for us in the house of his servant David, 70as he spoke through the mouth of his holy prophets from of old, 71that we would be saved from our enemies and from the hand of all who hate us. 72Thus he has shown the mercy promised to our ancestors, and has remembered his holy covenant, 73the oath that he swore to our ancestor Abraham, to grant us 74that we, being rescued from the hands of our enemies, might serve him without fear, 75in holiness and righteousness before him all our days. 76And you, child, will be called the prophet of the Most High; for you will go before the Lord to prepare his ways, 77to give knowledge of salvation to his people by the forgiveness of their sins. 78By the tender mercy of our God, the dawn from on high will break upon us, 79to give light to those who sit in darkness and in the shadow of death, to guide our feet into the way of peace." 80The child grew and became strong in spirit, and he was in the wilderness until the day he appeared publicly to Israel.

Reflection

Zechariah was a man who dedicated his life to the service of God; praying and offering sacrifices on behalf of his people and himself. He must have prayed earnestly for God to give him and his barren wife a son.

God had answered his prayers and it was all done in a glorious revelation at the holy sanctuary where he was serving. What was his reaction? Doubt. As Christians, when we doubt that God can do miracles in our lives, we also doubt the greatest miracles of all – the incarnation and the resurrection.

Church of St. John in the Mountains, Ein Karem

Zechariah was also the kind of man who repented his doubts. He was given a great gift, and once he learned to accept it, his tongue was released and he uttered the most wonderful words of praise to God.

When we look deeper into our lives, we find out that miracles happen all the time.

Prayer

In times of doubt and despair, I pray to you, Lord; strengthen my faith in you. Take my hand and guide my way. I trust you, I give you praise now and forever more. Amen.

> But you, O Bethlehem of Ephrathah, who are one of the little clans of Judah,
> from you shall come forth for me one who is to rule in Israel,
> whose origin is from of old, from ancient days.
>
> Micah 5:2

BETHLEHEM

HISTORY

Bethlehem is first mentioned in the 14th century BC in one of the Amarna letters.[1] The King of Jerusalem addressed his overlord, the King of Egypt, asking for archers to be sent to help recapture Bethlahmi that had seceded from his authority.

In the Bible, Bethlehem first appears in Genesis 35. Jacob was traveling with his wife Rachel from Bethel when she went into labor. She bore Benjamin, but did not survive. "*So Rachel died, and she was buried on the way to Ephrata (that is Bethlehem), and Jacob set up a pillar at her grave.*"[2]

Bethlehem was also the hometown of Elimelech and his wife Naomi. The Book of Ruth tells about their story. They were both from the tribe of Ephraim and lived in Bethlehem. When there was famine in the land, Elimelech chose to move with his family and settled in Moab. After finding Moabite wives for both his sons, Elimelech died. Ten years later his sons also died, leaving Naomi alone with her daughters-in-law.

Hearing that the famine in her homeland was over, Naomi embarked on a journey to return to Bethlehem. She told her daughters-in-law to stay with their tribes. One of them accepted. But the other, named Ruth, decided to follow Naomi. And so it was, they both returned to Bethlehem. Ruth catered for her mother-in-law. She started to go and glean the ears of grain in the fields of Boaz, a descendent of Elimelech. After Boaz met her and heard of her good conduct towards her mother-in-law, he took her as his wife. They had a son, Obed, who became father of Jesse, father of David, from whose lineage the Messiah was to come.[3]

David, while an outlaw, led attacks on the Philistines who were garrisoned in Bethlehem.[4] It was then that he cried, "*O that someone would give me water to drink from the well of Bethlehem which is by the gate!*" King David did not choose Bethlehem as capital of his kingdom, but Jebus (Jerusalem), mainly because it did not belong to any of the tribes of Israel.

In the eighth century BC, Bethlehem was an insignificant city, but the prophet Micah had a saying about Bethlehem's fortune saying, "*But you, O Bethlehem of Ephrathah, who are one of the little clans of Judah, from you shall come forth for me one who is to rule in Israel, whose origin is from of old, from ancient days.*"[5]

The birth of Jesus fulfilled Micah's prophecy and crowned the history of Bethlehem. "*In those days, a decree went out from Emperor Augustus that all the world should be registered. This was the first registration and was taken while Quirinius was governor of Syria. All went to their own towns to be registered. Joseph also went from*

the town of Nazareth in Galilee to Judea, to the city of David called Bethlehem, because he was descended from the house and family of David. He went to be registered with Mary, to whom he was engaged and who was expecting a child."[6]

According to St. Jerome who was writing in Bethlehem in AD 395, Roman Emperor Hadrian had the Jews expelled from Bethlehem. The town was overshadowed by a grove to the pagan god Thammuz. In the cave where Jesus was born the pagan goddess Venus was venerated. It was only in the fourth century AD, under a decree from Byzantine Emperor Constantine that such a tradition was stopped. Emperor Constantine ordered that a basilica church be built in honor of the nativity of Jesus to venerate the cave.

St. Jerome, and later St. Paula and her

daughter, took up residence in Bethlehem. Besides a tremendous amount of literary work, St. Jerome translated the Bible from Greek into Latin, in what is known today as the Vulgate. Both he and St. Paula turned Bethlehem into a center for monastic life.

The church of Constantine was destroyed by the Samaritans in AD 529, only to be rebuilt by Emperor Justinian soon after; this church is essentially the same one that stands today. Muslim Caliph Omar visited Bethlehem and promised that the church would be protected.

The Crusader period was very flourishing for Bethlehem, and pilgrims came from afar. After the Crusaders followed the Muslim Mamlukes, then the Ottoman Turks ruled the town for 400 years, which had many ups and downs in Christian-Muslim relations. Later, Bethlehem and the rest of Palestine fell to the British, then passed under Jordanian rule. In 1967, it was occupied by Israel with the rest of the West Bank. In 1995, under the Oslo peace agreement, Bethlehem fell under the rule of the Palestinian National Authority (PNA). Following the second intifada (shaking off or uprising) September 29, 2000, there were clashes with the Israeli army all over the West Bank. In the spring of 2002, Bethlehem and the Church of the Nativity was besieged during the Israeli army operation, "Defensive Shield." Since that time there has been general calm, yet Bethlehem is still segregated from the separation wall (barrier).

CHURCH OF THE NATIVITY

You would expect that the Church of the Nativity, one of the most important in Christian history and revered by all Christians around the world, to be very rich in architecture, décor and ornamentation. The fact is it is simple, poor and to some, totally unattractive.

But maybe, this is what makes this church so special. To see its real beauty, think of looking at it through your heart, contemplating the miracle of Christ's birth and the church's long history. Doing so will enrich the simplistic beauty with enough detail to make every ornament and piece of architecture narrate its own story.

"When they saw that the star had stopped, they were overwhelmed with joy. On entering the house, they saw the child with Mary his mother; and they knelt down and paid him homage. Then opening their treasure chests, they offered him gifts of gold, frankincense, and myrrh."[7]

The gospels are not very clear about the actual birthplace of Jesus. However, since the earliest centuries of Christianity, a firm tradition based on biblical texts and oral traditions has evolved, recounting the birth of Jesus in a cave in Bethlehem.

St. Justin in the middle of the second century wrote *"And the child being then born in Bethlehem, when Joseph had nowhere to lodge in that village he lodged in a certain cave close to the village; and it was then, while they were there, that Mary brought forth the Christ and laid him in a manger, where the wise men coming from Arabia found him."*[8]

The Christian scholar Origen, stated in the middle of the third century, *"as to Jesus having been born in Bethlehem, if any would have other proof beside the account that has been recorded in the Gospels by the disciples of Jesus, let him consider that in agreement with the account of his birth in the gospel, they still show the cave in Bethlehem where he was born and the manger in the cave*

Birthplace of our Lord, Church of the Nativity, Bethlehem

where he was wrapped in swaddling bands. And this which is shown is notorious in the district, even amongst strangers to the faith, namely that in this cave he who is worshipped and revered by Christians, namely Jesus, was born."[9]

Origen first came to Palestine about AD 215. He likely visited Bethlehem and the birthplace soon after. According to his testimony, the cave was shown to pilgrims and visitors. Once the connection was made with an actual cave in the town, it is not likely that people in general and devout Christians in particular would have misplaced the location. It is, therefore, plausible to conclude that the cave he referred to is identical to the one shown to Queen Helena early in the fourth century when she built, under orders from her son, Emperor Constantine, the first Basilica of the Nativity.

Ruins of that basilica were uncovered in the early 1930s. Its outline was sketched and verified. Today, part of the fourth century AD mosaic floor is shown in different parts beneath the floor of the current floor.

Constantine's basilica was visited by thousands of pilgrims from all over the world. Pilgrim hospices spread around the church and in the vicinity. The small town of Bethlehem enjoyed fame and fortune. Among its inhabitants were St. Jerome and St. Paula who lived on the grounds of the church.

In AD 395, St. Jerome wrote, *"From Hadrian's time until the reign of Constantine, for about 180 years [...] Bethlehem, now ours, and the earth's most sacred spot... was overshadowed by a grove of Thammuz, which is Adonis, and in the cave where the infant Messiah once cried, the paramour of Venus was bewailed."*[10]

Emperor Justinian was ruling the Byzantine Empire. His reign was one of material expansion for Christianity, but of hardship and oppression to non-Christians. The Samaritans expressed their rage against the emperor by staging a revolt. In AD 529, they destroyed the Church of the Nativity. The emperor brutally quelled the uprising and rebuilt the church, changing the scale and appearance from a small basilica to a larger cruciform structure.

The Persians ravaged the land in AD 614 with the destruction of almost all churches and monasteries. They spared the Church of the Nativity. A ninth-century Greek document stated, "when they [the Persians] arrived at Bethlehem, they saw with awe the figures of the Persian Wise Men, star-gazers, their country folk. For the respect and love towards their ancestors, they revered them as if they were still alive and spared the church. That is why it is still standing today."[11]

On Christmas Day 1100, Baldwin I, the first king of the Latin Kingdom was crowned in Bethlehem. Saladin, the Muslim sultan, defeated the Crusaders in 1187. He nevertheless allowed some priests to remain in the church of Bethlehem. Baybars, the Mamluke Sultan destroyed Bethlehem but somehow the church was not damaged. Soon after, the church was used as a source of political and economic income to the different occupiers leading to Christian quarrels. As a result, the Ottomans imposed a status quo in the 18th century, which to this day effectively perpetuates a schedule of rights and possessions in the Church of the Nativity.

Notes

1. Mostly diplomatic correspondence between the Egyptian administration and its representatives in Canaan (name of the land of Israel and Palestine before Joshua's conquest) and Amurru (contemporary western and north-western Syria and northern Lebanon, which made up northern Syria between the 14th and 12th centuries BC) during the New Kingdom. The letters were found in Upper Egypt at Amarna, the modern name for the Egyptian capital of Akhetaten (el-Amarna), founded by pharaoh Akhenaten (1350s-1330s BC) during the 18th Dynasty of Egypt.
2. Genesis 35:19.
3. I Samuel 16.
4. II Samuel 23:14-15.
5. Micah 5:2.
6. Luke 2:1-5.
7. Matthew 2:10-11.
8. http://www.titusinstitute.com/defendingfaith jesusbornbethlehem.php
9. Catholic Encyclopedia online - Bethlehem.
10. http://www.christusrex.org/www1/ofm/sites/ TSbtjust.html
11. http://www.christusrex.org/www1/ofm/sites/ TSbtmed.html

Cloister of the Catholic Church of St. Catherine, Church of the Nativity, Bethlehem

SHEPHERDS' FIELDS

ANGELS ANNOUNCE THE BIRTH OF JESUS

The Church of the Shepherds' Fields was built by the Italian architect Antonio Barluzzi in 1954 with funds from the Government of Canada. On the Franciscan property are also historical caves used by shepherds for millennia and some ruins of Byzantine churches from the fourth to the sixth centuries.

LUKE 2:8-20

[8] *In that region there were shepherds living in the fields, keeping watch over their flock by night.* [9] *Then an angel of the Lord stood before them, and the glory of the Lord shone around them, and they were terrified.* [10] *But the angel said to them, "Do not be afraid; for see – I am bringing you good news of great joy for all the people:* [11] *to you is born this day in the city of David a Saviour, who is the Messiah, the Lord.* [12] *This will be a sign for you: you will find a child wrapped in bands of cloth and lying in a manger."* [13] *And suddenly there was with the angel a multitude of the heavenly host, praising God and saying,* [14] *"Glory to God in the highest heaven, and on earth peace among those whom he favors!"*

[15] *When the angels had left them and gone into heaven, the shepherds said to one another, "Let us go now to Bethlehem and see this thing that has taken place, which the Lord has made known to us."* [16] *So they went with haste and found Mary and Joseph, and the child lying in the manger.* [17] *When they saw this, they made known what had been told them about this child;* [18] *and all who heard it were amazed at what the shepherds told them.* [19] *But Mary treasured all these words and pondered them in her heart.* [20] *The shepherds returned, glorifying and praising God for all they had heard and seen, as it had been told them.*

Reflection

The marginalized and outcast have become the privileged and the chosen to witness the birth of the prince of peace and the saviour of the world. Was it a coincidence? Couldn't God have chosen more prominent people to announce such good news? Jewish elite circles of the time were desperately anticipating the coming of the Messiah. Why didn't God choose them?

Could it be that God was telling us that the age of the privileged yielded to the age of the blessed? The elite of Israel were privileged in many ways, but failed to appreciate the blessings of their privileges. They were given the law to bless their lives, but they boasted about the privilege of being elected and forgot the blessing of the law of God. They boasted about the law and they lost the message of God. In contrast, the outcasts of Israel were less privileged,

Franciscan Church of the Shepherds' Fields,
Beit Sahour near Bethlehem

but accepted the blessing of the announcement with humble joy; only then were they able to understand how privileged they were. They went to Bethlehem and saw for themselves the true blessing of the infant God just born.

Prayer

Lord, it is no coincidence that I am today in this place. I ask you to open my heart to your love, and to be able to know that with you in my life, there are no coincidences, but only blessings. Bless me with your love and care, as you have blessed the shepherds before me. This I ask humbly, now and forever. Amen.

Shepherds' fountain, Shepherds' Fields, Beit Sahour

Byzantine ruins, fourth to fifth century AD

CHRISTMAS CYCLE

PASSIVE VOICE OF CHRISTMAS

The commercialization of Christmas is unfortunately eclipsing its spiritual message. During the Christmas season, the streets and neighborhoods are usually full of vivid colors, decorations and ornaments. Santa Claus is ringing his bells and carrying presents, bringing happiness and joy to children. Christmas commercials run around the clock, advertising gifts and prizes that become people's preoccupation.

There is nothing wrong with such additives that accompany the Christmas season. On the contrary, they fulfill their function, which is to add joy and happiness to people – one of the messages of Christmas. But somehow, they overshadow the real spirit of Christmas that the church laid out in the form of a Christmas cycle since the earliest centuries of Christian history. The cycle comprises preparation, acceptance then confirmation that God has become one of us in Jesus through the incarnation. Unfortunately, the Christmas cycle has become the passive voice of Christmas.

The Christmas cycle introduced by the church centuries ago, is divided into three parts, each with its own objectives. Advent is the time for preparation for the coming of Jesus. On Christmas day, Jesus is accepted as the Son of God and our saviour. Finally, at Epiphany, confirmation and dedication to live by his doctrine and become children of God is primarily acknowledged by baptism through the grace of the Holy Spirit.

Advent is celebrated differently in various churches, but essentially has the same message. It is the preparation for the coming of the Word of God, the incarnation. It ranges from about 30 to 40 days before Christmas Day, depending on whether the church follows the Western (Gregorian) or Eastern (Julian) calendar.

During Advent, prayers concentrate on readings from the book of Isaiah and the gospel of John. The focus is to link the Old and New Testaments. The book of Isaiah is considered to be a gospel of the Old Testament, for it concentrates on the coming of the Messiah and his proclamation. Readings are given and interpreted such as, "*a shoot shall come out from the stump of Jesse, and a branch shall grow out from his roots. The spirit of the Lord shall rest on him, the spirit of wisdom and understanding […] Righteousness shall be the belt around his waist and faithfulness the belt around his loins,*"[1].

The divinity of Jesus, manifestations and testimonies of his glory are abundant in the gospel of John, for example, "*And the Word became flesh and lived among us, and we have seen his glory the glory as of a father's only son, full of grace and truth.*"[2]

Readings from John and Isaiah, in addition to others, are meant to prepare the way for Christmas, to "*make straight the way of the Lord*"[3] like John the Baptist, who did so "*by proclaiming a baptism of repentance for the forgiveness of sin.*"[4] Similarly, Christians are to prepare their hearts for the birth of Christ.

Advent is crowned on Christmas Day, the wonder of the incarnation fulfilled. It is the Word of God becoming one of us. Celebrating Christmas needs a vivid contemplation on that mystery. The story of the birth in Bethlehem is read with joy and praise to God. Like the shepherds,

Christians rejoice and sing the Gloria. *"Glory to God in the highest heaven, and on earth peace among those whom he favors."*[5] Yet, accepting the Word to live within us means that we fully accept to live by the Word, by pouring out our lives for others; it is the spiritual acceptance of Christ.

The cycle concludes with Epiphany, which literally means manifestation from above. It is Christ becoming manifest as the Divine King for all humankind. This is confirmed by remembering the visit of the magi who paid him homage and presented him with their gifts. *"The Gentiles are fellow heirs, members of the same body, and partakers of the promise in Jesus Christ through the Gospel."*[6] Other manifestations of Jesus are also remembered. At the wedding ceremony in Cana of Galilee, Jesus manifested his divine glory and his disciples believed in him. At Jesus' baptism in the Jordan River, John testified that he had seen the Holy Spirit in the form of a dove that rested on Jesus' shoulder and heard the words of the Father, *"This is my son, the beloved, with whom I am well pleased."*[7] For many centuries, it has become customary for believers to confirm their dedication and confirmation to live in, with and through Jesus by accepting baptism or renewing their baptismal vows at Epiphany.

The Christmas cycle is a time for spiritual revival. It demands internal transformation that eventually leads to real joy. Christians need to look beyond the superficial and physical aspects of Christmas. Through acts of generosity, gentleness and charity, Christians can become witnesses to the miracle of the incarnation and transmit the real message of Christmas, which is the message of love.

Notes

1. Isaiah 11:1-10.
2. John 1:14.
3. John1:23.
4. Mark 1:4.
5. Luke 2:14.
6. Ephesians 3: 5-6.
7. Matthew 3:17.

Interior, Church of the Shepherds' Fields, Beit Sahour

*If ever a soul was lost, it was never from a sin too big
but only from too little trust in God's mercy and forgiveness.*

St. Francis Xavier

RIVER JORDAN

BAPTISM OF JESUS

It is not clear where along the banks of the River Jordan Jesus was baptized. However, historically it seems to have occurred closer to Jericho. From the fourth to the sixth centuries, churches were built in that area to commemorate the event.

Baptism is perceived in two different ways. As a sacrament, it is an act in which God is present and conveying his grace. As an ordinance, it is the testimony of one who believes, and God is only overseeing his work being commemorated. To the average person, indulging in these doctrines and trying to determine right from wrong will probably lead to confusion.

In his letters to the Romans, Paul offers an explanation: *"Should we continue in sin in order that grace may abound? By no means! How can we who died to sin go on living in it? Do you not know that all of us who have been baptized into Christ Jesus were baptized into his death? Therefore, we have been buried with him by baptism into death, so that, just as Christ was raised from the dead by the glory of the Father, so we too might walk in newness of life […] For whoever has died is freed from sin. But if we have died with Christ we believe that we will also live with him […] So you also must consider yourselves dead to sin and alive to God in Christ Jesus."*[1]

Christ carried the sins of humanity, and as a result, baptism is a celebration of the death of sin and the rebirth into Christ. In

the gospel of Matthew, John was hesitant to baptize Jesus, but Jesus insisted saying it was necessary to fulfill all righteousness. Once Jesus was baptized, the dove rested on his shoulder and the Father said, *"This is my son, with whom I am well pleased."*

JOHN 1:29-34
[29]*The next day he [John the Baptist] saw Jesus coming toward him and declared, "Here is the Lamb of God who takes away the sin of the world!* [30]*This is he of whom I said, 'After me comes a man who ranks ahead of me because he was before me.'* [31]*I myself did not know him; but I came baptizing with water for this reason, that he might be revealed to Israel."* [32]*And John testified, "I saw the Spirit descending from heaven like a dove, and it remained on him.* [33]*I myself did not know him, but the one who sent me to baptize with water said to me, 'He on whom you see the Spirit descend and remain is the one who baptizes with the Holy Spirit.'* [34]*And I myself have seen and have testified that this is the Son of God.*

MATTHEW 3:13-17
[13]*Then Jesus came from Galilee to John at the Jordan, to be baptized by him.* [14]*John would have prevented him, saying, "I need to be baptized by you, and do you come to me?"* [15]*But Jesus answered him, "Let it be so now; for it is proper for us in this way to fulfill all righteousness." Then he consented.* [16]*And when Jesus had*

River Jordan

been baptized, just as he came up from the water, suddenly the heavens were opened to him and he saw the Spirit of God descending like a dove and alighting on him. [17] *And a voice from heaven said, "This is my Son, the Beloved, with whom I am well pleased."*

Reflection

To fulfill the requirements of the law, Moses was commanded to ordain Aaron and his sons to the priesthood by washing them with water in front of the Tent of Meeting.[2] Then they were anointed with oil to complete the ordination. Similarly, John the Baptist, the last of the prophets before the coming of the Son of God, the bridge chosen by God to link the old covenant with the new covenant, had to wash (baptize) Jesus with water to fulfill his function as the ultimate High Priest. Moses knew whom he had to ordain to the office. John did not, yet God instructed him that it would be the one on whom the dove would rest. The anointing with oil under the old covenant is a pre-figure of the ordination of the Holy Spirit in the new covenant.

Priests were expected to offer daily sacrifices for sin on behalf of the people. Jesus Christ, the ultimate High Priest, carried the sins of all humanity and offered himself, a suffering servant, to take away the sins of the world. It is no coincidence that John was inspired to call him the Lamb of God.

Sin is the reason for our death. The Lamb of God, who took in his body the sins of all humanity, washed us of our sins in his baptism and gave us new birth by his rising from the water, a foreshadow of his resurrection.

View from the west bank of the Jordan, Qasr Al-Yahud baptismal site near Jericho

Prayer

Holy Father, on the day of our baptism, we receive a divine grace into your only son's death and into a new life through his resurrection. Grant us the will and the power to be worthy heirs of your kingdom.

Some of us were baptized as children without recollection. Loving parents and godparents concerned for our spiritual well-being and salvation made the decision for our baptism. More were baptized as adults out of personal conviction. Still others are yet to be baptized.

We pray today that, on the banks of the Jordan River, with water blessed by your son's baptism, that you bestow on us your righteousness and spirit, so that we live in a new creation in your son's body. We pray that one day, when we are in your presence again, you will finally reveal to us the true meaning of your word. This we pray in the name of the Father, the Son and the Holy Spirit. Amen.

> All authority in heaven and on earth has been given to me. Go therefore and make disciples of all nations, baptizing them in the name of the Father and of the Son and of the Holy Spirit, and teaching them to obey everything that I have commanded you. And remember, I am with you always, to the end of the age.
>
> Matthew 28:18-20

Notes

For a renewal of baptismal vows, see Annex 2.

1. Romans 6:1-11.
2. Exodus 29:1-7.

¹³No one, when tempted, should say, "I am being tempted by God;"
for God cannot be tempted by evil and he himself tempts no one.
¹⁴But one is tempted by one's own desire, being lured and enticed by it.

James 1:13-14

MOUNT OF TEMPTATION

DEVIL TEMPTING JESUS

One of the topographical features of the Jericho area is a high mountain with a monastery stretching from its bedrock. The monastery was first built in the fourth century on the traditional Mount of Temptation in memory of the Lord's fasting for 40 days and facing the temptation by the Devil.

MATTHEW 4:1-11

¹Then Jesus was led up by the Spirit into the wilderness to be tempted by the devil. ²He fasted forty days and forty nights, and afterwards he was famished. ³The tempter came and said to him, "If you are the Son of God, command these stones to become loaves of bread." ⁴But he answered, "It is written, 'One does not live by bread alone, but by every word that comes from the mouth of God.'" ⁵Then the devil took him to the holy city and placed him on the pinnacle of the temple, ⁶saying to him, "If you are the Son of God, throw yourself down; for it is written, 'He will command his angels concerning you,' and 'On their hands they will bear you up, so that you will not dash your foot against a stone.'" ⁷Jesus said to him, "Again it is written, 'Do not put the Lord your God to the test.'" ⁸Again, the devil took him to a very high mountain and showed him all the kingdoms of the world and their splendor; ⁹and he said to him, "All these I will give you, if you will fall down and worship me." ¹⁰Jesus said to him, "Away with you, Satan! For it is written, 'Worship the Lord your God, and serve only him.'" ¹¹Then the devil left him, and suddenly angels came and waited on him.

Reflection

At his baptism, Jesus' identity as Son of God is proclaimed publicly. The devil, always ready to tempt into sin, decides to put famished Jesus to the test. For him, success means dominion over the Son of God.

In the first temptation, the devil wants Jesus to prove to him he is the Son of God by a misuse of his strength. Jesus was obviously hungry. The devil asks him to prove that he is the Son of God and use his divine power to make bread. The devil tries to turn divine strength into a trap for sin; God's gift is to be used for selfish acts to satisfy human needs. But Jesus

Mount of Temptation, Jericho

answers that true bread comes not from the physical world but from the Word of God. As the Son of God, Jesus could have cast the devil wherever he wished for daring to tempt him. But as a regular human, he tells us that we have a weapon to resist temptation. For him, true bread, the ultimate strength lies in the scriptures.

In the second temptation, the devil aims to tempt God the Father by trying to force him to act supernaturally to protect his son. This time, he tries to use the weapon Jesus used. However, he deliberately left out *"in all your ways"* from Psalm 91:11 that he was quoting. He purposely creates a situation in which Jesus needs the Father's protection. The way of the son is to fulfill the Father's will and not to force (tempt) the Father to reveal his glory. The devil takes the scripture out of context to deceive rather than to reveal. Jesus answered him from scripture, *"I know the Father and trust him, I do not need to test him to reveal his glory."*

As humans, we always put God to the test, most of the time unreasonably. We desire to have God prove to us that our life matters to him. Jesus teaches us that we are unreasonable when we do that. The ultimate test of God was sending his only son to save us from sin because we matter to him.

Many of us put our trust in some people because they excel at quoting scripture. Jesus' second temptation is all about the manipulation of scripture by misquoting it or taking it out of context. *"I know the slander on the part of those who say that they are Jews and are not, but are a Synagogue of Satan."*[1] Jesus teaches us to be careful of those who misquote scripture by equipping ourselves with good knowledge of scripture as well.

In the third temptation, the devil attempts to have Jesus worship him by giving him power over material possessions. He entices Jesus to commit the sin by giving him kingdoms and splendors. Jesus answers him in no uncertain terms to worship only God. He tells us that the devil can be resisted, if we trust ourselves and trust the true power of God revealed in the Bible.

"Submit yourselves therefore to God. Resist the devil, and he will flee from you."[2]

Prayer

In the 21st century, no matter where I turn, I face all sorts of temptations. Depending on my physical, emotional and spiritual well-being, I might give in to some of them. Sometimes, I might even think they are vital.

Lord, grant me the wisdom to see temptations for what they are – lies and deceits. Give me the will to resist them. Equip my heart with your truth now are forever. Amen.

Notes
1. Revelations 2:9.
2. James 4:7.

Judean Desert, near Jericho

> After two days will he revive us: in the third day he will raise us up,
> and we shall live in his site.
>
> Hosea 6:2

CANA, GALILEE

North of Nazareth 10 km away, you will find the village of Cana with its beautiful churches. It was the home of Nathaniel who expressed his astonishment about Jesus saying: *"Can anything good come out of Nazareth."*

Cana's fame, however, evolved only following Jesus' first sign (or miracle) during a wedding ceremony. Today, the Franciscan church marking the site of the event is the place visited by most pilgrims. Built in 1879 then restored and inaugurated in 1999, the Wedding Church stands above the ruins of two older sanctuaries of the Byzantine and Crusader eras.

JOHN 2:1-12

[1]*On the third day there was a wedding in Cana of Galilee, and the mother of Jesus was there.* [2]*Jesus and his disciples had also been invited to the wedding.* [3]*When the wine gave out, the mother of Jesus said to him, "They have no wine."* [4]*And Jesus said to her, "Woman[1], what concern is that to you and to me? My hour has not yet come."* [5]*His mother said to the servants, "Do whatever he tells you."* [6]*Now standing there were six stone water-jars for the Jewish rites of purification, each holding twenty or thirty gallons.* [7]*Jesus said to them, "Fill the jars with water." And they filled them up to the brim.* [8]*He said to them, "Now draw some out, and take it to the chief steward." So they took it.* [9]*When the steward tasted the water that had become wine, and did not know where it came from (though the servants who had drawn the water knew), the steward called the bridegroom* [10]*and said to him, "Everyone serves the good wine first, and then the inferior wine after the guests have become drunk. But you have kept the good wine until now."* [11]*Jesus did this, the first of his signs, in Cana of Galilee, and revealed his glory; and his disciples believed in him.*

[12]*After this he went down to Capernaum with his mother, his brothers, and his disciples; and they remained there for a few days.*

Franciscan Wedding Church, Cana

Reflection

As the servants noticed that the wine supply was running short, they needed to tell somebody to do something about it before it became an embarrassment to the hosts. The sensible thing for them to do was to either tell the steward in charge of the banquet, or the groom, if not, a family member. The steward in charge must have been unavailable at the time, and the groom sitting at the center of the table with his bride did not need to be bothered by such bad news. A family member was their best choice; Mary must have been known to them, so they told her about the problem. It was clear to her that she needed to resolve this issue as discreetly as possible to avoid embarrassment in front of the guests. It was only logical that she request the assistance of a trustworthy person, her son.

Mary must have been eager to see him start his divine work. At the annunciation, the angel told her that Jesus was the son of the Most High. She had raised the Son of God and witnessed him growing in wisdom and spirit. She believed it was time for him to start his mission. Maybe she did not know exactly what Jesus was about to do, but she had total trust that he would resolve the matter somehow. Otherwise, why did she instruct the servants to follow his command? If she did not believe in her son's capabilities, this meant that her willingness to be part of the divine plan was meaningless, that she had learned nothing from some 30 years of raising the Son of God, and that she was unworthy of bearing the Son of God. At the request of his mother, Jesus turned water into wine.

Prayer

Lord Jesus, here at Cana of Galilee you have revealed your glory and the disciples believed in you. I ask that you continue filling the jars of my spirit with your wine and that I continue sharing it with others with a praising heart. Amen.

Notes

For a renewal of wedding vows, see Annex 3.

1. In Greek, the original language of the text, and in Aramaic, the original culture of the setting, Jesus' answer to his mother was respectful and in line with social norms of the time. It is always best to imagine that he addressed her with a hidden smile and a wink of the eye. Indeed, Mary felt she accomplished her mission, and she knew that her son's mission was just beginning.

> God's action is ever new. It never retraces its steps,
> but always marks out new paths.
>
> Jean-Pierre de Caussade

JACOB'S WELL, SAMARIA

THE WOMAN AT THE WELL

Jacob's Well is found in the heart of the northern West Bank, near Nablus. The current church was built in the 1990s on the ruins of Crusader and Byzantine churches by Father Ioustinos (Greek for Justin) who is its architect, builder and iconographer.

JOHN 4:1-42

[1]*Now when Jesus learned that the Pharisees had heard, "Jesus is making and baptizing more disciples than John" –* [2]*although it was not Jesus himself but his disciples who baptized –* [3]*he left Judea and started back to Galilee.* [4]*But he had to go through Samaria.* [5]*So he came to a Samaritan city called Sychar, near the plot of ground that Jacob had given to his son Joseph.* [6]*Jacob's well was there, and Jesus, tired out by his journey, was sitting by the well. It was about noon.*

[7]*A Samaritan woman came to draw water, and Jesus said to her, "Give me a drink."* [8]*(His disciples had gone to the city to buy food.)* [9]*The Samaritan woman said to him, "How is it that you, a Jew, ask a drink of me, a woman of Samaria?" (Jews do not share things in common with Samaritans.)* [10]*Jesus answered her, "If you knew the gift of God, and who it is that is saying to you, 'Give me a drink,' you would have asked him, and he would have given you living water."* [11]*The woman said to him, "Sir, you have no bucket, and the well is deep. Where do you get that living water?* [12]*Are you greater than our ancestor Jacob, who gave us the well, and with his sons and his flocks drank from*

it?" [13]*Jesus said to her, "Everyone who drinks of this water will be thirsty again,* [14]*but those who drink of the water that I will give them will never be thirsty. The water that I will give will become in them a spring of water gushing up to eternal life."* [15]*The woman said to him, "Sir, give me this water, so that I may never be thirsty or have to keep coming here to draw water."*

[16]*Jesus said to her, "Go, call your husband, and come back."* [17]*The woman answered him, "I have no husband." Jesus said to her, "You are right in saying, 'I have no husband;'* [18]*for you have had five husbands, and the one you have now is not your husband. What you have said is true!"* [19]*The woman said to him, "Sir, I see that you are a prophet.* [20]*Our ancestors worshipped on this mountain, but you say that the place where people must worship is in Jerusalem."* [21]*Jesus said to her, "Woman, believe me, the hour is coming when you will worship the Father neither on this mountain nor in Jerusalem.* [22]*You worship what you do not know; we worship what we know, for salvation is from the Jews.* [23]*But the hour is coming, and is now here, when the true worshippers will worship the Father in spirit and truth, for the Father seeks such as these to worship him.* [24]*God is spirit, and those who worship him must worship in spirit and truth."* [25]*The woman said to him, "I know that Messiah is coming" [who is called Christ]. "When he comes, he will proclaim all things to us."* [26]*Jesus said to her, "I am he, the one who is*

speaking to you."

27Just then his disciples came. They were astonished that he was speaking with a woman, but no one said, "What do you want?" or, "Why are you speaking with her?" 28Then the woman left her water-jar and went back to the city. She said to the people, 29"Come and see a man who told me everything I have ever done! He cannot be the Messiah, can he?" 30They left the city and were on their way to him.

31Meanwhile the disciples were urging him, "Rabbi, eat something." 32But he said to them, "I have food to eat that you do not know about." 33So the disciples said to one another, "Surely no one has brought him something to eat?" 34Jesus said to them, "My food is to do the will of him who sent me and to complete his work. 35Do you not say, 'Four months more, then comes the harvest?' But I tell you, look around you, and see how the fields are ripe for harvesting. 36The reaper is already receiving wages and is gathering fruit for eternal life, so that sower and reaper may rejoice together. 37For here the saying holds true, 'One sows and another reaps.' 38I sent you to reap that for which you did not labour. Others have laboured, and you have entered into their labour."

39Many Samaritans from that city believed in him because of the woman's testimony, "He told me everything I have ever done." 40So when the Samaritans came to him, they asked him to stay with them; and he stayed there for two days. 41And many more believed because of his word. 42They said to the woman, "It is no longer because of what you said that we believe, for we have heard for ourselves, and we know that this is truly the Saviour of the world."

When was the last time you had a serious conversation with a stranger or an outsider?

_____

_____

_____

Reflection

Could the Samaritan woman have imagined that on that particular day she would encounter not only the saviour of the Samaritan people, but the saviour of the world?

She went out to the well at noon, contrary to the customs of the time, hoping that she would escape the local women's contempt.[1] She arrived at the well carrying her water jar, and there was a stranger, an outsider to her community and to her people. He was a Jew seated at the edge of the well, blocking her source of water.

It became clear to her that he was not going to move to a socially acceptable distance for her to approach and get water. She moved closer hoping that he would move away. But to her surprise, he moved closer and spoke to her with a request. *Give me a drink,* he said.

There is so much strength in weakness. Why would God want to become a fragile baby? Why would God place himself at the whim of human beings? Does God really need our help? Jesus, the Son of God had occasionally but deliberately put himself in a situation of need. Only the strongest visionaries have this humble trait. Jesus was ready to serve, and his self-emptying was so total that he needed to be served.[2] Those who accepted to serve Jesus

Greek Orthodox Church of Jacob's Well, Nablus

Josef Von Hempel, *Christ and the Samaritan Woman*

with a humble heart received great gifts, such as his mother Mary as well as apostles Peter and Paul.

When Jesus asked the Samaritan woman for water, she was taken aback, her response akin to, "Why are you, a Jew, talking to me? Have you forgotten who you are, and who I am? Don't your laws forbid you to talk to women in public? Do you really want to have a drink from my defiled jar? Have you forgotten what your people have done to us, Samaritans, in the name of your religion?"

Jesus answered her, *"If you knew the gift of God, and who it is that is saying to you, 'Give me a drink,' you would have asked him, and he would have given you living water."* In the woman's mindset, God had given Moses the greatest gift of all, the Torah. In an average Jewish mindset, the Torah and the prophets were the gift of God. But Jesus here identified himself as the gift of God. He reaffirmed an old tradition that Isaiah had once mentioned, *"I have given you as a covenant to the people, a light to the nations."*[3] In other words, the gift, the covenant of God was not any word written in a book, or a set of laws, but Jesus himself. God knew that presenting his incarnated word in the form of his only son would be hard to believe. Therefore, he divided the process into stages until the manifestation of his word, through the incarnation of his son. Without that process, God's master plan of saving the world from sin would have been impossible to comprehend, even by the first few who believed in Jesus, and the depth of his message would have been lost.

The Samaritan woman obviously did not understand what Jesus meant, but it was apparent that she started to respect Jesus, *"Sir, you have no bucket! Are you greater than our father Jacob?"* Jesus' answer was crucial to the conversation, *"Those who drink of the water that I will give them will never be thirsty. The water that I will give will become in them a spring of water gushing up to eternal life."* Again she did not grasp the depth of these words. Jesus told her of the possibility of her becoming a spring of water welling up to eternal life, yet she was still thinking about the burden of daily chores. But Jesus did not give up on her as she received the grace of becoming living water without her knowledge.

Living water lives because it flows, gives and receives. It is not stagnant. The living gospel also lives because the one who shares it receives as much joy as the one who receives it. The Samaritan woman was asked to do exactly that, *"Go, call your husband and come back to share the living water I give!"* Though she had no husband at present, Jesus knew that she had had five husbands.

A stranger's knowledge of such a private detail in her life brought her closer to identifying the true character of Jesus, *"You are a prophet!"* Her private life was another topic she did not want to discuss, but by changing the subject she accidentally raised a deep theological question – where are we to worship?

At this point Jesus rendered obsolete the Samaritan temple on Mount Gerazim and more importantly the Jewish temple in Jerusalem. Instead, he said, *"The hour is coming, and is now here, when the true worshippers will worship the Father in spirit and truth, for the Father seeks such as these to worship him."* To the woman, such a sentence was like dropping a huge stone on a piece of glass. It not only shattered her religious worldview, but also the Jewish worldview of which the strange prophet was a part.

She did not know how to react. Jesus challenged all of her understandings and religious perceptions. Therefore, she reverted to the only person she knew of who could explain it all: the Messiah. And Jesus said to her, *"I am!"*

Only then did the grace of the living water that Jesus bestowed on her start to flow, and she became the first woman to preach the gospel of Jesus Christ.

Are you a source of living water yet?

_____

_____

_____

_____

Prayer

Lord Jesus, to the Samaritan woman, you said that the water you gave was living water. You are like the Sea of Galilee, you have given so much of yourself, deeds of tremendous effect on many people from physical healing to spiritual transformation. Each beneficiary became a source of living water, giving out what he had received from you with joyful proclamation.

By totally abandoning yourself to the whim of my sin, by allowing yourself to be brutally crushed on the cross, you have set the bar so high. You have given up your life so that I would receive salvation.

Lord, grant me an open and giving heart so that I become living water, _"gushing up to eternal life"_ for myself and for others. Amen.

Notes

1. It was customary for women to get the water for the household, either early in the morning or late in the evening before dark. Usually they would go at noon to avoid contact with other women on social or religious grounds or to meet someone.
2. Bailey, K. _Jesus through Middle Eastern Eyes_, IVP Academic, 2008, p. 205.
3. Isaiah 42:6.

Iconostasis, Greek Orthodox Church of Jacob's Well, Nablus

> Abraham's faith constitutes the beginning of the old covenant;
> Mary's faith at the annunciation inaugurates the new covenant.
>
> St. John Paul II

NAZARETH, GALILEE

Nazareth was the hometown of Jesus. It was also the hometown of his mother Mary, where she had received the message of the angel announcing her pregnancy with the Son of God. It can be inferred from the gospels that most events of the Lord's 30 concealed years would have happened in Nazareth. He probably worked as a skilled builder of stone and wood, the profession of his earthly father, Joseph, travelling from one city to another. His best work opportunities were probably in the nearby Roman city of Sepphoris, whose population was over 30,000. He may have also engaged in planting, farming and harvesting like the rest of the village of Nazareth, with its 300-500 inhabitants.

Nazareth must have had a bad reputation at the time to have merited Nathanael of Cana's words of astonishment. Hearing of a righteous teacher from the town, he said, *"Can anything good come out of Nazareth!"*

According to Luke 4, Jesus had already a routine when he entered the synagogue and was presented the book of Isaiah. He chose a text, read it and commented on it in town, causing an upheaval that almost cost him his life.

Today, Nazareth is a hometown for some 80,000 people, 25% of which are Christian and the rest, Muslim.

GREEK ORTHODOX CHURCH OF THE ANNUNCIATION

Also known as Mary's well or St. Gabriel's Church. According to an ancient tradition originating from the apocryphal gospel of James, Mary was at the spring when the angel first appeared. After her initial panic, he disappeared only to reappear again when she was at home.

The current church was built in the 17th century over the ruins of an earlier Crusader structure. At the heart is a crypt that holds the historical source of water of the ancient hometown of Jesus and his mother.

Iconostasis, Greek Orthodox Church of the Annunciation (St. Gabriel's), Nazareth

CATHOLIC CHURCH OF THE ANNUNCIATION

The current Franciscan Church is the last of a series of churches built from as early as the second century around the house of Mary where she accepted the angel Gabriel's announcement of her pregnancy with the Son of God. The last church was inaugurated in the 1960s, the idea of which was blessed by Pope John XXIII in 1959; the church itself was built under the auspices of Pope Paul VI.

ANNUNCIATION

LUKE 1:26-38

[26]*In the sixth month the angel Gabriel was sent by God to a town in Galilee called Nazareth, [27]to a virgin engaged to a man whose name was Joseph, of the house of David. The virgin's name was Mary. [28]And he came to her and said, "Greetings, favored one! The Lord is with you." [29]But she was much perplexed by his words and pondered what sort of greeting this might be. [30]The angel said to her, "Do not be afraid, Mary, for you have found favor with God. [31]And now, you will conceive in your womb and bear a son, and you will name him Jesus. [32]He will be great, and will be called the Son of the Most High, and the Lord God will give to him the throne of his ancestor David. [33]He will reign over the house of Jacob forever, and of his kingdom there will be no end." [34]Mary said to the angel, "How can this be, since I am a virgin?" [35]The angel said to her, "The Holy Spirit will come upon you, and the power of the Most High will overshadow you; therefore the child to be born will be holy; he will be called Son of God. [36]And now, your relative Elizabeth in her old age has also conceived a son; and this is the sixth month for her who was said to be barren. [37]For nothing will be impossible with God." [38]Then Mary said, "Here am I, the servant of the Lord; let it be with me according to your word." Then the angel departed from her.*

Reflection

"One day, I was…" and "Someday, I will be…" These are words that we keep reflecting on in our lives. Mary must have been pondering these words when the divine messenger appeared to her with his strange message. Her answer would certainly change everything she thought she knew about herself and everything that would happen to her in the future. Like Abraham, Mary was invited to experience the "I am" revelation.

How is God's love so different from human love? One thing is for sure, his love is for everything he has created, especially for us. God's love is abundant, omnipresent and infinite.

We keep misplacing his love with our sin. We keep misinterpreting his love with our zeal. Yet he never gives up on us. With his constant reminders, sending one angel after another, presenting one opportunity after another, he wants to bring us back to him and enjoy his love.

Our human ego refuses to see; we often live in the past and worry about the future. Some of us are even eccentric, trying to make him reveal himself "now" and forgetting that only he decides when that should be; there is nothing we do can change that.

Yet, divine wisdom never gives up on us. God sent his angel to a young woman, telling her that his love is eternal and boundless. He had a plan for the salvation of humanity, but it could only happen with her acceptance of his love. In the case of Mary, God was saying that he needed her love for his love, his word, to take a physical form on earth.

Does God love us? Do we love God? God's surrender to human will is the ultimate act of divine love. *"For God so loved the world that he gave his only Son, so that everyone who believes in him may not perish but may have eternal life."[1]* If God was willing to surrender himself to the will of a young woman to incarnate his love, how much more do we need

Franciscan Church of the Annunciation, Nazareth

to surrender to his love? We can only realize how much we love him, to the extent that we appreciate how much he loves us.

He was the one to make a covenant with our forefathers in the faith. But it is always we who deviate from his love. Sometimes, we do so because we make a big break in our lives and we think we do not need his love anymore. Other times, we think that he has abandoned us because we are trying to judge his love according to our human standards.

Mary's consent to accept God's "I am" revelation made her understand her past and gave her a future that she never could have conceived.

God always offers his "I am" revelation. Accepting it, gives us a better sense of the past and a worry-free outlook on the future.

It is time for us to emulate Mary now.

Do you remember meeting an angel in your life? How did you react?

Lord Jesus, Mary was not the first to give herself up to serve you; many did so before, and many others after. But Mary received what none other did: the honor of having the womb that would carry you for nine months. Because she accepted your love, your word was incarnated and you needed no more mediators to convey on your behalf your divine spirit and truth. Through her, you humbly became like us, sharing our joys and sorrows.

With her consent came a series of challenges; at times joyous, ultimately painful and heartfelt. She followed you everywhere. She was so concerned for your earthly being and witnessed the challenges you had to face. Her heart was torn apart when she saw you on that cross. Yet, she stood fast and never faltered. She trusted you with every beat of her heart.

Lord, as a blessed mother, Mary has set an example for me to be blessed with your word in my heart. I am more than honored at every opportunity you knock on my door. I humbly repeat her words, *"Here am I, the servant of the Lord; let it be with me according to your word!"*

Lord, grant me the wisdom to be able to *"ponder these things in my heart,"* to let your love live within me and grow; ultimately, to shine all around.

Lord, grant me the patience and the courage to endure to the end, as Mary did, and let me be a living stream and determined witness to your endless love. Amen.

Christ Church (Episcopal), Nazareth

Stained glass, Church of the Annunciation, Nazareth

Note
1. John 3:16.

Grotto, Church
of the Annunciation,
Nazareth

> The purpose of all major religious traditions is not to construct big temples on the outside, but to create temples of goodness and compassion inside, in our hearts.
>
> 14th Dalai Lama[1]

MELKITE (GREEK CATHOLIC) SYNAGOGUE CHURCH

A local tradition has identified the site as the synagogue of Jesus' day where he read the prophecy of Isaiah. The structure itself dates back to Crusader times and is maintained by the Melkite congregation of Nazareth.

INAUGURATION OF JESUS' MINISTRY[2]

There are various sources of Jewish origins and a wealth of Aramaic Arabic commentary that can help us have a deeper understanding of the prophecy of Isaiah 61, which Jesus read in the Nazareth synagogue. In addition, knowledge of the practices and beliefs of Jews in Jesus' day can all lead to a safe assumption that there was a general idea among Jews that they were to settle in the area of Galilee to invalidate the title of "Galilee of the Gentiles" and replace it with "Galilee of the Jews." As a result, many of them moved from the Judean region to settle in Galilee as early as the second century BC. That is most likely the reason behind the creation of Nazareth. The settlers' purpose was to build and plant on the land. Some Jews viewed these actions as redemption of the land, while they waited for the Messiah. This coming would release them from all burdens of hard labor, bring them wealth and allow them to fully devote themselves to the worship of God. All hard labor would befall on the Gentiles, who would become servants of the Jews.

LUKE 4:14-30

[14]*Then Jesus, filled with the power of the Spirit, returned to Galilee, and a report about him spread through all the surrounding country.* [15]*He began to teach in their synagogues and was praised by everyone.* [16]*When he came to Nazareth, where he had been brought up, he went to the synagogue on the Sabbath day, as was his custom. He stood up to read,* [17]*and the scroll of the prophet Isaiah was given to him. He unrolled the scroll and found the place where it was written:* [18]*"The Spirit of the Lord is upon me, because he has anointed me to bring good news to the poor. He has sent me to proclaim release to the captives and recovery of sight to the blind, to let the oppressed go free,* [19]*to proclaim the year of the Lord's favor."* [20]*And he rolled up the scroll, gave it back to the attendant, and sat down. The eyes of all in the synagogue were fixed on him.* [21]*Then he began to say to them, "Today this scripture has been fulfilled in your hearing."* [22]*All spoke well of him and were amazed at the gracious words that came from his mouth. They said, "Is not this Joseph's son?"* [23]*He said to them, "Doubtless*

Melkite (Greek Catholic) Synagogue Church, Nazareth

you will quote to me this proverb, 'Doctor, cure yourself!' And you will say, 'Do here also in your hometown the things that we have heard you did at Capernaum.'" ²⁴And he said, "Truly I tell you, no prophet is accepted in the prophet's hometown. ²⁵But the truth is, there were many widows in Israel in the time of Elijah, when the heaven was shut up three years and six months, and there was a severe famine over all the land; ²⁶yet Elijah was sent to none of them

except to a widow at Zarephath in Sidon. ²⁷There were also many lepers in Israel in the time of the prophet Elisha, and none of them was cleansed except Na'aman the Syrian." ²⁸When they heard this, all in the synagogue were filled with rage. ²⁹They got up, drove him out of the town, and led him to the brow of the hill on which their town was built, so that they might hurl him off the cliff. ³⁰But he passed through the midst of them and went on his way.

Jesus had great courage going back to his hometown, not only undermining the very reason for the foundation of Nazareth, but also claiming to be the Messiah whose message contradicted every belief that his fellow Nazarenes held.

Instead of appeasing, he was displeasing. Instead of endorsing, he was contradicting. And instead of surrendering, he was leading. He was leading his synagogue audience to a different approach of self-understanding and self-evaluation. Instead of fulfilling what they expected from the Messiah, he demanded what he expected from them. He required them to extend brotherhood, compassion and justice towards the Gentiles. In proving his point, he quoted examples of Elijah and Elisha who were sent to Gentiles.

In I Kings 17, God sent Elijah to the Gentile widow of Zarephath in Sidon. She was a poor woman facing the doom of hunger, together with her son at a time the land was confronted with an extended drought. Her only remaining food sustenance was a loaf of bread that she was about to bake when Elijah arrogantly asked her to give it to him. Knowing that the God of Elijah had no authority in her land,[3] she still trusted the prophet and his God and gave him the bread. Her leap of faith from the narrow national religious concept into the unknown world of the God of Israel was rewarded with an endless supply of oil that could sustain her and her son indefinitely. She exhibited a radical change of faith that became a model in all Israel.

Elisha, in II Kings 5, had a knock at his door. It was the Gentile commander of the Aram king's army. Na'aman the Syrian was struck by leprosy and advised to seek treatment in the land of Israel. Despite Elisha's inhospitable attitude towards him by sending a servant to talk to him and Na'aman's initial hesitation to fulfill Elijah's command, the Gentile bathed in the Jordan seven times to be healed from his leprosy. This exhibition of faith in the God of Israel, against all odds was highly exalted by Jesus and set the premise for what he deemed to be an exhibition of true faith.

Jesus showed his listeners that as chosen people, they needed to follow the path of those prophets and reach out with compassion to the Gentiles. They also had to exhibit the same kind of extraordinary faith in God that those Gentiles had vividly shown against all odds.

For Jesus, faith in God does not necessarily mean following the written word to the letter, but to surrender to the will of God and to trust in him, even when circumstances dictate otherwise. If outsiders were capable of that leap of faith, insiders were expected to exhibit faith even more. Unfortunately, Jesus' intended lesson found deaf ears or blind eyes. The ears of some were attached to misconceptions of the day, and the eyes of others were unable to see the way of the Messiah: to exhibit total trust in God and openness and compassion to the Gentiles. Such a message that upgraded the status of Gentiles and downgraded that of the Jews, infuriated them from the beginning.

Jesus spoke his word and showed that there was no set way for God to reveal his love. Instead of closing themselves up, Jews were to go out as Elijah did, and to invite others as Elisha did to partake in and share the love of God.

"For this is the message that you have heard from the beginning, that we should love one another…, let us love, not in word or speech, but in truth and action. And by this we will know that we are from the truth and will reassure our hearts before him whenever our hearts condemn us; for God is greater than our hearts, and he knows everything. Beloved, if our hearts

do not condemn us, we have boldness before God; and we receive from him whatever we ask, because we obey his commandments and do what he pleases."[4]

St. Benedict opened his rule saying, "*Listen and attend with the ear of your heart.*" We can only hope and pray that the ears of our hearts are ready to receive, unlike those in the Nazareth synagogue in Jesus' day.

Prayer

Lord Jesus, You provoked many to think differently as you did in the synagogue of Nazareth. What you wanted to do for the people of your hometown was to make them better, full of justice, compassion and love. But, they were too busy with *their* religion and practices that they forgot that their religion was based on your word and not on their interpretation of it. When you tried to reveal the truth to them, they chose to misunderstand you and it almost cost you your life.

Lord, I keep falling in a similar trap. Sometimes, I close myself from hearing your voice, because it is being heard in a different tone than the one I am used to. Sometimes, I exclude others from hearing your voice, thinking that I am so special and others are not worthy.

I pray that from today, I will be more open and receptive to others, especially when they talk about you. Let your will be done unto me, and save me from my pre-conceptions of myself and of others.

Here, in Nazareth, you have inaugurated your ministry with a daring challenge. Help me face my challenges with an open and a loving heart. Amen.

Notes

1. Tomlinson Dave, ibid. p. 23.
2. For more on this topic, see Bailey, 2008, pp. 147-169.
3. People believed that their gods could not act outside of their territory. This woman was willing to set that aside and changed course.
4. I John 3:11-22.

Jesus in the Synagogue,
Melkite Synagogue
Church, Nazareth

Πνεῦμα Κυρίου ἐπ᾿ ἐμέ, οὗ ἕνεκεν ἔχρισέ με, ἐυαγ
γελίσασθαι πτωχοῖς ἀπέσταλκέ με, ἰάσασθαι τοὺς
συντετριμμένους τὴν καρδίαν, κηρῦξαι αἰχμαλώτοις
ἄφεσιν καὶ τυφλοῖς ἀνάβλεψιν, ἀποστεῖλαι τεθραυσμένους
ἐν ἀφέσει, ἐν ἑαυτοῦ Κυρίου ἑαυτόν·

الشيخ يعلم في المجمع

ان روح الرب علي واجل ذلك مسحني يلي ابشر المساكين وارسلني يشفى
القلوب ولاداوي المأسورين بالغفلة والعميان بالبصر والطلق
الله يشير الي الخلاص واكرز يمنه الرب المقبولة
ويصير الدواء

115

> If a man wishes to be sure of the road he treads on,
> he must close his eyes and walk in the dark.
>
> St. John of the Cross

CHURCH OF ST. ANNE, JERUSALEM

POOL OF BETHESDA

At the entrance of St. Stephen's Gate (Lions' Gate) lie a beautiful garden and ancient ruins of Greco-Roman temples to gods of healing. There stands the majestic Church of St. Anne next to the remains of Byzantine and Crusader churches built over the Pool of Bethesda. An old tradition puts the birthplace of Mary, mother of Jesus, in a cave of St. Anne's crypt.

The Romanesque style church was built by the Crusaders around 1135 and converted to a Muslim school by Saladin in 1192 until it fell into disuse hundreds of years later.

In recognition of French support for the Ottomans in the Crimean War, Sultan Abdülmecid I presented the church to Napoleon III in 1856. France commissioned the Missionary Fathers of Africa, also known as the White Fathers because of the color of their garments, to run the property.

JOHN 5:1-16

5After this there was a festival of the Jews, and Jesus went up to Jerusalem. 2Now in Jerusalem by the Sheep Gate there is a pool, called in Hebrew Beth-zatha, which has five porticoes. 3In these lay many invalids – blind, lame, and paralyzed. 5One man was there who had been ill for thirty-eight years. 6When Jesus saw him lying there and knew that he had been there a long time, he said to him, "Do you want to be made well?" 7The sick man answered him, "Sir, I have no one to put me into the pool when the water is stirred up; and while I am making my way, someone else steps down ahead of me." 8Jesus said to him, "Stand up, take your mat and walk." 9At once the man was made well, and he took up his mat and began to walk. Now that day was a Sabbath. 10So the Jews said to the man who had been cured, "It is the Sabbath; it is not lawful for you to carry your mat." 11But he answered them,

Church of St. Anne and ruins at the Pool of Bethesda, Jerusalem

"The man who made me well said to me, 'Take up your mat and walk.'" [12]*They asked him, "Who is the man who said to you, 'Take it up and walk?'"* [13]*Now the man who had been healed did not know who it was, for Jesus had disappeared in the crowd that was there.* [14]*Later Jesus found him in the temple and said to him, "See, you have been made well! Do not sin anymore, so that nothing worse happens to you."* [15]*The man went away and told the Jews that it was Jesus who had made him well.* [16]*Therefore the Jews started persecuting Jesus, because he was doing such things on the Sabbath.*

Reflection

It seems from the first response of the paralytic to Jesus that he had neither friends nor family to take care of him. He must have tried so many times to plunge in the water, suffering and begging for help and compassion from others for as long as he could remember, but to no avail.

Yet, this paralytic never gave up hope. His strength to confront his suffering had come from within. He had faith, tucked deep inside his heart, which he never thought he had. After being miserable for 38 years, he was still hopeful for a miracle someday and he would be healed. He must have found a way to endure his suffering and live with his physical paralysis. He was helpless, not hopeless. So he stayed near the pool renowned for its healing power.

Then God knocked at his door without him knowing it. A total stranger had the decency and the heart to ask him, *"Do you want to be made well?"* The man may have been shocked but he believed in the honesty of the gesture.

God knows our needs. In response to our prayers, sometimes he speaks to us through others, but we may be so absorbed in our ways, that we fail to raise our eyes and see his outstretched hand prompting us to rise, take our mat and walk.

Jesus knew what the man at the pool wanted. But he went even further than the apparent physical and social want of 38 years. He restored the man's dormant hope in God and empowered his faith in him.

Prayer

Lord, how many times have we asked you why? Why am I born so poor? What did I do to deserve this? Why must I suffer? In the face of world atrocities, where are you, God? Why don't you do something, why don't you help us? How often have we seen the wrongs of those who claim to be your devoted disciples? Why do you let them use your name in such ways?

So sad are we when we ask such questions and never hear him answer – but maybe he does. In Revelations, you said, [9]*"I know your affliction and your poverty, even though you are rich. I know the slander on the part of those who say that they are Jews and are not, but are a synagogue of Satan.* [10]*Do not fear what you are about to suffer. Beware, the devil is about to throw some of you into prison so that you may be tested, and for ten days you will have affliction. Be faithful until death, and I will give you the crown of life."*[1]

Lord, help us endure our suffering and transform it into growth by focusing on you and your glorious resurrection, like the man at the Pool of Bethesda. Grant us the wisdom to feel the warmth of your presence in our suffering and recognize the moment when you tell us to rise, take our mat and walk your way. Amen.

Challenge: Truly say, "Jesus, I trust in you."

Note
1. Revelations 2:9-10.

At funerals we were allowed to recite the Lord's Prayer. As a young child I heard those strange words and had no idea who we were talking to, what the words meant, where they came from or why we were reciting them. When freedom came at last, I had the opportunity to search for their meaning. When you are in total darkness, the tiniest point of light is very bright. For me the Lord's Prayer was that point of light. By the time I found its meaning I was a Christian.

Young woman from Riga, Latvia[1]

CHURCH OF THE PATER NOSTER, JERUSALEM

The Carmelite Cloistered Nuns were entrusted with the care of the Pater Noster Church when the French government received it from the Turkish authorities, following the Crimean War. The convent's main shrine is the traditional grotto where Jesus taught the Lord's Prayer. The gospels of Luke and Matthew refer to his teaching.

LUKE 11: 1-4

[11]*He was praying in a certain place, and after he had finished, one of his disciples said to him, "Lord, teach us to pray, as John taught his disciples."* [2]*He said to them, "When you pray, say: 'Father, hallowed be your name. Your kingdom come.* [3]*Give us each day our daily bread.* [4]*And forgive us our sins, for we ourselves forgive everyone indebted to us. And do not bring us to the time of trial.'"*

MATTHEW 6: 7-15

[7]*"When you are praying, do not heap up empty phrases as the Gentiles do; for they think that they will be heard because of their many words.* [8]*Do not be like them, for your Father knows what you need before you ask him.*

[9]*"Pray then in this way: 'Our Father in heaven, hallowed be your name.* [10]*Your kingdom come. Your will be done, on earth as it is in heaven.* [11]*Give us this day our daily bread.* [12]*And forgive us our debts, as we also have forgiven our debtors.* [13]*And do not bring us to the time of trial, but rescue us from the evil one.'* [14]*For if you forgive others their trespasses, your heavenly Father will also forgive you;* [15]*but if you do not forgive others, neither will your Father forgive your trespasses.'"*

Church of the Pater Noster, Mount of Olives, Jerusalem

Our Father. It is both daring and innovative for Jesus at the time he lived to teach a prayer that started with these words. He probably had two intentions with this beginning.

First, he wanted those who used that prayer to have the courage and the confidence to call God the Almighty, as Father; the fear of God and obedience to his commandments was central to the Judaism of Jesus' time, and still is. Instead of a fearful God, Jesus presents him as a compassionate Father; this can be inferred from the context of all of Jesus' teachings. He had always portrayed God as merciful, compassionate and loving. From the gospel, we also know that Jesus referred to God as his own Father, which suggests that those who recite the Lord's Prayer can consider the Father their own. It is an invitation to have a personal and direct relationship with God, the Father, without introduction or fear.

The second intention is that anyone praying these words, regardless of location and time, shares the Father with everyone else praying the same words. God, our Father, is no longer restricted to a group of people, but he is universal, of all humanity.

While Jesus wants us to have a personal relationship with God, some limits have to be set. This is done by reminding us that we are humans living on earth, while the Father is in heaven. The second of the Ten Commandments reads, "honor thy father and mother." If we need to honor our earthly parents, how much more should we honor and respect our heavenly Father?

Hallowed be thy name. We ask the Father to do his marvelous works that hold us in awe, even for the simplest of things – a beautiful sunset, the softness of cool breeze on a hot summer's day, the beauty of a flower, the feeling of home thousands of miles away from home.

Thy kingdom come. All Christians pray for the return of Jesus in God's glorious kingdom. The gospel does not clearly state the definition or the time of the coming of God's kingdom. However, it is clear that God's kingdom is ruled by his unconditional love, for which we pray in this life – in sacrament, in each other, in nature.

Thy will be done, on earth as it is in heaven. Jesus teaches us to surrender our ego and will to the Father – one of the hardest things to do. And yet, this surrender is not requested to be done before a tyrant or a bully, but to a loving and caring Father. The will of the Father in heaven is the extension of the love that already exists in the heavenly kingdom towards earth and humanity. God sent his only son to proclaim the message of love and gave his life unconditionally. Jesus so vividly portrayed this image in many of his parables, like the prodigal son. He only wants the best for us. The problem is that sometimes we are so absorbed in our own ways, that we forget to see whether they are really good for us and are in line with God's commandments.

In his darkest hour, in agony and distress, Jesus prayed, "*Father, let the cup pass away from me, yet not my will, but yours be done!*" Nobody wants to suffer, not even Jesus in his humanity, but he accepted his fate with a loving heart, for it was the will of the Father. The focus of Jesus' surrender to suffering was on the glorious resurrection; a new life and our salvation.

Give us this day our daily bread. Maybe out of sheer determination, can we withstand days of hunger, but when we see our child hungry, the rules change. Despair and anger may overcome any resolve and any man-God relationship may be threatened. Aware of this

The Lord's Prayer in different languages, Church of the Pater Noster, Jerusalem

worry, Jesus taught us to pray to the Father to give us today and every day bread that sustains us physically, spiritually and metaphysically. The physical bread sustains the functions of the body, the spiritual bread sustains the soul, and the metaphysical bread takes us to a different spiritual dimension in our relationship with God and society. Jesus said, *"Love your God and your neighbor as yourself."* All three aspects of the bread of life nourish that love and keep relationships between us and God and between us and society undisturbed and balanced.

Forgive us our trespasses as we forgive those who trespass against us. Here, Jesus introduced another key innovation. He made the Father's forgiveness of sin conditional to our own forgiveness of the sin of others. In the parable of the wicked servant, the master forgave his servant a serious debt, but when he went out and saw another servant who owed him much less, he refused to forgive him. The master punished him severely. It is very hard to forgive, and we need the love of God to do so. While Jesus was on the cross, he said, *"Forgive them father, for they do not know what they do."* The Lord's Prayer calls us to open our eyes to God's way of perfect forgiving love.

Lead us not into temptation. Jesus teaches us to resist all temptation. When he withdrew to the desert for 40 days, he was hungry and an easy prey for the tempter. But he proved resilient and overcame all temptation.

And deliver us from evil. Like temptation, there is no escape from evil. If there is good, there must be evil. Jesus taught us to pray to the Father to preserve us from the yoke of becoming slaves to evil and evildoers.

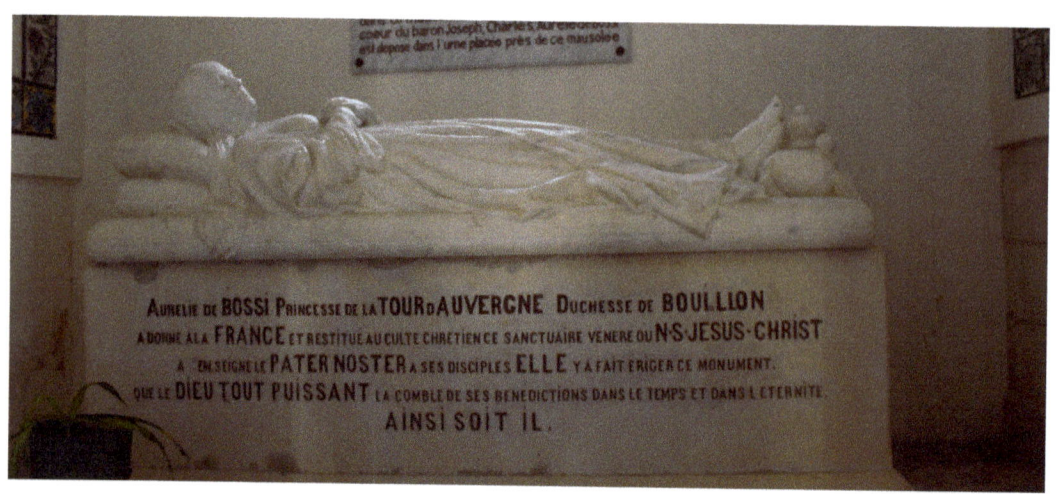

Tomb of Aurélie de Bossi, Church of the Pater Noster, Jerusalem

The Lord's Prayer

Our Father, who art in heaven,

hallowed be thy name, thy kingdom come,

thy will be done, on earth as it is in heaven.

Give us this day our daily bread,

and forgive us our trespasses

as we forgive those who trespass against us,

and lead us not into temptation,

but deliver us from evil.

For thine is the kingdom,

the power and the glory forever and ever. Amen.

Chapel, convent for Carmelite Sisters, Church of the Pater Noster, Jerusalem

---

Note

1. Bailey K. 2008. Ibid. The answer of a young woman, member of the Riga Lutheran Church in Latvia, to a question by Kenneth Bailey about how she came to the Christian faith, in spite of the communist state that sought to indoctrinate atheism. This encounter was after the fall of the Soviet Union.

> Be beautiful inside, in your hearts, with the lasting charm of a gentle
> and quiet spirit which is so precious to God.
>
> I Peter 3:4

MOUNT OF BEATITUDES, GALILEE

SERMON ON THE MOUNT

One of the features near the western shore of the Sea of Galilee is a hill where stands an octagonal building surrounded by eucalyptus trees and a beautiful garden. The Church of the Beatitudes, built in 1936, is administered by Franciscan nuns, who also provide hotel services to pilgrims in adjacent quarters.

According to a fourth century record, it was on this mount that Jesus gave his famous sermon that comprised the heart of his teachings.

MATTHEW 5-7

Chapter 5: ¹*When Jesus saw the crowds, he went up the mountain; and after he sat down, his disciples came to him.* ²*Then he began to speak, and taught them, saying:*

³*"Blessed are the poor in spirit, for theirs is the kingdom of heaven.* ⁴*Blessed are those who mourn, for they will be comforted.* ⁵*Blessed are the meek, for they will inherit the earth.* ⁶*Blessed are those who hunger and thirst for righteousness, for they will be filled.* ⁷*Blessed are the merciful, for they will receive mercy.* ⁸*Blessed are the pure in heart, for they will see God.* ⁹*Blessed are the peacemakers, for they will be called children of God.* ¹⁰*Blessed are those who are persecuted for righteousness' sake, for theirs is the kingdom of heaven.* ¹¹*Blessed are you when people revile you and persecute you and utter all kinds of evil against you falsely on my account.* ¹²*Rejoice and be glad, for your reward is great in heaven, for in the same way they persecuted the prophets who were before you.*

¹³*You are the salt of the earth; but if salt has lost its taste, how can its saltiness be restored? It is no longer good for anything, but is thrown out and trampled under foot.* ¹⁴*You are the light of the world. A city built on a hill cannot be hid.* ¹⁵*No one after lighting a lamp puts it under the bushel basket, but on the lamp stand, and it gives light to all in the house.* ¹⁶*In the same way, let your light shine before others, so that they may see your good works and give glory to your Father in heaven.*

¹⁷*Do not think that I have come to abolish the law or the prophets; I have come not to abolish but to fulfill.* ¹⁸*For truly I tell you, until heaven and earth pass away, not one letter, not one stroke of a letter, will pass from the law until all is accomplished.* ¹⁹*Therefore, whoever breaks one of the least of these commandments, and teaches others to do the same, will be called least in the kingdom of heaven; but whoever does them and teaches them will be called great in the kingdom of heaven.* ²⁰*For I tell you, unless your righteousness exceeds that of the scribes and Pharisees, you will never enter the kingdom of heaven.*

²¹*You have heard that it was said to those of ancient times, 'You shall not murder'; and 'whoever murders shall be liable to judgment.'* ²²*But I say to you that if you are*

Church of the Beatitudes, near Tabgha

angry with a brother or sister, you will be liable to judgment; and if you insult a brother or sister, you will be liable to the council; and if you say, 'You fool,' you will be liable to the hell of fire. 23So when you are offering your gift at the altar, if you remember that your brother or sister has something against you, 24leave your gift there before the altar and go; first be reconciled to your brother or sister, and then come and offer your gift. 25Come to terms quickly with your accuser while you are on the way to court with him, or your accuser may hand you over to the judge, and the judge to the guard, and you will be thrown into prison. 26Truly I tell you, you will never get out until you have paid the last penny.

27You have heard that it was said, 'You shall not commit adultery.' 28But I say to you that everyone who looks at a woman with lust has already committed adultery with her in his heart. 29If your right eye causes you to sin, tear it out and throw it away; it is better for you to lose one of your members than for your whole body to be thrown into hell. 30And if your right hand causes you to sin, cut it off and throw it away; it is better for you to lose one of your members than for your whole body to go into hell. 31It was also said, 'Whoever divorces his wife, let him give her a certificate of divorce.' 32But I say to you that anyone who divorces his wife, except on the ground of unchastity, causes her to commit adultery; and whoever marries a divorced woman commits adultery.

33Again, you have heard that it was said to those of ancient times, 'You shall not swear falsely, but carry out the vows you have made to the Lord.' 34But I say to you, do not swear at all, either by heaven, for it is the throne of God, 35or by the earth, for it is his footstool, or by Jerusalem, for it is the city of the great King. 36And do not swear by your head, for you cannot make one hair white or black. 37Let your word be 'Yes, yes' or 'No, no;' anything more than this comes from the evil one.

38You have heard that it was said, 'An eye for an eye and a tooth for a tooth.' 39But I say to you, do not resist an evildoer. But if anyone strikes you on the right cheek, turn the other also; 40and if anyone wants to sue you and take your coat, give your cloak as well; 41and if anyone forces you to go one mile, go also the second mile. 42Give to everyone who begs from you, and do not refuse anyone who wants to borrow from you.

43You have heard that it was said, 'You shall love your neighbor and hate your enemy.' 44But I say to you, love your enemies and pray for those who persecute you, 45so that you may be children of your Father in heaven; for he makes his sun rise on the evil and on the good, and sends rain on the righteous and on the unrighteous. 46For if you love those who love you, what reward do you have? Do not even the tax collectors do the same? 47And if you greet only your brothers and sisters, what more are you doing than others? Do not even the Gentiles do the same? 48Be perfect, therefore, as your heavenly Father is perfect."

Chapter 6: 1"Beware of practicing your piety before others in order to be seen by them; for then you have no reward from your Father in heaven. 2So whenever you give alms, do not sound a trumpet before you, as the hypocrites do in the synagogues and in the streets, so that they may be praised by others. Truly I tell you, they have received their reward. 3But when you give alms, do not let your left hand know what your right hand is doing, 4so that your alms may be done in secret; and your Father who sees in secret will reward you.

5And whenever you pray, do not be like the hypocrites; for they love to stand and pray in

Altar, Church of the Beatitudes, near Tabgha

the synagogues and at the street corners, so that they may be seen by others. Truly I tell you, they have received their reward. ⁶But whenever you pray, go into your room and shut the door and pray to your Father who is in secret; and your Father who sees in secret will reward you. ⁷When you are praying, do not heap up empty phrases as the Gentiles do; for they think that they will be heard because of their many words. ⁸Do not be like them, for your Father knows what you need before you ask him.

⁹Pray then in this way: Our Father in heaven, hallowed be your name. ¹⁰Your kingdom come. Your will be done, on earth as it is in heaven. ¹¹Give us this day our daily bread. ¹²And forgive us our debts, as we also have forgiven our debtors. ¹³And do not bring us to the time of trial, but rescue us from the evil one. ¹⁴For if you forgive others their trespasses, your heavenly Father will also forgive you; ¹⁵but if you do not forgive others, neither will your Father forgive your trespasses.

¹⁶And whenever you fast, do not look dismal, like the hypocrites, for they disfigure their faces so as to show others that they are fasting. Truly I tell you, they have received

their reward. ¹⁷But when you fast, put oil on your head and wash your face, ¹⁸so that your fasting may be seen not by others but by your Father who is in secret; and your Father who sees in secret will reward you.

¹⁹Do not store up for yourselves treasures on earth, where moth and rust consume and where thieves break in and steal; ²⁰but store up for yourselves treasures in heaven, where neither moth nor rust consumes and where thieves do not break in and steal. ²¹For where your treasure is, there your heart will be also. ²²"The eye is the lamp of the body. So, if your eye is healthy, your whole body will be full of light; ²³but if your eye is unhealthy, your whole body will be full of darkness. If then the light in you is darkness, how great is the darkness! ²⁴No one can serve two masters; for a slave will either hate the one and love the other, or be devoted to the one and despise the other. You cannot serve God and wealth.

²⁵Therefore I tell you, do not worry about your life, what you will eat or what you will drink, or about your body, what you will wear. Is not life more than food, and the body more than clothing? ²⁶Look at the birds of

Interior, Church of the Beatitudes, near Tabgha

the air; they neither sow nor reap nor gather into barns, and yet your heavenly Father feeds them. Are you not of more value than they? 27And can any of you by worrying add a single hour to your span of life? 28And why do you worry about clothing? Consider the lilies of the field, how they grow; they neither toil nor spin, 29yet I tell you, even Solomon in all his glory was not clothed like one of these. 30But if God so clothes the grass of the field, which is alive today and tomorrow is thrown into the oven, will he not much more clothe you – you of little faith? 31Therefore do not worry, saying, 'What will we eat?' or 'What will we drink?' or 'What will we wear?' 32For it is the Gentiles who strive for all these things; and indeed your heavenly Father knows that you need all these things. 33But strive first for the kingdom of God and his righteousness, and all these things will be given to you as well. 34So do not worry about tomorrow, for tomorrow will bring worries of its own. Today's trouble is enough for today."

Chapter 7: 1"Do not judge, so that you may not be judged. 2For with the judgment you make you will be judged, and the measure you give will be the measure you get. 3Why do you see the speck in your neighbor's eye, but do not notice the log in your own eye? 4Or how can you say to your neighbor, 'Let me take the speck out of your eye,' while the log is in your own eye? 5You hypocrite, first take the log out of your own eye, and then you will see clearly to take the speck out of your neighbor's eye. 6Do not give what is holy to dogs; and do not throw your pearls before swine, or they will trample them under foot and turn and maul you.

7Ask, and it will be given you; search, and you will find; knock, and the door will be opened for you. 8For everyone who asks receives, and everyone who searches finds, and for everyone who knocks, the door will be opened. 9Is there anyone among you who, if your child asks for bread, will give a stone? 10Or if the child asks for a fish, will give a snake? 11If you then, who are evil, know how to give good gifts to your children, how much more will your Father in heaven give good things to those who ask him!

12In everything do to others as you would have them do to you; for this is the law and the prophets. 13Enter through the narrow gate; for the gate is wide and the road is easy that leads to destruction, and there are many who take it. 14For the gate is narrow and the road is hard that leads to life, and there are few who find it.

15Beware of false prophets, who come to you in sheep's clothing but inwardly are ravenous wolves. 16You will know them by their fruits. Are grapes gathered from thorns, or figs from thistles? 17In the same way, every good tree bears good fruit, but the bad tree bears bad fruit. 18A good tree cannot bear bad fruit, nor can a bad tree bear good fruit. 19Every tree that does not bear good fruit is cut down and thrown into the fire. 20Thus you will know them by their fruits.

21Not everyone who says to me, 'Lord, Lord,' will enter the kingdom of heaven, but only the one who does the will of my Father in heaven. 22On that day many will say to me, 'Lord, Lord, did we not prophesy in your name, and cast out demons in your name, and do many deeds of power in your name?' 23Then I will declare to them, 'I never knew you; go away from me, you evildoers.' 24Everyone then who hears these words of mine and acts on them will be like a wise man who built his house on rock. 25The rain fell, the floods came, and the winds blew and beat on that house, but it did not fall, because it had been founded on rock. 26And everyone who hears these words of mine and does not act on them will be like a foolish man who built his house on sand.

[27]The rain fell, and the floods came, and the winds blew and beat against that house, and it fell – and great was its fall!" [28]Now when Jesus had finished saying these things, the crowds were astounded at his teaching, [29]for he taught them as one having authority, and not as their scribes.

Reflection

"The days are surely coming, says the Lord, when I will establish a new covenant with the house of Israel and with the house of Judah; not like the covenant that I made with their ancestors, on the day when I took them by the hand to lead them out of the land of Egypt; for they did not continue in my covenant, and so I had no concern for them, says the Lord. This is the covenant that I will make with the house of Israel after those days says the Lord: I will put my laws in their hearts, and I will be their God, and they shall be my people. And they shall not teach one another or say to each other, 'Know the Lord,' for they shall all know me, from the least of them to the greatest. For I will be merciful toward their iniquities, and I will remember their sins no more."[1]

On the Mount of the Beatitudes, God established a new covenant with his people. Unlike the old covenant filled with threats of death, the new covenant was built on words of life. The Sermon on the Mount is the cornerstone of the new law, which can be summarized in one word – love – with the binding sign being faith in the one who made it.

Jesus understood the dynamics of Jewish society. For him, the law that advocated external behavioral and physical sacrifice had run its course. He tried to go beyond those physical features into a deeper and a more spiritual realm. He wanted a law that advocated justice, compassion, mercy, forgiveness and the all-encompassing law of love as an inseparable guideline in our life.

God's omnipresent law of love found in each one of these was overshadowed, even obliterated by stressing some of its physical practices. Jesus tried to reintroduce the spiritual dimension of the law and the prophets through his beatitudes and his sermon. For him, the physical practices of the law were no guarantee for salvation. It was the spiritual sacrifice and not the physical one that was so crucial to a healthy relationship with God. It was the spiritual circumcision and not the physical one that was important to God. He was telling the golden rule: *"In everything, do to others as you would have them do to you; for this is the law and the prophets."[2]*

In this context, the covenant of love, to the people of his day, was to be viewed as an uprising in the way of teaching the law. It was the same spiritual uprising that led to the persecution and killing of all the prophets. Instead of reiterating *"An eye for an eye and a tooth for a tooth,"* Jesus said, *"Blessed are the merciful, for they will receive mercy."* And instead of reminding, *"You shall love your neighbor and hate your enemy,"[3]* Jesus said: *"Love your enemies and pray for those who persecute you, so that you may be children of your Father in Heaven."[4]*

This new covenant remains as long we have the necessary faith in the one who made it; the faith that helps us keep and continue the law of love. Otherwise, we are no different than our predecessors under the old covenant. The apostle Paul explained this point in his letters to the Romans: *[13]"Now I am speaking to you Gentiles. Inasmuch then as I am an apostle to the Gentiles, I glorify my ministry [14]in order to make my own people jealous, and thus save some of them. [15]For if their rejection is the reconciliation of the world, what will their acceptance be but life from the dead! [16]If the part of the dough offered as first fruits is holy, then the whole batch is holy; and if the root is holy, then the branches also are holy. [17]But if some of the branches were broken off, and you, a wild olive shoot, were grafted in their place to share the rich root of the olive tree, [18]do not boast over the branches. If you do boast, remember that it is not you that support the root, but the root that supports you. [19]You will say, 'Branches were broken off so that I might be grafted in.' [20]That is true. They were broken off because of their unbelief, but you stand only through faith. So do not become proud, but stand in awe. [21]For if God did not spare the natural branches, perhaps he will not spare you. [22]Note then the kindness and the severity of God: severity toward those who have fallen, but God's kindness toward you, provided you continue in his kindness; otherwise you also will be cut off. [23]And even those of Israel, if they do not persist in unbelief, will be grafted in, for God has the power to graft them in again."[5]*

The Mount of Beatitudes is the mount of love and faith. It is a place to feel spiritual pleasure and satisfaction with one's faith in God. It is a place of contemplation, a place of remembrance of the eternal gift of God's love.

Prayer

Lord, to live my life in the spirit of your sermon on the mount is a serious challenge, but not impossible. I ask you to strengthen my heart and open my mind.

Lord, for my church and community, it is also hard to live by your sermon. Bless our souls with a deeper understanding so that the challenge becomes a joy and a code for a life to be shared with others. Amen.

Notes
1. Jeremiah 31:31-34.
2. Matthew 7:12.
3. Matthew 5:43.
4. Matthew 5:44-45.
5. Romans 11:13-24.

At once his fame began to spread throughout
the surrounding region of Galilee.

Mark 1:28

CAPERNAUM

Some 2,000 people lived in Capernaum in Jesus' day. But being near a major crossroad known as the Via Maris, and as a prime fishing town, this city would have been visited by hundreds, if not thousands, daily. There is no doubt that if rocks could talk, each one on every street corner would have a story to tell about Jesus when he was there.

Having been rejected from his hometown of Nazareth, Jesus moved to Capernaum, which became the center of his Galilean public ministry. Archaeological evidence from the 19th and 20th centuries strongly suggests a veneration to a special room within a sacred *insula* complex.[1] The city and its house were built in the first century BC and continued to exist until roughly the 11th century. The room's flooring was changed more than once. In the fourth century AD, it was enclosed with an octagonal wall and served as a *domus ecclesia* (house church) by a Christian community. In the fifth century, the whole structure was enlarged as a Byzantine church, adorned with mosaics and domes. Graffiti inscriptions on its inner walls mention the name of Peter.

Of all Christian sites in the Holy Land venerated throughout the ages, Capernaum, the synagogue and the house of Peter stand out as some of the most authentic. It was here where Jesus lived, preached, taught and healed, where he prayed at sunrise and sunset, where he gave some of his most important teachings.

There are many events that happened in Capernaum or in its immediate vicinity. Here are some gospel references.

MARK 1:16-20

16 As Jesus passed along the Sea of Galilee, he saw Simon and his brother Andrew casting a net into the lake—for they were fishermen. 17And Jesus said to them, 'Follow me and I will make you fish for people.' 18And immediately they left their nets and followed him. 19As he went a little farther, he saw James son of Zebedee and his brother John, who were in their boat mending the nets. 20Immediately he called them; and they left their father Zebedee in the boat with the hired men, and followed him.

MARK 1:21-28

[21]They went to Capernaum; and when the Sabbath came, he entered the synagogue and taught. [22]They were astounded at his teaching, for he taught them as one having authority, and not as the scribes. [23]Just then there was in their synagogue a man with an unclean spirit, [24]and he cried out, "What have you to do with us, Jesus of Nazareth? Have you come to destroy us? I know who you are, the Holy One of God." [25]But Jesus rebuked him, saying, "Be silent, and come out of him!" [26]And the unclean spirit, throwing him into convulsions and crying with a loud voice, came out of him. [27]They were all amazed, and they kept on asking one another, "What is this? A new teaching – with authority! He commands even the unclean spirits, and they obey him." [28]At once his fame began to spread throughout the surrounding region of Galilee.

MARK 1:29-34

[29]As soon as they left the synagogue, they entered the house of Simon and Andrew, with James and John. [30]Now Simon's mother-in-law was in bed with a fever, and they told him about her at once. [31]He came and took her by the hand and lifted her up. Then the fever left her, and she began to serve them.

[32]That evening, at sunset, they brought to him all who were sick or possessed with demons. [33]And the whole city was gathered around the door.

[34]And he cured many who were sick with various diseases, and cast out many demons; and he would not permit the demons to speak, because they knew him.

MARK 2:1-12

[1]When he returned to Capernaum after some days, it was reported that he was at home. [2]So many gathered around that there was no longer room for them, not even in front of the door; and he was speaking the word to them. [3]Then some people came, bringing to him a paralyzed man, carried by four of them. [4]And when they could not bring him to Jesus because of the crowd, they removed the roof above him; and after having dug through it, they let down the mat on which the paralytic lay. [5]When Jesus saw their faith, he said to the paralytic, "Son, your sins are forgiven." [6]Now some of the scribes were sitting there, questioning in their hearts, [7]"Why does this fellow speak in this way? It is blasphemy! Who can forgive sins but God alone?" [8]At once Jesus perceived in his spirit that they were discussing these questions among themselves; and he said to them, "Why do you raise such questions in your hearts? [9]Which is easier, to say to the paralytic, 'Your sins are forgiven,' or to say, 'Stand up and take your mat and walk?' [10]But so that you may know that the Son of Man has authority on earth to forgive sins." He said to the paralytic, [11]"I say to you, stand up, take your mat and go to your home." [12]And he stood up, and immediately took the mat and went out before all of them; so that they were all amazed and glorified God, saying, "We have never seen anything like this!"

MARK 3:1-6

[1]Again he entered the synagogue, and a man was there who had a withered hand. [2]They watched him to see whether he would cure him on the Sabbath, so that they might accuse him. [3]And he said to the man who had the withered hand, "Come forward." [4]Then he said to them, "Is it lawful to do good or to do harm on the Sabbath, to save life or to kill?" But they were silent. [5]He looked around at them with anger; he was grieved at their hardness of heart and said to the man, "Stretch out your hand." He stretched it out, and his hand was restored. [6]The Pharisees went out and immediately conspired with the Herodians against him, how to destroy him.

Synagogue, first century AD, Magdala

MARK 3:31-34

[31]*Then his mother and his brothers came; and standing outside, they sent to him and called him. * [32]*A crowd was sitting around him; and they said to him, "Your mother and your brothers and sisters are outside, asking for you."* [33]*And he replied, "Who are my mother and my brothers?"* [34]*And looking at those who sat around him, he said, "Here are my mother and my brothers!"*

MATTHEW 17:24-27

[24]*When they reached Capernaum, the collectors of the temple tax came to Peter and said, "Does your teacher not pay the temple tax?"* [25]*He said, "Yes, he does." And when he came home, Jesus spoke of it first, asking, "What do you think, Simon? From whom do kings of the earth take toll or tribute? From their children or from others?"* [26]*When Peter said, "From others," Jesus said to him, "Then the children are free.* [27]*However, so that we do not give offence to them, go to the lake and cast a hook; take the first fish that comes up; and when you open its mouth, you will find a coin; take that and give it to them for you and me."*

MATTHEW 8:5-13

[5]*When he entered Capernaum, a centurion came to him, appealing to him* [6]*and saying, "Lord, my servant is lying at home paralyzed, in terrible distress."* [7]*And he said to him, "I will come and cure him."* [8]*The centurion answered, "Lord, I am not worthy to have you come under my roof; but only speak the word, and my servant will be healed.* [9]*For I also am a man under authority, with soldiers under me; and I say to one, 'Go,' and he goes, and to another, 'Come,' and he comes, and to my slave, 'Do this,' and the slave does it."* [10]*When Jesus heard him, he was amazed and said to those who followed him, "Truly I tell you, in no one in Israel have I found such faith.* [11]*I tell you, many will come from east and west and will eat with Abraham and Isaac and Jacob in the kingdom of heaven,* [12]*while the heirs of the kingdom will be thrown into the outer darkness, where there will be weeping and gnashing of teeth."* [13]*And to the centurion Jesus said, "Go; let it be done for you according to your faith." And the servant was healed in that hour.*

JOHN 6:22-71

[22]*The next day the crowd that had stayed on the other side of the sea saw that there had been only one boat there. They also saw that Jesus had not got into the boat with his disciples, but that his disciples had gone away alone.* [23]*Then some boats from Tiberias came near the place where they had eaten the bread after the Lord had given thanks.* [24]*So when the crowd saw that neither Jesus nor his disciples were there, they themselves got into the boats and went to Capernaum looking for Jesus.* [25]*When they found him on the other side of the sea, they said to him, "Rabbi, when did you come here?"* [26]*Jesus answered them, "Very truly, I tell you, you are looking for me, not because you saw signs, but because you ate your fill of the loaves.* [27]*Do not work for the food that perishes, but for the food that endures for eternal life, which the Son of Man will give you. For it is on him that God the Father has set his seal."*

[28]*Then they said to him, "What must we do to perform the works of God?"* [29]*Jesus answered them, "This is the work of God, that you believe in him whom he has sent."* [30]*So they said to him, "What sign are you going to give us then, so that we may see it and believe you? What work are you performing?* [31]*Our ancestors ate the manna in the wilderness; as it is written, 'He gave them bread from heaven to eat.'"* [32]*Then Jesus said to them, "Very truly, I tell you, it was not Moses who gave you the bread from heaven, but it is my Father who gives you*

the true bread from heaven. [33]For the bread of God is that which comes down from heaven and gives life to the world." [34]They said to him, "Sir, give us this bread always." [35]Jesus said to them, "I am the bread of life. Whoever comes to me will never be hungry, and whoever believes in me will never be thirsty. [36]But I said to you that you have seen me and yet do not believe. [37]Everything that the Father gives me will come to me, and anyone who comes to me I will never drive away; [38]for I have come down from heaven, not to do my own will, but the will of him who sent me. [39]And this is the will of him who sent me, that I should lose nothing of all that he has given me, but raise it up on the last day. [40]This is indeed the will of my Father, that all who see the Son and believe in him may have eternal life; and I will raise them up on the last day." [41]Then the Jews began to complain about him because he said, "I am the bread that came down from heaven." [42]They were saying, "Is not this Jesus, the son of Joseph, whose father and mother we know? How can he now say, 'I have come down from heaven?'" [43]Jesus answered them, "Do not complain among yourselves. [44]No one can come to me unless drawn by the Father who sent me; and I will raise that person up on the last day. [45]It is written in the prophets, 'And they shall all be taught by God.' Everyone who has heard and learned from the Father comes to me. [46]Not that anyone has seen the Father except the one who is from God; he has seen the Father. [47]Very truly, I tell you, whoever believes has eternal life. [48]I am the bread of life. [49]Your ancestors ate the manna in the wilderness, and they died. [50]This is the bread that comes down from heaven, so that one may eat of it and not die. [51]I am the living bread that came down from heaven. Whoever eats of this bread will live forever; and the bread that I will give for the life of the world is my flesh." [52]The Jews then disputed among themselves, saying, "How can this man give us his flesh to eat?" [53]So Jesus said to them, "Very truly, I tell you, unless you eat the flesh of the Son of Man and drink his blood, you have no life in you. [54]Those who eat my flesh and drink my blood have eternal life, and I will raise them up on the last day; [55]for my flesh is true food and my blood is true drink. [56]Those who eat my flesh and drink my blood abide in me, and I in them. [57]Just as the living Father sent me, and I live because of the Father, so whoever eats me will live because of me. [58]This is the bread that came down from heaven, not like that which your ancestors ate, and they died. But the one who eats this bread will live forever." [59]He said these things while he was teaching in the synagogue at Capernaum.

[60]When many of his disciples heard it, they said, "This teaching is difficult; who can accept it?" [61]But Jesus, being aware that his disciples were complaining about it, said to them, "Does this offend you? [62]Then what if you were to see the Son of Man ascending to where he was before? [63]It is the spirit that gives life; the flesh is useless. The words that I have spoken to you are spirit and life. [64]But among you there are some who do not believe." For Jesus knew from the first who were the ones that did not believe, and who was the one that would betray him. [65]And he said, "For this reason I have told you that no one can come to me unless it is granted by the Father." [66]Because of this many of his disciples turned back and no longer went about with him. [67]So Jesus asked the twelve, "Do you also wish to go away?" [68]Simon Peter answered him, "Lord, to whom can we go? You have the words of eternal life. [69]We have come to believe and know that you are the Holy One of God." [70]Jesus answered them, "Did I not choose you, the twelve? Yet one of you is a devil." [71]He was speaking of Judas son of Simon Iscariot, for he, though

Late fourth-century A.D. synagogue, built over the first one there in Jesus' time, Capernaum

one of the twelve, was going to betray him.

MATTHEW 11:20-24
[20] *Then he began to reproach the cities in which most of his deeds of power had been done, because they did not repent.* [21] *"Woe to you, Chorazin! Woe to you, Bethsaida! For if the deeds of power done in you had been done in Tyre and Sidon, they would have repented long ago in sackcloth and ashes.* [22] *But I tell you, on the day of judgment it will be more tolerable for Tyre and Sidon than for you.* [23] *And you, Capernaum, will you be exalted to heaven? No, you will be brought down to Hades. For if the deeds of power done in you had been done in Sodom, it would have remained until this day.* [24] *But I tell you that on the day of judgment it will be more tolerable for the land of Sodom than for you."*

Reflection

People were so eager for somebody like Jesus. Talking the way he did, with captivating authority, was unlike any teaching they had ever heard before. Finally they had found somebody to whom they could entrust their life and future. He performed miracles and exhibited signs that only an anointed person of God could do. What a joy it must have been to be in his presence.

But the moment people started admiring his words and focusing their attention on him, Jesus often decided to add some radical teaching that would upset and confuse most Jews. Take for example his discourse on the bread of life in the synagogue at Capernaum when he said, *"Those who eat my flesh and drink my blood have eternal life."* Jesus' words were at times so blasphemous and outrageous that even some of his own disciples abandoned him. Others, though, remained to acknowledge the true nature of Jesus. In the words of Peter talking on behalf of the twelve disciples, Jesus was the Holy One of God and his radical teaching, in spite of how shocking it sounded to some at the time, amounted to nothing less than eternal life.

It is impossible to understand Jesus' words if we take them literally. Jesus always challenged his audience to think outside the box. When he spoke about something in spiritual and metaphysical terms, some listeners misunderstood them in their physical and material meaning. In the case of the bread of life discourse, he was setting the stage for the eucharistic meal. Such news, which seemed outrageous then, became a cornerstone of Christianity.

Prayer

Lord, in this hometown of your Galilean ministry you performed so many miracles and taught so much. I am here today, focusing my whole attention on your words and trying to hear you with my inner senses. Grant me the will and the power, to stand fast against those evils that are meant to destroy your image as the eternal source of spiritual bread. Amen.

Note

1. An *insula* is a block or group of rooms used as homes located on three sides of a central courtyard. The forth side of the courtyard opens on a street within the city. This kind of housing is typical of Capernaum, Bethsaida, Chorazin and other Galilean cities in Jesus' day.

Church of Capernaum over the sacred insula and ruins, Capernaum

> The privilege that we have to adore Him every day is one of His greatest gifts. If you have a clean heart, you will be able always to see that wonderful connection between
> the Bread of Life and the broken body of Christ in the Poor.
>
> Mother Theresa

TABGHA

CHURCH OF THE MULTIPLICATION OF THE LOAVES AND FISH

Tabgha's original name comes from the Greek word Heptapegon, or seven springs. Some of these are still visible today near the church and the road that leads north to Capernaum. Heptapegon – often misread and mispronounced over the years in Arabic, replacing the Ps with Bs – changed to Tabgha.

A story of Egeria, a pilgrim in the late forth century, tells how Jesus placed the basket of loaves and fish on a rock before he performed the miracle. Later, the same rock was slightly moved and its angle adjusted to serve as the altar of a fifth-century Byzantine church built in memory of the miracle. The rock sits under a modern altar today.

The church had a beautiful mosaic floor depicting different plants and animals characteristic of Nile area flora and fauna. The church and its mosaics sustained much destruction and burned at the hands of the Persians during their short-lived conquest of AD 614. They fell into historical darkness, only to be re-discovered in the 1930s. The current German Benedictine church was built in 1982. In June 2015, buildings on the grounds sustained serious damage from a fire allegedly torched by a radical Jewish group; fortunately the

sanctuary and the beautiful mosaics were spared.

MARK 6:7-13

[7] *He called the twelve and began to send them out two by two, and gave them authority over the unclean spirits.* [8] *He ordered them to take nothing for their journey except a staff; no bread, no bag, no money in their belts;* [9] *but to wear sandals and not to put on two tunics.* [10] *He said to them, "Wherever you enter a house, stay there until you leave the place.* [11] *If any place will not welcome you and they refuse to hear you, as you leave, shake off the dust that is on your feet as a testimony against them."* [12] *So they went out and proclaimed that all should repent.* [13] *They cast out many demons, and anointed with oil many who were sick and cured them.*

MARK 6:30-44

[30] *The apostles gathered around Jesus, and told him all that they had done and taught.* [31] *He said to them, "Come away to a deserted place all by yourselves and rest a while." For many were coming and going, and they had no leisure even to eat.* [32] *And they went away in the boat to a deserted place by themselves.* [33] *Now many saw them going and recognized*

Benedictine Church of the Multiplication of the Loaves and Fish, Tabgha

them, and they hurried there on foot from all the towns and arrived ahead of them. ³⁴As he went ashore, he saw a great crowd; and he had compassion for them, because they were like sheep without a shepherd; and he began to teach them many things. ³⁵When it grew late, his disciples came to him and said, "This is a deserted place, and the hour is now very late; ³⁶send them away so that they may go into the surrounding country and villages and buy something for themselves to eat." ³⁷But he answered them, "You give them something to eat." They said to him, "Are we to go and buy two hundred denarii worth of bread, and give it to them to eat?" ³⁸And he said to them, "How many loaves have you? Go and see." When they had found out, they said, "Five, and two fish." ³⁹Then he ordered them to get all the people to sit down in groups on the green grass. ⁴⁰So they sat down in groups of hundreds and of fifties. ⁴¹Taking the five loaves and the two *fish, he looked up to heaven, and blessed and broke the loaves, and gave them to his disciples to set before the people; and he divided the two fish among them all. ⁴²And*

all ate and were filled; ⁴³and they took up twelve baskets full of broken pieces and of the fish. ⁴⁴Those who had eaten the loaves numbered five thousand men.

Reflection 1

Earlier in the gospel, Jesus sent out the Twelve two by two with the mission of proclaiming repentance, and he empowered them with some of his authority to cast out demons. A few days later, they returned, feeling proud and showing no gratitude towards Jesus. Ironically, they thought of themselves as teachers, forgetting who the real teacher was. Jesus decided to teach them a lesson about discipleship. He demanded that they feed the hungry crowds. The disciples did not know what to do as Jesus had stripped them of his authority and rendered them worthless.

In John 6:35, Jesus said, *"I am the bread of life."* He gave the bread of life, through the twelve apostles, to the twelve tribes of Israel. Shortly after this feeding miracle, Jesus set out to teach and heal in Gentile cities of Tyre, Sidon and Decapolis on the east bank of the Jordan and the Sea of Galilee. Here the story is given a new perspective. Jesus the Messiah, who was to come exclusively for the Jews, was now healing and teaching Gentiles as well, which was unacceptable for the chosen ones. Moreover, Jesus gave Gentiles the same bread he gave the Jews when he performed another feeding miracle for 4,000 people.[1]

Comparing the two miracles in their original Greek language indicates that there are a few intended distinctions. In the first, twelve baskets remained, one for each tribe of Israel. In the second, seven baskets were left, one for each Gentile nation that existed in the land of Canaan before the Israelite conquest.

Jesus also used different blessings of the meal. When he blessed the bread on Jewish land, he used a Jewish blessing; on Gentile land, he gave a Gentile blessing. In order to convey a message of sharing of the bread for Jews and Gentiles, he blessed the fish using the Jewish blessing. The lesson to remember here is that God's bread is not just for the chosen ones, but for all peoples. Jesus said, *"I have other sheep that do not belong to this fold. I must bring them also, and they will listen to my voice. So there will be one flock, one shepherd."*[2]

Reflection 2

Men, women and children were willing to leave everything behind to stay with Jesus. Based on accounts from the gospels, crowds were with him for days. What would make them leave the convenience of home and livelihood to spend days in the fields at the risk of hunger? Is being physically hungry less of a risk than satisfying another hunger? If so, what were they hungry for?

Were they hungry for healing? Witnessing people being healed from all kinds of sickness must have been quite a sight to behold.

Were they hungry for preaching and teaching? Jews heard daily preaching from scribes and Pharisees. Every Sabbath, they went to synagogues to hear rabbis preach about the law. Up to three times a year, they could hear high priests at the Jerusalem temple. Was Jesus preaching

Mosaic, Church of the Multiplication of the Loaves and Fish, Tabgha

and teaching anything different and was it enough to leave everything behind at the risk of being physically hungry?

If you were living in the times of Jesus, would you risk being hungry for him? Why?

_____

_____

_____

_____

What are you hungry for today?

_____

_____

_____

_____

145

What are you doing to satisfy that hunger?

Sea of Galilee from the Church of Tabgha

A DIFFERENT INTERPRETATION OF THE MIRACLE

Father Jean-Claude Sauzet, from the Diocese of St. Denis in France, lived in Mexico around the 1990s for 10 years. As part of his mission, he visited once a year a small community known as Raramuri or Tarahumara at the limits of the Chihuahua desert. On one occasion, after he read and discussed John's classical version of the feeding of the five thousand, the community could not accept his interpretation; that Jesus actually multiplied the loaves and the fish to feed hungry crowds. For them, it was inconceivable that people in Jesus' day could have been so irresponsible. The only reasonable thing to do when going on a desert trip was to have enough food and water.

Father Jean-Claude accepted and adopted the Raramuri interpretation of John's story. It is an existential, not intellectual, perspective that is based on human experience. Therefore, it can be classified under liberation theology in which a live analysis of human experience can interpret the presence of God and his works on earth.

JOHN 6:1-15

⁶After this Jesus went to the other side of the Sea of Galilee, also called the Sea of Tiberias. ²A large crowd kept following him, because they saw the signs that he was doing for the sick. ³Jesus went up the mountain and sat down there with his disciples. ⁴Now the Passover, the festival of the Jews, was near. ⁵When he looked up and saw a large crowd coming toward him, Jesus said to Philip, "Where are we to buy bread for these people to eat?" ⁶He said this to test him, for he himself knew what he was going to do. ⁷Philip answered him, "Six months' wages would not buy enough bread for each of them to get a little." ⁸One of his disciples,

Andrew, Simon Peter's brother, said to him, ⁹"There is a boy here who has five barley loaves and two fish. But what are they among so many people?" ¹⁰Jesus said, "Make the people sit down." Now there was a great deal of grass in the place; so they sat down, about five thousand in all. ¹¹Then Jesus took the loaves, and when he had given thanks, he distributed them to those who were seated; so also the fish, as much as they wanted. ¹²When they were satisfied, he told his disciples, "Gather up the fragments left over, so that nothing may be lost." ¹³So they gathered them up, and from the fragments of the five barley loaves, left by those who had

Sea of Galilee from the Church of Tabgha

eaten, they filled twelve baskets. [14] *When the people saw the sign that he had done, they began to say, "This is indeed the prophet who is to come into the world."*

[15] *When Jesus realized that they were about to come and take him by force to make him king, he withdrew again to the mountain by himself.*

Reflection

Families that had enough food were not willing to share for fear of exhausting theirs provisions too soon. But a little boy in his innocence was willing to share the little he had. Blessed by Jesus, the boy set the example and all took out their food. Some had more than others so they shared and were blessed.

Jesus, not only healed the sick and the paralyzed, but his teachings reached deep into the heart of people's lives and transformed them. Through his blessing of the little food that the boy had, he let the word of God free people from their selfishness and share goodness with others. The crowds wanted to make him king, but he left them and retreated to the mountain.

Prayer

Father, you have shown many times that the little we have, if used properly, can have a great positive effect on the lives of so many around us.

I ask you today to help me let go of my selfishness and fill me with your Holy Spirit. Build me, Father, and bless me so that I can share your bread with the rest of the world. Amen.

Notes
1. Mark 8:1-10.
2. John 10:16.

Grilled St. Peter's fish - Tiberias

Ceramic plate - Loaves and Fish

CAESAREA PHILIPPI

BANIAS SPRING

Caesarea Philippi is an archaeological park and nature reserve in the Golan Heights. It is known today by its Arabic name, Banias, a derivative of the Greek name, Paneas. According to an ancient Greek myth, it was there that Pan, god of the shepherds, pursued Eco, the beautiful nymph, who, not wishing to be with him, slipped off a cliff and died. Under the precipice and the acropolis below runs one of the three main springs that feeds the Jordan River.

MATTHEW 16:13-20
[13]*Now when Jesus came into the district of Caesarea Philippi, he asked his disciples, "Who do people say that the Son of Man is?"*

Waterfall, Banias (Caesarea Philippi)

[14]*And they said, "Some say John the Baptist, but others Elijah, and still others Jeremiah or one of the prophets." [15]He said to them, "But who do you say that I am?" [16]Simon Peter answered, "You are the Messiah, the Son of the living God." [17]And Jesus answered him, "Blessed are you, Simon son of Jonah! For flesh and blood has not revealed this to you, but my Father in heaven. [18]And I tell you, you are Peter, and on this rock I will build my church, and the gates of Hades will not prevail against it. [19]I will give you the keys of the kingdom of heaven, and whatever you bind on earth will be bound in heaven, and whatever you loose on earth will be loosed in heaven." [20]Then he sternly ordered the disciples not to tell anyone that he was the Messiah.*

Reflection

Who do you say Jesus is, and who is he to you? Believing that Jesus is the Messiah and the Son of God is one thing, but living with, in and through him is quite another. Is he there when you conduct your business? Is he there when you have your meals? Is he there when you are reading or watching TV? Is he there in your intimate relationships? Is he there when you make your decisions? Is Jesus truly part of your life?

Prayer

Lord Jesus, in this place you asked the question of all questions. The apostle Peter identified your true nature, son of the living God. Sometime later, he rebuked you when you proclaimed your death and resurrection.

Lord, I pray that I never rebuke you, whether in my moments of joy or of trial.

I totally abandon myself to you, I pray, "Here I am, Lord.

Is it I, Lord? I have heard you calling in the night.

I will go, Lord. If you lead me, I will hold your people in my heart. Amen." [1]

Note

1. http://artists.letsingit.com/daniel-odonnell-lyrics-here-i-am-lord-t3xtzlf#axzz3OMBP0aVS

> ...then he sat down, and taught the crowds from the boat...
>
> Luke 5:3

SEA OF GALILEE

It was in Galilee that the Lord chose to live most of his earthly life – he swam and fished in the sea, scaled the mountains, walked on the paths and strolled through the fields. Here he preached, taught and performed amazing miracles.

MARK 4:1-9

[4]*Again he began to teach beside the sea. Such a very large crowd gathered around him that he got into a boat on the sea and sat there, while the whole crowd was beside the sea on the land.* [2]*He began to teach them many things in parables, and in his teaching he said to them:* [3]*"Listen! A sower went out to sow.* [4]*And as he sowed, some seed fell on the path, and the birds came and ate it up.* [5]*Other seed fell on rocky ground, where it did not have much soil, and it sprang up quickly, since it had no depth of soil.* [6]*And when the sun rose, it was scorched; and since it had no root, it withered away.* [7]*Other seed fell among thorns, and the thorns grew up and choked it, and it yielded no grain.* [8]*Other seed fell into good soil and brought forth grain, growing up and increasing and yielding thirty and sixty and a hundredfold."* [9]*And he said, "Let anyone with ears to hear listen!"*

MARK 4:35-41

[35]*On that day, when evening had come, he said to them, "Let us go across to the other side."* [36]*And leaving the crowd behind, they took him with them in the boat, just as he was. Other boats were with him.* [37]*A great windstorm arose, and the waves beat into the boat, so that the boat was already being swamped.* [38]*But he was in the stern, asleep on the cushion; and they woke him up and said to him, "Teacher, do you not care that we are perishing?"* [39]*He woke up and rebuked the wind, and said to the sea, "Peace! Be still!" Then the wind ceased, and there was a dead calm.* [40]*He said to them, "Why are you afraid? Have you still no faith?"* [41]*And they were filled with great awe and said to one another, "Who then is this, that even the wind and the sea obey him?"*

MATTHEW 14: 22-36

[22]*Immediately he made the disciples get into the boat and go on ahead to the other side, while he dismissed the crowds.* [23]*And after he had dismissed the crowds, he went up the mountain by himself to pray. When evening came, he was there alone,* [24]*but by this time the boat, battered by the waves, was far from the land, for the wind was*

Sea of Galilee from the Mount of Beatitudes

against them. ²⁵And early in the morning he came walking toward them on the sea. ²⁶But when the disciples saw him walking on the sea, they were terrified, saying, "It is a ghost!" And they cried out in fear. ²⁷But immediately Jesus spoke to them and said, "Take heart, it is I; do not be afraid." ²⁸Peter answered him, "Lord, if it is you, command me to come to you on the water." ²⁹He said, "Come." So Peter got out of the boat, started walking on the water, and came toward Jesus. ³⁰But when he noticed the strong wind, he became frightened, and beginning to sink, he cried out, "Lord, save me!" ³¹Jesus immediately reached out his hand and caught him, saying to him, "You of little faith, why did you doubt?" ³²When they got into the boat, the wind ceased. ³³And those in the boat worshiped him, saying, "Truly you are the Son of God."

³⁴When they had crossed over, they came to land at Gennesaret. ³⁵After the people of that place recognized him, they sent word throughout the region and brought all who were sick to him, ³⁶and begged him that they might touch even the fringe of his cloak; and all who touched it were healed.

LUKE 8:26-39

²⁶Then they arrived at the country of the Gerasenes, which is opposite Galilee. ²⁷As he stepped out on land, a man of the city who had demons met him. For a long time he had worn no clothes, and he did not live in a house but in the tombs. ²⁸When he saw Jesus, he fell down before him and shouted at the top of his voice, "What have you to do with me, Jesus, Son of the Most High God? I beg you, do not torment me" – ²⁹for Jesus had commanded the unclean spirit to come out of the man. (For many times it had seized him; he was kept under guard and bound with chains and shackles, but he would break the bonds and be driven by the demon into the wilds.) ³⁰Jesus then asked him, "What is your name?" He said, "Legion;" for many demons had entered him. ³¹They begged him not to order them to go back into the abyss. ³²Now there on the hillside a large herd of swine was feeding; and the demons begged Jesus to let them enter these. So he gave them permission. ³³Then the demons came out of the man and entered the swine, and the herd rushed down the steep bank into the lake and was drowned. ³⁴When the swineherds saw what had happened, they ran off and told it in the city and in the country. ³⁵Then people came out to see what had happened, and when they came to Jesus, they found the man from whom the demons had gone sitting at the feet of Jesus, clothed and in his right mind. And they were afraid. ³⁶Those who had seen it told them how the one who had been possessed by demons had been healed. ³⁷Then all the people of the surrounding country of the Gerasenes asked Jesus to leave them; for they were seized with great fear. So he got into the boat and returned. ³⁸The man from whom the demons had gone begged that he might be with him; but Jesus sent him away, saying, ³⁹"Return to your home, and declare how much God has done for you." So he went away, proclaiming throughout the city how much Jesus had done for him.

Pilgrim boats on the Sea of Galilee

Reflection

The Two Seas, by Bruce Barton[1]

There are two seas in Palestine. One is fresh, and fish are in it. Splashes of green adorn its banks. Trees spread their branches over it, and stretch out their thirsty roots to dip of its healing water. Along its shore the children play.

The River Jordan makes this sea with sparkling water from the hills. So it laughs in the sunshine. Men build their houses near it, and birds their nests, and every kind of life is happier because it is there.

The River Jordan flows on south into another sea. Here there is no splash of fish, no fluttering leaf, no song of birds, no children's laughter. Travelers choose another route, unless on urgent business. The air hangs heavy above its waters and neither man nor beast nor foul will drink. What makes this mighty difference in the neighbor seas? Not the River Jordon, it empties the same good water into both. Not the soil in which they lie; not the country round about.

This is the difference. The Sea of Galilee receives but does not keep the Jordan. For every drop that flows into it, another drop flows out. The giving and receiving go on in equal measure. The other sea is shrewder, hoarding its income jealously. It will not be tempted into any generous impulse. Every drop it gets it keeps. The Sea of Galilee gives and lives. The other sea gives nothing. It is named the Dead.

There are two seas in Palestine and there are two kinds of people in this world.

Which kind are we?

Prayer

The church is like a boat flowing on water. In its hull, are many people. They all hope that the boat will get them ashore to safety. Yet every boat needs a skipper, and every church needs a pastor.

When you were asleep on the boat, your disciples were finding it hard to struggle with the winds and the waves on their own. When the pastor is asleep, the community will also struggle against the winds and waves of life.

Lord Jesus, I pray for priests and pastors so that they are strengthened in you and stay alert and focused on you. I pray that they do not boast over anything but their belonging to you as their prime pastor. I pray that you grant them wisdom as they lead their communities to eternal safety.

From your church by the Sea of Galilee, I lift my heart in prayer. Amen.

Note

1. Originally published in McCall's, 1928. Republished in Fr. Stephen Doyle's *The new pilgrim guide to the Holy land*, The Liturgical Press, 1985.

Sea of Galilee and Golan Heights

> This is my Son, the Beloved; with him I am well pleased;
> listen to him!
>
> Matthew 17:5

MOUNT TABOR

TRANSFIGURATION

Above the crypt, in the central apse is a representation of the transfiguration. The divine figure of Jesus is raised and suspended in the sky. His eyes and face retell the glory that bathed his soul in the vision of the Father and the Holy Spirit. Moses and Elijah are flooded by the splendor; their look is one of stupor and ecstasy. Peter, James and John are struck with awe and wonder. The portrayal of each person brings to mind the words of Peter: *"Lord, how good it is for us to be here."*

ARCHITECTURE OF THE BASILICA

Approaching the basilica, you notice that it is divided into three parts, reminding us of Peter's intention to build three tents, one for Jesus, Moses and Elijah. Before entering the church, we pass under an open arch richly sculptured and supported by two towers that form a narthex.

Italian architect Antonio Barluzzi chose to represent the transfiguration over the central apse altar in glowing mosaic. He wanted visitors, to forget everything around them and be overwhelmed by the mystery of the event. The divine figure of Jesus is raised and suspended in the limped sky, with his garments moved by a gentle breeze.

You cannot fail to notice the high ceiling and roof, which today is covered with metal. When the basilica was first built, it had a glass roof, so that rays of sunshine could penetrate and light the interior; Barluzzi wanted to convey the feeling of a radiating Jesus, when *"the appearance of his face changed, and his clothes became dazzling white."*

Twelve steps descend to the crypt, where the ancient Crusader altar is still used today. In this arched room is a beautiful mosaic depicting the revelation of the Holy Trinity through four symbolic transfigurations:

- The nativity of Jesus, *"And the Word that was made flesh, and dwelt among us."*[1]
- The Eucharist, the body (bread) and blood (wine) of Christ given for our salvation.
- The crucifixion and death of Jesus, the Paschal Lamb sacrificed for our sins.
- His resurrection, the new life given to us through Christ.

On either side of the main entrance of the church are two chapels built over Byzantine ruins; they are dedicated to Moses and Elijah, as Peter intended.

Main altar, Church of the Transfiguration,
Mount Tabor

Symbolic tranfiguration, *Death of Jesus*,
Church of the Transfiguration

Chapel of Elijah, Church of the Transfiguration

Chapel of Moses, Church
of the Transfiguration

Interior, Church of the Transfiguration, Mount Tabor

East of Nazareth, in the heart of the fertile Jezreel valley stands the bell-shaped Mount Tabor.

In the book of Joshua, when the Israelites entered the Promised Land and started dividing among the 12 tribes, Mount Tabor formed the border between the tribes of Issachar and Zebulun.[2]

Mount Tabor is also remembered for its connection with a decisive battle that took place between Israelites, General Barak and Deborah the prophetess, and Sisera, commander of the King of Hazor's army.[3]

King David described it, with Mount Hermon, as symbols of strength of the divine arm: *"Tabor and Hermon joyously praise your name."*[4]

Jeremiah compared the mighty entrance of Nebuchadnezzar to Egypt, *"like Tabor among the mountains."*[5]

Hosea, foretelling the impending judgment on Israel and Judah, compared the wickedness of the priests and the house of Israel as *"a net spread upon Tabor."*[6]

Josephus Flavius, governor of Galilee, withdrew to Tabor to escape the advancing armies of Vespasian in AD 67. He fortified the summit by building a wall in 40 days.

Cyril of Jerusalem inaugurated the commemoration of the transfiguration of the Lord on Mount Tabor in AD 348. Supported by St. Jerome and St. Epiphanius, the commemoration continues, and thousands of pilgrims visit the mount every year.

Following the inauguration of the mount, Byzantine churches and chapels were built, as recorded by different pilgrims in the early and late Byzantine centuries. Tancred, Prince of Galilee, built a Benedictine monastery in 1100. In 1187, following the defeat of the Crusaders by Saladin, the fortress monastery capitulated. Malek Al-Adel ruler of Damascus fortified the mountain, but later because its presence constituted a continuous threat of the Crusaders' return, he dismantled it. Later, a truce allowed Christian pilgrims to visit the mountain until 1263 when the Mamluke Sultan Baybars stopped them.

Today, custody of the summit is divided between the Greek Orthodox and the Catholic Franciscan churches.

MATTHEW 17:1-9

[1]*Six days later, Jesus took with him Peter and James and his brother John and led them up a high mountain, by themselves.* [2]*And he was transfigured before them, and his face shone like the sun, and his clothes became dazzling white.* [3]*Suddenly there appeared to them Moses and Elijah, talking with him.* [4]*Then Peter said to Jesus, "Lord, it is good for us to be here; if you wish, I will make three dwellings here, one for you, one for Moses, and one for Elijah."* [5]*While he was still speaking, suddenly a bright cloud overshadowed them, and from the cloud a voice said, "This is my Son, the Beloved; with him I am well pleased; listen to him!"* [6]*When the disciples heard this, they fell to the ground and were overcome by fear.* [7]*But Jesus came and touched them, saying, "Get up and do not be afraid."* [8]*And when they looked up, they saw no one except Jesus himself alone.* [9]*As they were coming down the mountain, Jesus ordered them, "Tell no one about the vision until after the Son of Man has been raised from the dead."*

Mount Tabor

Reflection

It will always remain a mystery to us how the disciples truly felt as the transfiguration of the Lord transpired. What words can describe the awe at the apparition of the Holy Spirit that overshadowed them all, the astonishment upon hearing the voice of God proclaiming his beloved son, the moment when Jesus' face shone and his clothes became dazzling white?

What a privilege it was for Peter, James and John to witness God's wondrous divine world in which they saw the past, present and future – all in the blink of an eye. They saw the great prophets Moses and Elijah, the Son of God cloaked in the dazzling heavenly armor that he would wear until the end of time. From where they were standing, they had a role to pursue in the present. The three disciples had to fulfill God's command of listening to him; only then could they become true witnesses and share in the glory of his son.

They were terrified when they finally knew the true identity of Jesus. If they doubted earlier who he was, the voice of the Father identified him as the beloved son. Their reaction was to fall to the ground. Jesus touched them saying, *"Get up, do not be afraid!"* They looked up and saw him alone; they now felt free and comforted, because they trusted him.

God is always at our side, if we allow ourselves to see him.

Prayer

Lord, the disciples were struck with fear when they knew your true identity. In spite of being your follower for so long, I still do not know how to put all my trust in you. I am struck with fear for the things I have done and their consequences. I am afraid of the future. These feelings prevent me from truly living with you.

Lord, I am in so much need of your tender touch, as you touched the disciples. I want to hear your soothing voice telling me to get up and not be afraid. I want to see your beloved face shine upon me.

Father grant me these privileges, I ask you with the full appreciation of the Holy Spirit and the power of your son, Jesus Christ. Amen.

Notes
1. John 1:14.
2. Joshua 19:22.
3. Judges 4.
4. Psalm 89:12.
5. Jeremiah 46:18.
6. Hosea 5:1.

ON THE ROAD
TO JERUSALEM

LUKE 18

[1]*Then Jesus told them a parable about their need to pray always and not to lose heart.* [2]*He said, "In a certain city there was a judge who neither feared God nor had respect for people.* [3]*In that city there was a widow who kept coming to him and saying, 'Grant me justice against my opponent.'* [4]*For a while he refused; but later he said to himself, 'Though I have no fear of God and no respect for anyone,* [5]*yet because this widow keeps bothering me, I will grant her justice, so that she may not wear me out by continually coming.'"* [6]*And the Lord said, "Listen to what the unjust judge says.* [7]*And will not God grant justice to his chosen ones who cry to him day and night? Will he delay long in helping them?* [8]*I tell you, he will quickly grant justice to them. And yet, when the Son of Man comes, will he find faith on earth?"*

[9]*He also told this parable to some who trusted in themselves that they were righteous and regarded others with contempt:* [10]*"Two men went up to the temple to pray, one a Pharisee and the other a tax collector.* [11]*The Pharisee, standing by himself, was praying thus, 'God, I thank you that I am not like other people: thieves, rogues, adulterers, or even like this tax collector.* [12]*I fast twice a week; I give a tenth of all my income.'* [13]*But the tax collector, standing far off, would not even look up to heaven, but was beating his breast and saying, 'God, be merciful to me,*

Dome of the Rock and Al-Aqsa Mosque, Jerusalem

a sinner!' ¹⁴*I tell you, this man went down to his home justified rather than the other; for all who exalt themselves will be humbled, but all who humble themselves will be exalted."*

¹⁵*People were bringing even infants to him that he might touch them; and when the disciples saw it, they sternly ordered them not to do it.* ¹⁶*But Jesus called for them and said, "Let the little children come to me, and do not stop them; for it is to such as these that the kingdom of God belongs.* ¹⁷*Truly I tell you, whoever does not receive the kingdom of God as a little child will never enter it."*

¹⁸*A certain ruler asked him, "Good Teacher, what must I do to inherit eternal life?"* ¹⁹*Jesus said to him, "Why do you call me good? No one is good but God alone.* ²⁰*You know the commandments: 'You shall not commit adultery; You shall not murder; You shall not steal; You shall not bear false witness; Honor your father and mother.'"* ²¹*He replied, "I have kept all these since my youth."* ²²*When Jesus heard this, he said to him, "There is still one thing lacking. Sell all that you own and distribute the money to the poor, and you will have treasure in heaven; then come, follow me."* ²³*But when he heard this, he became sad; for he was very rich.* ²⁴*Jesus looked at him and said, "How hard it is for those who have wealth to enter the kingdom of God.* ²⁵*Indeed, it is easier for a camel to go through the eye of a needle than for someone who is rich to enter the kingdom of God."* ²⁶*Those who heard it said, "Then who can be saved?"* ²⁷*He replied, "What is impossible for mortals is possible for God."* ²⁸*Then Peter said, "Look, we have left our homes and followed you."* ²⁹*And he said to them, "Truly I tell you, there is no one who has left house or wife or brothers or parents or children, for the sake of the kingdom of God,* ³⁰*who will not get back very much more in this age, and in the age to come eternal life."*

³¹*Then he took the twelve aside and said to them, "See, we are going up to Jerusalem, and everything that is written about the Son of Man by the prophets will be accomplished.* ³²*For he will be handed over to the Gentiles; and he will be mocked and insulted and spat upon.* ³³*After they have flogged him, they will kill him, and on the third day he will rise again."* ³⁴*But they understood nothing about all these things; in fact, what he said was hidden from them, and they did not grasp what was said.*

On the road to Jerusalem, photo by Marc Rock

JERICHO

At 300 meters below sea level, Jericho, one of the oldest cities in the world, is an oasis in the heart of the Judean Desert.

The shift from nomadic to sedentary livelihoods was first realized in Jericho. Tel Jericho, with its 25 archaeological strata, is a witness to the city's grand, rich history. From the Neolithic, through the Bronze to the Iron ages, one civilization after another lived there and left its archaeological mark.

In Joshua 6 of the Bible, the story of Joshua's conquest of Jericho would have taken place at the Tel. Elisha's purification of the spring water related in II Kings 2 would have also have happened here.

Tel Jericho in Jesus' day was considered only a part of the city, which extended further north to include King Herod's building projects and palaces. The New Testament stories about Jesus, Zacchaeus the tax collector, Bartimaeus the blind and others happened in this area, where also the devil tempted Jesus after fasting for 40 days on the Mount of Temptation.

LUKE 18:35-43

35As he approached Jericho, a blind man was sitting by the roadside begging. 36When he heard a crowd going by, he asked what was happening. 37They told him, "Jesus of Nazareth is passing by." 38Then he shouted, "Jesus, Son of David, have mercy on me!" 39Those who were in front sternly ordered him to be quiet; but he shouted even more loudly, "Son of David, have mercy on me!" 40Jesus stood still and ordered the man to be brought to him; and when he came near, he asked him, 41"What do you want me to do for you?" He said, "Lord, let me see again." 42Jesus said to him, "Receive your sight; your faith has saved you." 43Immediately he regained his sight and followed him, glorifying God; and all the people, when they saw it, praised God.

LUKE 19:1-10

19He entered Jericho and was passing through it. 2A man was there named Zacchaeus; he was a chief tax collector and was rich. 3He was trying to see who Jesus was, but on account of the crowd he could not, because he was short in stature. 4So he ran ahead and climbed a sycamore tree to see him, because he was going to pass that way. 5When Jesus came to the place, he looked up and said to him, "Zacchaeus, hurry and come down; for I must stay at your house today." 6So he hurried down and was happy to welcome him. 7All who saw it began to grumble and said, "He has gone to be the guest of one who is a sinner." 8Zacchaeus stood there and said to the Lord, "Look, half of my possessions, Lord, I will give to the poor; and if I have defrauded anyone of anything, I will pay back four times as much." 9Then Jesus said to him, "Today salvation has come to this house, because he too is a son of Abraham. 10For the Son of Man came to seek out and to save the lost."

Judean Desert, near Jericho

Reflection

The gospel stories of Jericho show a vivid picture that healing and saving accounts of the Lord's ministry were extended not only to the poor, but to the rich as well.

In the first, Jesus showed compassion for a blind beggar. This healing miracle follows the same stream of thought throughout the gospel in which ill-fortuned members of society like the poor, the sick and the dispossessed received most of Jesus' attention. Jesus heard the blind beggar's messianic shout and passionate prayer. In an amazing gesture, he turned the focus of his welcome party around, from welcoming him to welcoming the blind beggar. The people's prayer of wanting to see Jesus had been changed by his command to an action prayer by bringing a blind man, to see Jesus.

Jesus gave the blind man the choice between a relatively easy beggar's life or a life with sight and all its challenges. The man chose sight, and he and everybody who saw it praised God.

While the crowds were still cheering, Jesus passed through Jericho and was not stopping there. His welcome party must have been dismayed, as they were planning to offer him the customary dinner banquet.[1]

Just then, the story took a new dimension. Jesus changed his plans and decided to attend a banquet hosted by one of the most hated people of the city, its corrupt tax collector. To the community, anybody entering his house would be defiled. Another turning point took place when the collector's announcement, with all its consequences, brought him a new birth and his salvation.

Jesus' costly act of love had been repaid by another costly act of salvation.

Prayer

Lord Jesus, I am marveled by how things turn when we open the door to your love. The impossible becomes possible. I pray never to shut the door to your endless love. Amen.

Note

1. When an important guest came to a village, it was customary for leaders to prepare a dinner banquet for the guest, with seniors attending. Bailey, 2008, pp. 170-188.

Franciscan Church of Bethany, Al-Azariyeh

> You always have the poor with you, but you do not always have me.
>
> John 12:8

BETHANY

The modern Palestinian town of Al-Azariyeh is the old village of Bethany, two miles from Jerusalem on the southern boundary of the Mount of Olives.

There stands a 1950s Franciscan church built in the spirit and symbolism of burial and resurrection by Italian architect Antonio Barluzzi. The traditional tomb of Lazarus, venerated for centuries lies nearby.

JOHN 11:38-44

[38] *Then Jesus, again greatly disturbed, came to the tomb. It was a cave, and a stone was lying against it.* [39] *Jesus said, "Take away the stone." Martha, the sister of the dead man,* said to him, "Lord, already there is a stench because he has been dead four days." [40] *Jesus said to her, "Did I not tell you that if you believed, you would see the glory of God?"* [41] *So they took away the stone. And Jesus looked upward and said, "Father, I thank you for having heard me.* [42] *I knew that you always hear me, but I have said this for the sake of the crowd standing here, so that they may believe that you sent me."* [43] *When he had said this, he cried with a loud voice, "Lazarus, come out!"* [44] *The dead man came out, his hands and feet bound with strips of cloth, and his face wrapped in a cloth. Jesus said to them, "Unbind him, and let him go."*

JOHN 12:1-8

12Six days before the Passover Jesus came to Bethany, the home of Lazarus, whom he had raised from the dead. 2There they gave a dinner for him. Martha served, and Lazarus was one of those at the table with him. 3Mary took a pound of costly perfume made of pure nard, anointed Jesus' feet, and wiped them with her hair. The house was filled with the fragrance of the perfume. 4But Judas Iscariot, one of his disciples (the one who was about to betray him), said, 5"Why was this perfume not sold for three hundred denarii and the money given to the poor?" 6(He said this not because he cared about the poor, but because he was a thief; he kept the common purse and used to steal what was put into it.) 7Jesus said, "Leave her alone. She bought it so that she might keep it for the day of my burial. 8You always have the poor with you, but you do not always have me."

Church of Bethany, Al-Azariyeh

Reflection

Having witnessed the death and burial of her brother Lazarus, it must have been hard for Mary of Bethany to believe he came back to life. Only a few days before, she was weeping over his body. This celebration of new life from the dead must have proven beyond any doubt that all were in the presence of the long-awaited Messiah, son of David, son of man, Son of God!

Mary heard from Jesus himself of plots to kill him, but she felt helpless to stop them. So she brought from her room a jar of ointment perfume, broke it open and poured it on his feet to thank and honor him, wiping them with her hair. She prayed, "Thank you." Judas grumbled. The Lord said, *"let her be, she knows what she is doing! She is honoring me! She has anointed my body beforehand for its burial!"*

"Truly I tell you, wherever the good news is proclaimed in the whole world, what she has done will be told in remembrance of her."

Prayer

Lord Jesus,
I break open my heart,
and I humbly pray
"thank you"
for walking with me this far.
Amen.

BETHPHAGE

Bethphage is mentioned in the gospel narratives as the starting point of Jesus' triumphal entry into Jerusalem with his disciples. However, it is not clear whether Jesus entered Bethphage on that Palm Sunday or not. Nevertheless, over the centuries the day is commemorated with a procession that starts from the Bethphage Franciscan church, built in 1883 on Crusader ruins, and continues on the traditional Palm Sunday road on the Mount of Olives.

Franciscan Church of Bethphage, Jerusalem

MARK 11:1-7

[1]*When they were approaching Jerusalem, at Bethphage and Bethany, near the Mount of Olives, he sent two of his disciples* [2]*and said to them, "Go into the village ahead of you, and immediately as you enter it, you will find tied there a colt that has never been ridden; untie it and bring it.* [3]*If anyone says to you, 'Why are you doing this?' just say this, 'The Lord needs it and will send it back here immediately.'"* [4]*They went away and found a colt tied near a door, outside in the street. As they were untying it,* [5]*some of the bystanders said to them, "What are you doing, untying the colt?"* [6]*They told them what Jesus had said; and they allowed them to take it.* [7]*Then they brought the colt to Jesus and threw their cloaks on it; and he sat on it.*

Reflection

With full knowledge of different messianic expectations that various groups of people held, Jesus must have shattered the dreams of many by choosing to ride into Jerusalem on a donkey. He stated, "*I am not the army general Messiah but the prophetic Messiah […] I have come with a message of peace and not a message of war!*"

Prayer

Lord Jesus, most people are afraid to tread the path of peace. Many people read it as a sign of weakness and compromise. We pray that the path of humble self-sacrifice that you have demonstrated becomes a visionary path lighting our way – especially the way of the leaders of the world – so that your peace may prevail on us and on all God's creation. Amen.

Here is a fictional recreation of Jesus' Palm Sunday. It presents different views of Jewish sects on the Messiah in the same narrative style used for the telling of the earthly life of Jesus that appears in the front section of this guide; scripture and other extra biblical text are italicized.

There were three weeks to Passover. I packed my things, and as required in the law of Moses, I went to the holy city of Jerusalem with family and trusted friends. I scheduled our itinerary to overlap with that of Jesus of Nazareth, though I wanted to keep a low profile, lest others detected I was following him.

After a week of travelling, we arrived in Jericho where I saw some unusual events: Jesus healing a blind man and eating with the unpopular tax collector who repented for his sins and gave half his possessions to the poor.

The next morning, Jesus set out towards Jerusalem. Half way on the road, he and his disciples stopped to rest and prepare a meal. I seized the opportunity when he was left alone to get closer and offer him water. I asked, "Look at me, my son, do you remember me?"

Jesus looked into my eyes and said, "You are Joseph of Arimathea, the wise priest I met in the temple when I was a little boy." He stood up and kissed me warmly on the cheek.

"How are you my good friend?" he asked.

"Yes, it is me. I had no doubt you would recognize me, in spite of all these years and my white hair!"

"Where have you been?" he inquired. "How many years has it been since you last visited us at home?"

"Oh, many years my son, I stopped counting. But that does not mean that I forgot about you. After all, thanks to you, your father and I became good friends. I am really sorry that I wasn't there to pay my condolences to you when he died; may he rest in peace."

Jesus spoke sorrowfully, "Thank you my good friend. Yes, he was a wonderful man! He is already seated in my Father's kingdom."

The disciples would soon return, so I hastened to explain the point of our encounter: "My work and responsibilities at the temple have increased and I am living more in Jerusalem than in Arimathea."

"I see," acknowledged Jesus, "then that is why you haven't visited us for such a long time. A few days before he died, my father Joseph talked fondly about you and told me that I could trust you as much as I trusted him! Tell me, with whom are you travelling?"

"My family and close friends. I am to meet other friends you might also know, now that you have become so popular around Galilee."

"Like who?" asked Jesus.

"Nicodemus the Pharisee," I answered.

"Yes, I remember him. He is a wise man, but he still needs to discover his true nature!"

I assured Jesus, "You don't need to worry. I will talk to him. Now, I must speak to you of a pressing matter. I have been following you quietly in the hope of warning you. The religious authorities are afraid to lose what they have established over many years because of your teachings. I have been trying to be a bridging voice to subdue their fury towards you, but you know how stubborn they are to their ways. As for me, I trust you with my life." Jesus said, "Then you know what

I must accomplish in Jerusalem. You know how dearly I love all people, and that I must lay down my life for them!"

I continued, "I do not know what you must do, though I have never doubted your intentions. Do what you have to do, and I will be one step behind you. As much as I can, I will try to pave the way for you, but our relationship has to stay discreet for the time being."

"I understand, my friend, and you do not need to take any risks on my behalf. Tonight, I am lodging with friends of mine in Bethany, Lazarus and his two sisters Mary and Martha. That is where you will find me if you need me. I will stay there for a few days until I am ready to go up to the city. Be patient and read the signs of time."

At this point, some disciples returned and Jesus introduced them to me. "This is Simon Peter, son of John and his brother Andrew, John and James sons of Zebedee and their mother, Matthew, Bartholomew, and this is Simon the zealot, and Mary Magdalene." He continued, "Friends, this

Jesus on Palm Sunday, Church of Bethphage, Jerusalem

is Joseph of Arimathea, a trusted member of the Council. Our friendship goes back many years."

We exchanged greetings, then I returned to my family and friends to continue our journey, ahead of Jesus, towards Bethany.

There, we found lodging and waited patiently for Jesus' arrival. When he came, he learned the sad news that Lazarus had died and been in the tomb for four days. 18*Now Bethany was near Jerusalem, some two miles away,* 19*and many of the Jews had come to Martha and Mary to console them about their brother.* 20*When Martha heard that Jesus was coming, she went and met him, while Mary stayed at home.* 21*Martha said to Jesus, "Lord, if you had been here, my brother would not have died.* 22*But even now I know that God will give you whatever you ask of him."* 23*Jesus said to her, "Your brother will rise again."* 24*Martha said to him, "I know that he will rise again in the resurrection on the last day."* 25*Jesus said to her, "I am the resurrection and the life. Those who believe in me, even though they die, will live,* 26*and everyone who lives and believes in me will never die. Do you believe this?"* 27*She said to him, "Yes, Lord, I believe that you are the Messiah, the Son of God, the one coming into the world."*

28*When she had said this, she went back and called her sister Mary, and told her privately, "The Teacher is here and is calling for you."* 29*And when she heard it, she got up quickly and went to him.* 30*Now Jesus had not yet come to the village, but was still at the place where Martha had met him.* 31*The Jews who were with her in the house, consoling her, saw Mary get up quickly and go out. They followed her because they thought that she was going to the tomb to weep there.* 32*When Mary came where Jesus was and saw him, she knelt at his feet and said to him, "Lord, if you had been here, my brother would not have died."* 33*When Jesus saw her weeping, and the Jews who came with her also weeping, he was greatly disturbed in spirit and deeply moved.* 34*He said, "Where have you laid him?" They said to him, "Lord, come and see."* 35*Jesus began to weep.* 36*So the Jews said, "See how he loved him!"* 37*But some of them said, "Could not he who opened the eyes of the blind man have kept this man from dying?"*

38*Then Jesus, again greatly disturbed, came to the tomb. It was a cave, and a stone was lying against it.* 39*Jesus said, "Take away the stone." Martha, the sister of the dead man, said to him, "Lord, already there is a stench because he has been dead for four days."* 40*Jesus said to her, "Did I not tell you that if you believed, you would see the glory of God?"* 41*So they took away the stone. And Jesus looked upwards and said, "Father, I thank you for having heard me.* 42*I knew that you always hear me, but I have said this for the sake of the crowd standing here, so that they may believe that you sent me."* 43*When he had said this, he cried with a loud voice, "Lazarus, come out!"* 44*The dead man came out, his hands and feet bound with strips of cloth, and his face wrapped in a cloth. Jesus said to them, "Unbind him, and let him go"*

45*Many of the Jews therefore, who had come with Mary and had seen what Jesus did, believed in him.* 46*But some of them went to the Pharisees and told them what he had done.* 47*So the chief priests and the Pharisees called a meeting of the council, and said, "What are we to do? This man is performing many signs.* 48*If we let him go on like this, everyone will believe in him, and the Romans will come and destroy both our holy place and our nation."* 49*But one of them, Caiaphas, who was high priest that year, said to them, "You know nothing at all!* 50*You do not understand that it is better for you to have one man die for the people than to have the whole nation destroyed."* 51*He did not say this on his own, but being high* *priest that year he prophesied that Jesus was about to die for the nation, [52]and not for the nation only, but to gather into one the dispersed children of God. [53]So from that day on they planned to put him to death. [54]Jesus therefore no longer walked about openly among the Jews, but went from there to a town called Ephraim in the region near the wilderness; and he remained there with the disciples.*

[55]Now the Passover of the Jews was near, and many went up from the country to Jerusalem before the Passover to purify themselves. [56]They were looking for Jesus and were asking one another as they stood in the temple, "What do you think? Surely he will not come to the festival, will he?" [57]Now the chief priests and the Pharisees had given orders that anyone who knew where Jesus was should let them know, so that they might arrest him.[1]

Six days before the Passover, Jesus returned to Bethany, at the home of Lazarus, where there was to be a banquet. He sent one of his disciples to have me attend. *[2]There they gave a dinner for him. Martha served, and Lazarus was one of those at the table with him. [3]Mary took a pound of costly perfume made of pure nard, anointed Jesus' feet, and wiped them with her hair. The house was filled with the fragrance of the perfume. [4]But Judas Iscariot, one of his disciples (the one who was about to betray him), said, [5]"Why was this perfume not sold for three hundred denarii and the money given to the poor?" [6](He said this not because he cared about the poor, but because he was a thief; he kept the common purse and used to steal what was put into it.) [7]Jesus said, "Leave her alone. She bought it so that she might keep it for the day of my burial. [8]You always have the poor with you, but you do not always have me."*

[9]When the great crowd of the Jews learned that he was there, they came not only because of Jesus but also to see Lazarus, whom he had raised from the dead. [10]So the chief priests planned to put Lazarus to death as well, [11]since it was on account of him that many of the Jews were deserting and were believing in Jesus.

The next morning, Jesus set out to Jerusalem. I waited for him at Bethphage to catch his reaction to the city and its beautiful temple. He sent two of his disciples ahead. I followed them into town, where I saw them untie a donkey colt. As they lead it away, the owner rushed out yelling, "*Stop! where are you taking my donkey?*"

"*The Lord needs it,*" they answered. To my surprise, the owner let them take it.

They brought the colt to Jesus, and lay their cloaks on its back for him to sit for the rest of his journey into Jerusalem. The disciples followed Jesus, praising God and reciting words from Psalm 118: "*Blessed is the king who comes in the name of the Lord!*" Another one shouted, "*Peace in heaven and glory in the highest heaven!*"

As the procession drew nearer to the city, at the Mount of Olives, more people joined in what became a chorus of dialects: Galileans, Pereans and Judeans shouted, "*Blessed is the king who comes in the name of the Lord. Peace in heaven and glory in the highest heaven!*"[2]

A group of Pharisees murmured beside me. "This man has gone mad, he rides a donkey. He thinks he is the prophetic Messiah!"

"We do not need such Messiahs!" said a second.

A third protested, "Can't you hear that some people call him king! We need a real warrior king, a fighter and liberator, and this man does not show any sign that he is."

"Yes, where is his honorable horse?" yelled another. "He should be riding on a horse, not this pathetic colt!"

Then the one who started the debate warned, "If the Romans hear this now, we will all be in trouble, they will destroy us and our nation! We need to arrest him before he does more damage to our life and our temple and its livelihood. What shall we do?"

A Pharisee, who was silent during the exchange, told the others to follow him. He stopped in front of Jesus and yelled, *"Teacher, order your disciples to stop!"*[3]

Jesus replied with a loud joyous voice trying to overcome the crowds' voices, *"I tell you, if these were silent, the stones would shout out."*[4] And he continued on his way. The Pharisees then said to one another, *"You see, you can do nothing. Look, the world has gone after him!"*[5]

At last, the moment I had been waiting for was near. But strangely enough, I noticed that the closer Jesus got to the city, the sadder he became. I thought, "Finally, he can see the city, but why is he so sad all of a sudden." I was shocked to hear him say, *"Jerusalem, Jerusalem, the city that kills the prophets and stones those who are sent to it."*[6] *"If you, even you, had only recognized on this day the things that make for peace! But now they are hidden from your eyes.* [43]*Indeed, the days will come upon you, when your enemies will set up ramparts around you and surround you, and hem you in on every side.* [44]*They will crush you to the ground, you and your children within you, and they will not leave within you one stone upon another; because you did not recognize the time of your visitation from God."*[7]

His words touched deep in my soul, but I still did not fully understand. What is he talking about? Who is this Jesus? I thought I knew him. Then suddenly it all made sense. The scriptures were being fulfilled in front

Interior, Church of Bethphage, Jerusalem

of our eyes. He is riding on a donkey. He is telling us something! Seven hundred years ago, the prophet Isaiah talked about the Righteous King of Peace.[8] Could it be Jesus? I know he is righteous, I know his father was certainly righteous. But Zechariah the prophet also talked about a humble king for Jerusalem. He would ride on a donkey.[9] But what kind of king would he be if the city were to be destroyed? What does he mean? Who is this man?

The voice of my wife broke my trance, "Come on, we are far behind. Let us go. If we don't move now, we will lose track of him." We rushed among the crowd that held palm branches, our symbol of victory. "Where did all these palm branches come from?" I asked my wife. Then we saw him again, getting off the donkey and entering the temple. People shouted, *"Hosanna! Blessed is the one who comes in the name of the Lord!* [10]*Blessed is the coming kingdom of our ancestor David! Hosanna in the highest heaven!"*[10]

I had to confide to my wife, "This man is truly a son of David, but he is different. They misunderstand. They are proclaiming him as a warrior saviour like King David whose glorious days they wish to restore. But Jesus does not seek to establish a kingdom like King David. They are wrong about him, they are wrong. He is different. I should tell them."

"You're a fool," she replied. "Don't go against the crowd. Let everyone rejoice, if he is silent about it, you should be too. Either way, you cannot win. If you open your mouth, whatever you say will be held against you, if not by the crowd, it will be by the Pharisees and the elders. Give it up. The time is not right for you or for him! Give it up!" Of course, she was right.

[12]*Then Jesus entered the temple and drove out all who were selling and buying in the temple, and he overturned the tables of the money changers and the seats of those who sold doves.* [13]*He said to them, "It is written,*

'My house shall be called a house of prayer'; but you are making it a den of robbers." [14]*The blind and the lame came to him in the temple, and he cured them.* [15]*But when the chief priests and the scribes saw the amazing things that he did, and heard the children crying out in the temple, "Hosanna to the Son of David," they became angry* [16]*and said to him, "Do you hear what these are saying?" Jesus said to them,*

"Yes; have you never read, 'Out of the mouths of infants and nursing babies you have prepared praise for yourself'?" [17]*He left them, went out of the city to Bethany, and spent the night there.*[11]

Notes

1. John 11:18-57.
2. Luke 19:38.
3. Luke 19:39.
4. Luke 19:40.
5. John 12:19.
6. Matthew 23:37.
7. Luke 19:41-44.
8. Isaiah 9:6.
9. Zechariah 9:9.
10. Mark 11: 9-10.
11. Matthew 21:12-17.

View from the Mount of Olives
of the Temple Mount and the
old city of Jerusalem

DOMINUS FLEVIT CHURCH

Half way down the Mount of Olives, on the path of the traditional Palm Sunday road across from the old city of Jerusalem is the beautiful Church of Dominus Flevit, commemorating Jesus' weeping over Jerusalem as he foretold the destruction of the city and its temple.

The church built in 1954 has a roof in the shape of a teardrop. On its four corners are vases used to collect tears, a practice that dates back to antiquity as a sign of sorrow.[1]

The interior of the church has remains of a fifth-century Byzantine altar and some mosaics. On the walls are four beautiful sculptures depicting, Jesus sitting on a donkey on Palm Sunday among men and women no doubt asking, "Why is Jesus so sad on a joyous occasion?" Only Jesus knew of the forthcoming destruction of Jerusalem, as shown on the opposite wall.[2]

While digging for archeological remains, Franciscans uncovered outside the church a necropolis, an underground city for the dead. It was first used around 1600-1300 BC and again in 100 BC-AD 135. Most of it is buried today, except for a small part where three kinds of ancient tombs lie.

LUKE 19:41-44

[41]As he came near and saw the city, he wept over it, [42]saying, "If you, even you, had only recognized on this day the things that make for peace! But now they are hidden from your eyes. [43]Indeed, the days will come upon you, when your enemies will set up ramparts around you and surround you, and hem you in on every side. [44]They will crush you to the ground, you and your children within you, and they will not leave within you one stone upon another; because you did not recognize the time of your visitation from God."

MATTHEW 23:37-39

[37]"Jerusalem, Jerusalem, the city that kills the prophets and stones those who are sent to it! How often have I desired to gather your children together as a hen gathers her brood under her wings, and you were not willing! [38]See, your house is left to you, desolate. [39]For I tell you, you will not see me again until you say, 'Blessed is the one who comes in the name of the Lord.'"

View of Jerusalem from
Dominus Flevit Church

Franciscan Dominus Flevit Church, Jerusalem

Reflection

Israel was beyond any salvation that was based on revolution or war. Jesus, like many prophets before him, attacked the notion that God's choice of Israel guaranteed its protection, or that the obligations of a covenant could be discharged by cultic activity alone. Indeed, he declared that Israel's cults held no place for God.

This view could be understood from his cleansing of the temple, where he overturned tables and rebuked the people telling them, *"Isn't it written, my house of prayer shall be called a house of prayer for all nations,[3] but you have turned it into a den of robbers."[4]* In the gospel of Mark, Jesus also *"'would not allow anyone to carry anything through the temple;"* this meant animals intended for the burnt sacrifices. He abolished cultic activity and concentrated on personal deeds enshrined in peoples' hearts.

Israel needed another kind of salvation, one that would turn its values upside down to free itself from sin. It needed to acquire the righteousness of God that was based on truth and love, not the upholding of religious rituals with an empty heart. It was that kind of salvation that Jesus had come to offer. Societies could change and be saved if the hearts of people were changed. Therefore, instead of turning everything upside down, maybe Jesus was turning them right side up?

Jesus was not the anticipated warrior Messiah. He was another kind of Messiah, one that threatened the stability and power of the corrupt Jewish leadership. He was the kind they wanted to kill at all cost.

Prayer

Jesus, I accept you as my personal saviour. I love you and I will follow you as your disciple every day of my life. Amen.

Mosaic on altar of Franciscan
Dominus Flevit Church, Jerusalem

Notes
1. Psalm 56:9.
2. Matthew 23:37, Luke 19:41.
3. Isaiah 56:7
4. Jeremiah 7:11

> The Jewish people will be able to survive without the Holy Temple,
> but they will not survive without Torah....
> Woe unto us! If the Holy Temple is destroyed,
> it will be because my people did not want to live together in peace.
> It will be because we hated each other for no reason.
> We are one people, but we act so differently!
>
> Rabbi Yohannan Ben Zaccai[1]

TEMPLE MOUNT

ESPLANADE AND WESTERN WALL

The Temple Mount or the Al Haram Al-Sharif is the essence of the whole debate over the question of Jerusalem. Both Muslims and Jews claim sovereignty over the Temple Mount.

For Jews, it is the traditional location where Abraham offered his son Isaac (Genesis 22) and where once stood the holy temples of Solomon (II Chronicles 3:1) and Herod the Great. The former was destroyed by the Babylonians in 586 BC, while the latter was destroyed in AD 70 by the Romans.

For Muslims, the Al Haram Al Sharif is the traditional location of the Distant Mosque (Al Aqsa) where Prophet Mohammad travelled on the night of Al Isra' wal Miraj (from the Near Mosque of Mecca to the Distant Mosque and ascended to heaven and back). At this location stands the AD 705 mosque by the same name and the Dome of the Rock built in AD 691. To both religions, sovereignty over the Temple Mount is a symbol of religious importance and political dominance.

The lower stone strata of the Western Wall, believed to be the western retaining wall of the holy temple, dates to the time of Herod the Great in the first century BC.

LUKE 2:22-38

[22] When the time came for their purification according to the law of Moses, they brought him up to Jerusalem to present him to the Lord [23](as it is written in the law of the Lord, "Every firstborn male shall be designated as holy to the Lord"), [24]and they offered a sacrifice according to what is stated in the law of the Lord, "a pair of turtle-doves or two young pigeons."

[25]Now there was a man in Jerusalem whose name was Simeon; this man was righteous and devout, looking forward to the consolation of Israel, and the Holy Spirit rested on him. [26]It had been revealed to him by the Holy Spirit that he would not see death before he had seen the Lord's Messiah. [27]Guided by the Spirit, Simeon came into the temple; and when the parents brought in the child Jesus, to do for him what was customary under the law, [28]Simeon took him in his arms and praised God, saying,

The Western Wall and Esplanade at the base of the Temple Mount, Jerusalem

29"Master, now you are dismissing your servant in peace, according to your word; 30for my eyes have seen your salvation, 31which you have prepared in the presence of all peoples ,32a light for revelation to the Gentiles and for glory to your people Israel."

33And the child's father and mother were amazed at what was being said about him. 34Then Simeon blessed them and said to his mother Mary, "This child is destined for the falling and the rising of many in Israel, and to be a sign that will be opposed 35so that the inner thoughts of many will be revealed – and a sword will pierce your own soul too."

36There was also a prophet, Anna the daughter of Phanuel, of the tribe of Asher. She was of a great age, having lived with her husband for seven years after her marriage, 37then as a widow to the age of eighty-four. She never left the temple but worshipped there with fasting and prayer night and day. 38At that moment she came, and began to praise God and to speak about the child to all who were looking for the redemption of Jerusalem.

LUKE 2:41-52

41Now every year his parents went to Jerusalem for the festival of the Passover. 42And when he was twelve years old, they went up as usual for the festival. 43When the festival was ended and they started to return, the boy Jesus stayed behind in Jerusalem, but his parents did not know it. 44Assuming that he was in the group of travellers, they went a day's journey. Then they started to look for him among their relatives and friends. 45When they did not find him, they returned to Jerusalem to search for him.

The shekel of Tyre
According to many historians, Judas received thirty of these pieces of silver for betraying Jesus. The value of one shekel was enough to pay the temple tax for two people
(Matthew 17:24-27)

Coin of Pontius Pilate (26-36 A.D.)
set in a gold Jerusalem cross

Roman (Herodian) oil lamp
(Matthew 5:15 and 25:1-13)

[46]*After three days they found him in the temple, sitting among the teachers, listening to them and asking them questions.* [47]*And all who heard him were amazed at his understanding and his answers.* [48]*When his parents saw him they were astonished; and his mother said to him, "Child, why have you treated us like this? Look, your father and I have been searching for you in great anxiety."* [49]*He said to them, "Why were you searching for me? Did you not know that I must be in my Father's house?"* [50]*But they did not understand what he said to them.* [51]*Then he went down with them and came to Nazareth, and was obedient to them. His mother treasured all these things in her heart.* [52]*And Jesus increased in wisdom and in years, and in divine and human favour.*

JOHN 7:10-31

[10]*But after his brothers had gone to the festival, then he also went, not publicly but as it were in secret.* [11]*The Jews were looking for him at the festival and saying,*

"Where is he?" [12]And there was considerable complaining about him among the crowds. While some were saying, "He is a good man," others were saying, "No, he is deceiving the crowd." [13]Yet no one would speak openly about him for fear of the Jews.

[14]About the middle of the festival Jesus went up into the temple and began to teach. [15]The Jews were astonished at it, saying, "How does this man have such learning, when he has never been taught?" [16]Then Jesus answered them, "My teaching is not mine but his who sent me. [17]Anyone who resolves to do the will of God will know whether the teaching is from God or whether I am speaking on my own. [18]Those who speak on their own seek their own glory; but the one who seeks the glory of him who sent him is true, and there is nothing false in him."

[19]"Did not Moses give you the law? Yet none of you keeps the law. Why are you looking for an opportunity to kill me?" [20]The crowd answered, "You have a demon! Who is trying to kill you?" [21]Jesus answered them, "I performed one work, and all of you are astonished. [22]Moses gave you circumcision (it is, of course, not from Moses, but from the patriarchs), and you circumcise a man on the Sabbath. [23]If a man receives circumcision on the Sabbath in order that the law of Moses may not be broken, are you angry with me because I healed a man's whole body on the Sabbath? [24]Do not judge by appearances, but judge with right judgment."

[25]Now some of the people of Jerusalem were saying, "Is not this the man whom they are trying to kill? [26]And here he is, speaking openly, but they say nothing to him! Can it be that the authorities really know that this is the Messiah? [27]Yet we know where this man is from; but when the Messiah comes, no one will know where he is from." [28]Then Jesus cried out as he was teaching in the temple, "You know me, and you know where I am from. I have not come on my own. But the one who sent me is true, and you do not know him. [29]I know him, because I am from him, and he sent me." [30]Then they tried to arrest him, but no one laid hands on him, because his hour had not yet come. [31]Yet many in the crowd believed in him and were saying, "When the Messiah comes, will he do more signs than this man has done?"

JOHN 10:22-39

[22]At that time the festival of the Dedication took place in Jerusalem. It was winter, [23]and Jesus was walking in the temple, in the portico of Solomon. [24]So the Jews gathered around him and said to him, "How long will you keep us in suspense? If you are the Messiah, tell us plainly." [25]Jesus answered, "I have told you, and you do not believe. The works that I do in my Father's name testify to me; [26]but you do not believe, because you do not belong to my sheep. [27]My sheep hear my voice. I know them, and they follow me. [28]I give them eternal life, and they will never perish. No one will snatch them out of my hand. [29]What my Father has given me is greater than all else, and no one can snatch it out of the Father's hand. [30]The Father and I are one."

[31]The Jews took up stones again to stone him. [32]Jesus replied, "I have shown you many good works from the Father. For which of these are you going to stone me?" [33]The Jews

answered, "It is not for a good work that we are going to stone you, but for blasphemy, because you, though only a human being, are making yourself God." ³⁴Jesus answered, "Is it not written in your law, 'I said, you are gods?' ³⁵If those to whom the word of God came were called gods – and the scripture cannot be annulled – ³⁶can you say that the one whom the Father has sanctified and sent into the world is blaspheming because I said, 'I am God's Son?' ³⁷If I am not doing the works of my Father, then do not believe me. ³⁸But if I do them, even though you do not believe me, believe the works, so that you may know and understand that the Father is in me and I am in the Father." ³⁹Then they tried to arrest him again, but he escaped from their hands.

MATTHEW 24:1-2

²⁴As Jesus came out of the temple and was going away, his disciples came to point out to him the buildings of the temple. ²Then he asked them, "You see all these, do you not? Truly I tell you, not one stone will be left here upon another; all will be thrown down."

MARK 11:15-19

¹⁵Then they came to Jerusalem. And he entered the temple and began to drive out those who were selling and those who were buying in the temple, and he overturned the tables of the money-changers and the seats of those who sold doves; ¹⁶and he would not allow anyone to carry anything through the temple. ¹⁷He was teaching and saying, "Is it not written, 'My house shall be called a house of prayer for all the nations?' But you have made it a den of robbers." ¹⁸And when the chief priests and the scribes heard it, they kept looking for a way to kill him; for they were afraid of him, because the whole crowd was spellbound by his teaching. ¹⁹And when evening came, Jesus and his disciples went out of the city.

JOHN 2:18-21

¹⁸The Jews then said to him, "What sign can you show us for doing this?" ¹⁹Jesus answered them, "Destroy this temple, and in three days I will raise it up." ²⁰The Jews then said, "This temple has been under construction for forty-six years, and will you raise it up in three days?" ²¹But he was speaking of the temple of his body.

Reflection

The prophet Isaiah spoke, ¹"Thus says the Lord: Heaven is my throne and the earth is my footstool; what is the house that you would build for me, and what is my resting-place? ²All these things my hand has made, and so all these things are mine, says the Lord."[2] The relevance of these verses for the New Testament were reiterated by the proto-martyr Stephen just before he was stoned to death![3]

God wants people to obey his word in a humble way and with a contrite spirit, not sacrifice animals and build temples as dwelling places. Isaiah continued, ²"But this is the one to whom I will look, to the humble and contrite in spirit, who trembles at my word. ³Whoever slaughters an ox is like one who kills a human being; whoever sacrifices a lamb, like one who breaks a *dog's neck; whoever presents a grain-offering, like one who offers swine's blood; whoever makes a memorial offering of frankincense, like one who blesses an idol. These have chosen their own ways, and in their abominations they take delight;* [4]*I also will choose to mock them, and bring upon them what they fear; because, when I called, no one answered, when I spoke, they did not listen; but they did what was evil in my sight, and chose what did not please me."*[4]

This is what Isaiah said some 700 years before Palm Sunday when Jesus entered the temple whose leadership took delight in it. Jesus cleansed the temple, repeating Isaiah's words, *"My house is a house of prayer, but you have turned it into a den of robbers!"*[5]

Temples, mosques and churches are places where God is present, but does not live. God is spirit and is everywhere. *"For where two or three are gathered in my name, I am there among them."*[6] Places of worship are places of prayer to God.

Jesus said to the Samaritan woman, *"The hour is coming when you will worship the Father neither on this mountain nor in Jerusalem [...] but the hour is coming when the true worshippers will worship the Father in spirit and truth, for the Father seeks such as these to worship him. God is Spirit, and those who worship Him must worship in spirit and truth."*[7]

Prayer[8]

God, grant me the serenity to accept the things I cannot change, courage to change the things I can, and wisdom to know the difference. Amen.

Why was the Second Holy Temple destroyed? Because needless hatred prevailed.

Babylonian Talmud Yoma 9b

Notes

1. Rabbi Ben Zaccai is a first-century rabbi to whom is attributed the prime survival of Judaism. On the eve of the destruction of the Second Temple, while Jerusalem was under Roman siege, he was smuggled out of the city in a coffin and requested that a Jewish school of theology be established in Yavneh. The Romans granted his wish.
2. Isaiah 66:1-2.
3. Acts 7:49-50.
4. Isaiah 66:3-4.
5. Matthew 21:13
6. Matthew 18:20.
7. John 4:21.
8. The Serenity Prayer which was originally written by Reinhold Niebuhr was later adopted by Alcoholics Anonymous, requoted in Tomlinson Dave, 2012.

CENACLE (UPPER ROOM)

The Gothic style cenacle leaves no doubt that this was not the Upper Room where the Lord gave the last supper. Archaeologists date the structure between the 12th century, before Saladin's invasion, and the 14th century, when Franciscans took possession of the building until their eviction by the Ottomans in 1552 to transform it into a mosque.

For 2,000 years at this location, there have existed multiple religious buildings. Pilgrims identified a synagogue and nearby, the octagonal Holy Zion church that was built by Roman Emperor Theodosius I in the late forth century. By then the synagogue was renamed the Church of the Apostles. Another reference identified the site as the Mother of all Churches, commemorating the descent of the Holy Spirit on the day of Pentecost. In the fifth century, the church was enlarged into a basilica only to be destroyed by the Persians in AD 614. It was rebuilt on a modest scale and destroyed again, this time by Muslim Caliph Al Hakim in AD 1009. The Crusaders replaced it with another church dedicated to Mary, Holy Mother. Part of the original church was incorporated into the Dormition Abbey. The historical building is owned by the state of Israel, with administrative control by the Franciscans through Vatican coordination. Under the Upper Room is a cenotaph dedicated to King David. A Yeshiva school and synagogue are nearby.

MARK 14:12-16

12On the first day of Unleavened Bread, when the Passover lamb is sacrificed, his disciples said to him, "Where do you want us to go and make the preparations for you to eat the Passover?" 13So he sent two of his disciples, saying to them, "Go into the city, and a man carrying a jar of water will meet you; follow him, 14and wherever he enters, say to the owner of the house, 'The Teacher asks, Where is my guest room where I may eat the Passover with my disciples?' 15He will show you a large room upstairs, furnished and ready. Make preparations for us there." 16So the disciples set out and went to the city, and found everything as he had told them; and they prepared the Passover meal.

MATTHEW 26: 26-28

26While they were eating, Jesus took a loaf of bread, and after blessing it he broke it, gave it to the disciples, and said, "Take, eat; this is my body." 27Then he took a cup, and after giving thanks he gave it to them, saying, "Drink from it, all of you; 28for this is my blood of the covenant, which is poured out for many for the forgiveness of sins."

JOHN 13:2-17

²*The devil had already put it into the heart of Judas son of Simon Iscariot to betray him. And during supper* ³*Jesus, knowing that the Father had given all things into his hands, and that he had come from God and was going to God,* ⁴*got up from the table, took off his outer robe, and tied a towel around himself.* ⁵*Then he poured water into a basin and began to wash the disciples' feet and to wipe them with the towel that was tied around him.* ⁶*He came to Simon Peter, who said to him, "Lord, are you going to wash my feet?"* ⁷*Jesus answered, "You do not know now what I am doing, but later you will understand."* ⁸*Peter said to him, "You will never wash my feet." Jesus answered, "Unless I wash you, you have no share with me."* ⁹*Simon Peter said to him, "Lord, not my feet only but also my hands and my head!"* ¹⁰*Jesus said to him, "One who has bathed does not need to wash, except for the feet, but is entirely clean. And you are clean, though not all of you."* ¹¹*For he knew who was to betray him; for this reason he said, "Not all of you are clean."* ¹²*After he had washed their feet, had put on his robe, and had returned to the table, he said to them, "Do you know what I have done to you?* ¹³*You call me Teacher and Lord – and you are right, for that is what I am.* ¹⁴*So if I, your Lord and Teacher, have washed your feet, you also ought to wash one another's feet.* ¹⁵*For I have set you an example, that you also should do as I have done to you.* ¹⁶*Very truly, I tell you, servants are not greater than their master, nor are messengers greater than the one who sent them.* ¹⁷*If you know these things, you are blessed if you do them.*

JOHN 13:18-30

¹⁸*"I am not speaking of all of you; I know whom I have chosen. But it is to fulfill the scripture, 'The one who ate my bread has lifted his heel against me.'* ¹⁹*I tell you this now, before it occurs, so that when it does occur, you may believe that I am he.* ²⁰*Very truly, I tell you, whoever receives one whom I send receives me; and whoever receives me receives him who sent me."* ²¹*After saying this Jesus was troubled in spirit, and declared, "Very truly, I tell you, one of you will betray me."* ²²*The disciples looked at one another, uncertain of whom he was speaking.* ²³*One of his disciples – the one whom Jesus loved – was reclining next to him;* ²⁴*Simon Peter therefore motioned to him to ask Jesus of whom he was speaking.* ²⁵*So while reclining next to Jesus, he asked him, "Lord, who is it?"* ²⁶*Jesus answered, "It is the one to whom I give this piece of bread when I have dipped it in the dish." So when he had dipped the piece of bread, he gave it to Judas son of Simon Iscariot.* ²⁷*After he received the piece of bread, Satan entered into him. Jesus said to him, "Do quickly what you are going to do."* ²⁸*Now no one at the table knew why he said this to him.* ²⁹*Some thought that, because Judas had the common purse, Jesus was telling him, "Buy what we need for the festival"; or, that he should give something to the poor.* ³⁰*So, after receiving the piece of bread, he immediately went out. And it was night.*

JOHN 13:31-35

³¹*When he had gone out, Jesus said, "Now the Son of Man has been glorified, and God has been glorified in him.* ³²*If God has been glorified in him, God will also glorify him in himself and will glorify him at once.* ³³*Little children, I am with you only a little longer. You will look for me; and as I said to the Jews so now I say to you, 'Where I am going, you cannot come.'* ³⁴*I give you a new commandment, that you love one another. Just as I have loved you, you also should love one another.* ³⁵*By this everyone will know that you are my disciples, if you have love for one another."*

Cenacle (Upper Room), Jerusalem

JOHN 13:36-38

[36]*Simon Peter said to him, "Lord, where are you going?" Jesus answered, "Where I am going, you cannot follow me now; but you will follow afterward."* [37]*Peter said to him, "Lord, why can I not follow you now? I will lay down my life for you."* [38]*Jesus answered, "Will you lay down your life for me? Very truly, I tell you, before the cock crows, you will have denied me three times."*

JOHN 16:5-8

[5]*"But now I am going to him who sent me; yet none of you asks me, 'Where are you going?'* [6]*But because I have said these things to you, sorrow has filled your hearts.* [7]*Nevertheless I tell you the truth: it is to your advantage that I go away, for if I do not go away, the Advocate will not come to you; but if I go, I will send him to you.* [8]*And when he comes, he will prove the world wrong about sin and righteousness and judgment."*

JOHN 20:19-31

[19]*When it was evening on that day, the first day of the week, and the doors of the house where the disciples had met were locked for fear of the Jews, Jesus came and stood among them and said, "Peace be with you."* [20]*After he said this, he showed them his hands and his side. Then the disciples rejoiced when they saw the Lord.* [21]*Jesus said to them again, "Peace be with you. As the Father has sent me, so I send you."* [22]*When he had said this, he breathed on them and said to them, "Receive the Holy*

Spirit. ²³*If you forgive the sins of any, they are forgiven; if you retain the sins of any, they are retained."* ²⁴*But Thomas (who was called the Twin), one of the twelve, was not with them when Jesus came.* ²⁵*So the other disciples told him, "We have seen the Lord." But he said to them, "Unless I see the mark of the nails in his hands, and put my finger in the mark of the nails and my hand in his side, I will not believe."*

²⁶*A week later his disciples were again in the house, and Thomas was with them. Although the doors were shut, Jesus came and stood among them and said, "Peace be with you."* ²⁷*Then he said to Thomas, "Put your finger here and see my hands. Reach out your hand and put it in my side. Do not doubt but believe."* ²⁸*Thomas answered him, "My Lord and my God!"* ²⁹*Jesus said to him, "Have you believed because you have seen me? Blessed are those who have not seen and yet have come to believe."* ³⁰*Now Jesus did many other signs in the presence of his disciples, which are not written in this book.* ³¹*But these are written so that you may come to believe that Jesus is the Messiah, the Son of God, and that through believing you may have life in his name.*

ACTS 1:12-26

¹²*Then they returned to Jerusalem from the mount called Olivet, which is near Jerusalem, a Sabbath day's journey away.* ¹³*When they had entered the city, they went to the room upstairs where they were staying, Peter, and John, and James, and Andrew, Philip and Thomas, Bartholomew and Matthew, James son of Alphaeus, and Simon the Zealot, and Judas son of James.* ¹⁴*All these were constantly devoting themselves to prayer, together with certain women, including Mary the mother of Jesus, as well as his brothers.*

¹⁵*In those days Peter stood up among the believers (together the crowd numbered about one hundred twenty persons) and said,* ¹⁶*"Friends, the scripture had to be fulfilled, which the Holy Spirit through David foretold concerning Judas, who became a guide for those who arrested Jesus – [...] 'Let another take his position of overseer.' [...]* ²³*So they proposed two, Joseph called Barsabbas, who was also known as Justus, and Matthias.* ²⁴*Then they prayed* [...] ²⁶*And they cast lots for them, and the lot fell on Matthias; and he was added to the eleven apostles.*

ACTS 2:1-13

¹*When the day of Pentecost had come, they were all together in one place.* ²*And suddenly from heaven there came a sound like the rush of a violent wind, and it filled the entire house where they were sitting.* ³*Divided tongues, as of fire, appeared among them, and a tongue rested on each of them.* ⁴*All of them were filled with the Holy Spirit and began to speak in other languages, as the Spirit gave them ability.*

⁵*Now there were devout Jews from every nation under heaven living in Jerusalem.* ⁶*And at this sound the crowd gathered and was bewildered, because each one heard them speaking in the native language of each.* ⁷*Amazed and astonished, they asked, "Are not all these who are speaking Galileans?* ⁸*And how is it that we hear, each of us, in our own native language?* ⁹*Parthians, Medes, Elamites, and residents of Mesopotamia, Judea and Cappadocia, Pontus and Asia,* ¹⁰*Phrygia and Pamphylia, Egypt and the parts of Libya belonging to Cyrene, and visitors from Rome, both Jews and proselytes,* ¹¹*Cretans and Arabs – in our own languages we hear them speaking about God's deeds of power."* ¹²*All were amazed and perplexed, saying to one another, "What does this mean?"*

The Eucharist, or Holy Communion, is a cornerstone of Christian faith. It reminds of the sacrificial lamb offered on behalf of the sins of humanity, Jesus' death and resurrection as well as the presence of the Lord in the offering itself. It was instituted by Jesus during the last supper when he took the bread and blessed it, saying it was his body. At the end of the meal, he took the cup and blessed it, saying it was his blood of the covenant shed for the forgiveness of sins. He concluded the institution by commanding, "*do this in memory of me.*"

I CORINTHIANS 11:23-26

[23]For I received from the Lord what I also handed on to you, that the Lord Jesus on the night when he was betrayed took a loaf of bread, [24]and when he had given thanks, he broke it and said, "This is my body that is for you. Do this in remembrance of me." [25]In the same way he took the cup also, after supper, saying, "This cup is the new covenant in my blood. Do this, as often as you drink it, in remembrance of me." [26]For as often as you eat this bread and drink the cup, you proclaim the Lord's death until he comes.

Reflection

In John 6, Jesus said, *[53]"Very truly, I tell you, unless you eat the flesh of the Son of Man and drink his blood, you have no life in you. [54]Those who eat my flesh and drink my blood have eternal life, and I will raise them up on the last day; [55]for my flesh is true food and my blood is true drink. [56]Those who eat my flesh and drink my blood abide in me, and I in them. [57]Just as the living Father sent me, and I live because of the Father, so whoever eats me will live because of me."*[1]

There is no doubt that Jesus spoke these words in preparation for the institution of the Eucharist at the last supper. Every time as Christians, we partake in the symbolic meal and repeat the words of Jesus, we share in, with and through the covenant of the incarnated Love of God.

Isaiah said, *"I have given you as a covenant to the people, a light to the nations."*[2] In Matthew 18:20, Jesus said, *"Where two or three are gathered in my name, I am there among them."* If Jesus' spirit is present at a gathering in his name, it is only natural that we encounter Jesus in person at a gathering fulfilling his commandment. Our faith becomes empty without his presence.

We, Christians, believe that *"the Word became flesh, and dwelt among us."*[3] To the same extent, we believe that Jesus' presence in our lives, revealed through the Bible, changes us. The effect is double for those who firmly believe that Jesus is actually present in the Eucharist. Eating of the word alone can be compared to eating fast food that becomes physically addictive, whereas, eating his flesh and drinking his blood provides a full meal of the word and the body, realizing the command of the Lord himself. Those who eat the full meal become more spiritually fulfilled with the word and the body of Christ. To reiterate what Jesus said, *"Those who eat my flesh and drink my blood abide in me, and I in them."* This is nothing less than living in eternal life now, since living in Christ is living forever.

The two disciples on the road to Emmaus did not recognize the Lord even after hearing all his interpretations of the scriptures. Interpretation caused their hearts to burn, but breaking the bread caused their hearts to see and fed their spirit.

UNITY WITHIN DIVERSITY

The Lord chose to reveal himself in a society full of social, political and religious divisions. He witnessed firsthand the consequences of division. Consequently, he concentrated his whole ministry on unity within diversity. His teachings and his miracles attest to that. Ultimately, his dying on the cross was meant to bring unity rather than division, because he died to save all humanity, not one particular group of people, from sin.

Divisions among Jews have caused serious suffering and destruction to Judaism. Divisions over fundamental principles of Christian faith, such as the Eucharist, could have dire consequences as well; Christianity as a whole would lose its essence, its message of love.

Prayer

Lord Jesus, though we often eat your flesh and drink your blood, we, the church, are still unable to live the fullness of your words. Feed us with your true word and your living body. Enlighten us with the fruits of unity around your cross rather than division, so that we become Christians, worthy of carrying your name.

Teach us Lord, unity within diversity, your way, every day and forever more. Amen.

Walter Rana, *The Last Supper*, Notre Dame Hotel, Jerusalem

Notes
1. John 6:53-57.
2. Isaiah 42:6.
3. John 1:14.

Then he said to the disciple, "here is your mother."
And from that hour the disciple took her to his own home.

John 19:27

DORMITION ABBEY

ASSUMPTION OF THE MOTHER OF JESUS INTO HEAVEN

On Mount Zion, stands the Church of the Dormition of Mary to commemorate the end of Mary's earthly life, her falling asleep. It was built by the German Benedictine order with funds from Czar Wilhelm II in 1900. In the crypt lies a beautiful wooden statue of the sleeping Holy Mother.

The scriptures are silent about Mary's death, and nobody knows when and where it happened, though an ancient tradition places her passing at John's home on Mount Zion. Her body was taken and laid in a tomb in the area of the Garden of Gethsemane. Three days later, her body disappeared and in its place a fragrance emerged. Early church tradition teaches that Mary was assumed into heaven, body and soul, a tradition affirmed as a dogma for Catholics by Pope Pious XII in 1950. What Western churches call the 'Feast of the Assumption of the Virgin Mary' is the 'Dormition of the Mother of God' to the Eastern churches.

Prayer

Lord, your mother Mary remained faithful and dedicated to your way all her life. I know that she is with you, sanctified by your presence. She has set a wonderful example for me to live by your love. Lord, help me become as dedicated to you as she was, so that I may be worthy of the promise of resurrection that you made to all of us who believe in you. Amen.

Hail Mary, full of Grace, the Lord is with you. Blessed are you among women, and blessed is the fruit of your womb, Jesus [...] Amen.

Benedictine Church of the Dormition of Mary, Jerusalem

ST. PETER IN GALLICANTU

HIGH PRIEST'S TRIAL OF JESUS AND PETER'S DENIAL

On Mount Zion, stands the Church of St. Peter in Gallicantu (St. Peter where the rooster crowed) built on the site of the high priest's home where Jesus was tried by the Jewish Council and where St. Peter denied him three times. The church, inaugurated in the late 1990s, belongs to the French Catholic order of the Assumptionist Fathers. It houses ruins of a Byzantine church and a pit that is believed to be the prison of Christ before his trial. Next to the church are first-century Roman steps that the Lord followed from Mount Zion, through Kidron, to Gethsemane and back.

Assumptionist Church of St. Peter in Gallicantu, Jerusalem

Reflection

PSALM 88[1]

[1]*O Lord, my God, by day, I cry out; at night I clamor in your presence,*

[2]*let my prayer come before you; incline your ear to my call for help.*

[3]*For my soul is surfeited with troubles, and my life draws near to the nether-world.*

[4]*I am numbered with those who go down to the pit; I am a man without strength.*

[5]*My couch is among the dead, like the slain that lie in the grave,*

whom you remember no longer, and who are cut off from your care.

[6]*You have plunged me into the bottom of the pit, into the dark abyss.*

[7]*Upon me your wrath lies heavy, and with all your billows you overwhelm me.*

[8]*You have taken my friends away from me; you have made me an abomination to them.*

I am imprisoned, and I cannot escape;

[9]*My eyes have grown dim through affliction. Daily I call upon you, O Lord;*

to you I stretch out my hands.

[10]*Will you work wonders for the dead? Will the shades arise to give you thanks?*

[11]*Do they declare your kingdom in the grave?*

Is your faithfulness among those who have perished?

[12]*Are your wonders made known in the darkness, or your justice in the land of oblivion?*

[13]*But I, O Lord, cry out to you; with my morning prayer I wait upon you.*

[14]*Why, O Lord, do you reject me? Why do you hide your face from me?*

[15]*I am afflicted and in agony from my youth;*

I am dazed with the burden of your dread.

[16]*Your furies have swept over me; your terrors have cut me off.*

[17]*They encompass me like water all the day; on all sides they close in upon me.*

[18]*Companions and neighbor you have taken from me; my only friend is darkness.*

MATTHEW 26:57-68

⁵⁷*Those who had arrested Jesus took him to Caiaphas the high priest, in whose house the scribes and the elders had gathered.* ⁵⁸*But Peter was following him at a distance, as far as the courtyard of the high priest; and going inside, he sat with the guards in order to see how this would end.* ⁵⁹*Now the chief priests and the whole council were looking for false testimony against Jesus so that they might put him to death,* ⁶⁰*but they found none, though many false witnesses came forward. At last two came forward* ⁶¹*and said, "This fellow said, 'I am able to destroy the temple of God and to build it in three days.'"* ⁶²*The high priest stood up and said, "Have you no answer? What is it that they testify against you?"* ⁶³*But Jesus was silent. Then the high priest said to him, "I put you under oath before the living God, tell us if you are the Messiah, the Son of God."* ⁶⁴*Jesus said to him, "You have said so. But I tell you, from now on you will see the Son of Man seated at the right hand of Power and coming on the clouds of heaven."* ⁶⁵*Then the high priest tore his clothes and said, "He has blasphemed! Why do we still need witnesses? You have now heard his blasphemy.* ⁶⁶*What is your verdict?" They answered, "He deserves death."* ⁶⁷*Then they spat in his face and struck him; and some slapped him,* ⁶⁸*saying, "Prophesy to us, you Messiah! Who is it that struck you?"*

Peter's denials,
Church of St. Peter in Gallicantu, Jerusalem

Jesus goes down the holy steps
to Gethsemane

Steps that the Lord followed from Mount
Zion, Church of St. Peter in Gallicantu,
Jerusalem

[69]*Now Peter was sitting outside in the courtyard. A servant-girl came to him and said, "You also were with Jesus the Galilean."* [70]*But he denied it before all of them, saying, "I do not know what you are talking about."* [71]*When he went out to the porch, another servant-girl saw him, and she said to the bystanders, "This man was with Jesus of Nazareth."* [72]*Again he denied it with an oath, "I do not know the man."* [73]*After a little while the bystanders came up and said to Peter, "Certainly you are also one of them, for your accent betrays you."* [74]*Then he began to curse, and he swore an oath, "I do not know the man!" At that moment the cock crowed.* [75]*Then Peter remembered what Jesus had said: "Before the cock crows, you will deny me three times." And he went out and wept bitterly.*

Prayer

Lord and Father, in this place, you needed companionship so dearly, but you could not find it. One of your disciples betrayed you and the others abandoned you. Your closest apostle, Peter, the one you considered a dear friend, denied you after he promised to defend you. Lord, being betrayed by an enemy hurts; even more so when it's done by friends and family. I cannot imagine the emotional stress you went through in this place.

I pray, Father, that you spare me from such trials. If it is your will that I go through them, then I will do so knowing that I am not alone. I trust in you and I know that you will carry me through. Amen.

Note
1. Liturgical translation as shown in the Church of St. Peter in Gallicantu.

Jesus said, 'I tell you, Peter, the cock will not crow this day,
until you have denied three times that you know me.'

Luke 22:34

Zaki Baboun, *The Last Supper* (on olive wood), Bethlehem

> Let your soul be at rest. God will not fail you if you keep your promises and abandon yourself to God's will.
>
> St. Teresa of Avila

GARDEN OF GETHSEMANE

CHURCH OF ALL NATIONS

At the foot of the Mount of Olives, overlooking the Kidron Valley stands the majestic Church of All Nations (also the Church of the Agony), one of the most beautiful in the Holy Land. The whole basilica is built over the rock of the agony at the Garden of Gethsemane where, on the night before he was betrayed and arrested, Jesus went down on his face and prayed: *"Father, if you are willing, remove this cup away from me; yet, not my will, but yours be done."*[1]

The church was built in 1924 by Italian architect Antonio Barluzzi on the ruins of a Byzantine church and a Crusader basilica.

MATTHEW 26:36-56

[36]*Then Jesus went with them to a place called Gethsemane; and he said to his disciples, "Sit here while I go over there and pray." [37]He took with him Peter and the two sons of Zebedee, and began to be grieved and agitated. [38]Then he said to them, "I am deeply grieved, even to death; remain here, and stay awake with me." [39]And going a little farther, he threw himself on the ground and prayed, "My Father, if it is possible, let this cup pass from me; yet not what I want but what you want." [40]Then he came to the disciples and found them sleeping; and he said to Peter, "So, could you not stay awake with me one hour? [41]Stay awake and pray that you may not come into the time of trial; the spirit indeed is willing, but the flesh is weak." [42]Again he went away for the second time and prayed, "My Father, if this cannot pass unless I drink it, your will be done." [43]Again he came and found them sleeping, for their eyes were heavy. [44]So leaving them again, he went away and prayed for the third time, saying the same words. [45]Then he came to the disciples and said to them, "Are you still sleeping and taking your rest? See, the hour is at hand, and the Son of Man is betrayed into the hands of sinners. [46]Get up, let us be going. See, my betrayer is at hand."*

[47]*While he was still speaking, Judas, one of the twelve, arrived; with him was a large crowd with swords and clubs, from the chief priests and the elders of the people. [48]Now the betrayer had given them a sign, saying, "The one I will kiss is the man; arrest him." [49]At once he came up to Jesus and said, "Greetings, Rabbi!" and kissed him. [50]Jesus said to him,*

Franciscan Church of All Nations (Agony) and Russian Orthodox Church
of St. Mary Magdalene, Jerusalem

"Friend, do what you are here to do." Then they came and laid hands on Jesus and arrested him. [51]*Suddenly, one of those with Jesus put his hand on his sword, drew it, and struck the slave of the high priest, cutting off his ear.* [52]*Then Jesus said to him, "Put your sword back into its place; for all who take the sword will perish by the sword.* [53]*Do you think that I cannot appeal to my Father, and he will at once send me more than twelve legions of angels?* [54]*But how then would the scriptures be fulfilled, which say it must happen in this way?"* [55]*At that hour Jesus said to the crowds, "Have you come out with swords and clubs to arrest me as though I were a bandit? Day after day I sat in the temple teaching, and you did not arrest me.* [56]*But all this has taken place, so that the scriptures of the prophets may be fulfilled." Then all the disciples deserted him and fled.*

Reflection

It was dark. After supper, Jesus walked with a heavy heart to the garden across the valley. The disciples followed, perplexed with grief about the things they learned. "How can this be?" they asked in their hearts.

"Sit down here, while I go there and pray," he said, "but you, Peter, John and James, you accompany me."

The soft wind whispered as we walked towards the trees. Jesus looked up to the skies and said to me, "The hour has come, my son." He could hear. In every tree we passed, branches surrendered to despair. To me, they glistened from the evening dew, as if sobbing with grief; they have a feeling too, I thought.

A little further, my Lord admitted, "I am distressed and deeply grieved. Remain here and keep awake, for at such times, I need my friends." Falling to his knees, overburdened with thoughts only he truly felt, I watched him with grieving eyes. I have to stay awake; his wish is for me to see. My eyes were turning back to the other two, but, I was trying hard to concentrate on what the Lord was doing, too. It was dark.

On his knees, I heard him pray, *"O Lord, Father of my salvation, this night I cry out in your presence, let my prayer come before you; incline your ear to my cry, let the cup pass away from me, but not my will, but yours be done."*

The moon shone as if focusing its rays on him. The Lord, still on his knees, his white robe dripping with grief, his hands clenched with sorrow, his sweat like blood drops overshadowing his marrow, and I, Peter, pondering silently. What was I to do in the face of such agony? Should I comfort him with a touch on the shoulder, or let him be with the Father? Suddenly, there was silence.

The breeze softened. The hour passed, and I with the other two could not resist. As much as we tried, the grief overtook us and we fell sound asleep. Sometime later, the Lord asked me, "Simon, are you asleep? Could you not keep awake one hour? Keep awake and pray that you may not fall into temptation; the spirit indeed is willing, but the flesh is weak."

Before I could answer, the Lord went away and fell again on his knees, even more earnestly. I heard him pray, "Father, the spirit is willing, but the flesh is weak. Let the cup pass away from me, but not my will, but yours be done, O Father, your will be done."

His grief was echoing deep in my soul. I knew his heart was torn apart by the way his people had closed their hearts, even to the true word of God. He was rejected and about to be betrayed by his closest of friends. Oh my Lord, what pain you must feel!

Interior, Church of All Nations, Jerusalem

Garden of Gethsemane, Jerusalem

Suddenly the wind stirred, as if wrapping us all in a heavenly blanket of the heavenly deed. An angel appeared. "Father, why should I?" asked my Lord.

"You are my son; with you I am well pleased!" was the reply.

"Father, why should I?" asked he again.

"So that every word written about you is fulfilled, my son."

"Father why should I?" asked he a third time.

"Because there is no greater love, than for you to put down your life for the ones you love! You are my beloved son."

My Lord woke me up again with a gentle nudge on the shoulder. His compassionate gaze penetrated my eyes and reached deep in my heart. I felt he knew what I did not dare say. I could still see the agony on his face. As he walked away, I alerted the other two, "The Lord needs us to be awake," but their eyes were too heavy. "Leave us alone, we are tired," they grumbled.

"Father, let the cup pass away," repeated my Lord, "but not my will, but yours be done!" Then there was silence.

My Lord awoke us once more, "Are you still sleeping and taking your rest? Enough! The hour has come." I looked at the Lord. There was no more agony, no more sorrow on his face. The Lord said, "The Son of Man is betrayed into the hands of sinners. Get up, let us be going. See, my betrayer is at hand."

Prayer

Dear Father, every day I am faced with tough decisions. I ask that you grant me the wisdom to distinguish good decisions from bad ones and help me make decisions with your loving presence at their core. Amen.

Note
1. Luke 22:42.

I call you by name and you are mine. From all eternity I have loved you and to eternity I shall love you. Your mind cannot comprehend this, but your heart can respond to it.

Hal M. Helms

VIA DOLOROSA

Walking the stations of the cross can be a spiritual exercise for every Christian and need not be restricted to any particular denomination. It is a symbolic walk that allows us to relive the passion of our saviour and revisit moments in our own lives.

The 14 stations of the cross are presented here with the support of scripture, reflection and prayer. You are invited to walk them, the way you find appropriate for you.

Opening prayer

Lord Jesus, I am privileged to be here and follow the traditional path you took towards Golgotha. Let this sorrowful walk with you – from your condemnation to your death – show me the truth of your freedom, compassion, love and resurrection that will guide me through my walk in life. Amen.

Munir Twemeh,
olive wood carving of Jesus
bearing the cross, Bethlehem

214

FIRST STATION

JESUS IS CONDEMNED TO DEATH

> I have come to this world to bear witness to the truth.
> Everyone who is of the truth hears my voice.
>
> John 18:37

Pages 225-247 and 254: Father Andrea Martini, *The Stations of the Cross*, Franciscan Chapel of the Blessed Sacrament, Church of the Holy Sepulchre, Jerusalem

JOHN 19:4-16

⁴Pilate went out again and said to them, "Look, I am bringing him out to you to let you know that I find no case against him." ⁵So Jesus came out, wearing the crown of thorns and the purple robe. Pilate said to them, "Here is the man!" ⁶When the chief priests and the police saw him, they shouted, "Crucify him! Crucify him!" Pilate said to them, "Take him yourselves and crucify him; I find no case against him." ⁷The Jews answered him, "We have a law, and according to that law he ought to die because he has claimed to be the Son of God." ⁸Now when Pilate heard this, he was more afraid than ever. ⁹He entered his headquarters again and asked Jesus, "Where are you from?" But Jesus gave him no answer. ¹⁰Pilate therefore said to him, "Do you refuse to speak to me? Do you not know that I have power to release you, and power to crucify you?" ¹¹Jesus answered him, "You would have no power over me unless it had been given you from above; therefore the one who handed me over to you is guilty

of a greater sin." ¹²From then on Pilate tried to release him, but the Jews cried out, "If you release this man, you are no friend of the emperor. Everyone who claims to be a king sets himself against the emperor." ¹³When Pilate heard these words, he brought Jesus

outside and sat on the judge's bench at a place called The Stone Pavement, or in Hebrew Gabbatha. ¹⁴Now it was the day of Preparation for the Passover; and it was about noon. He said to the Jews, "Here is your King!" ¹⁵They cried out, "Away with *him! Away with him! Crucify him!" Pilate asked them, "Shall I crucify your King?" The chief priests answered, "We have no king but the emperor." ¹⁶Then he handed him over to them to be crucified.*

Reflection

Lord, on the day when you were condemned to death, I was there shouting against you. I admit it, Lord, I still do so more often than I dare to think: every time I feed on hatred towards my brothers and sisters, every time I cheat and defraud others, every time I refuse to be generous to somebody in need, every time I sin, every time I distance my soul from your loving presence, I shout, "Away with him, Crucify him."

Prayer

Lord, I believe in your sacrifice on my behalf. Please forgive my sins as my spirit walks with you every step, every station on this way of the cross – the *via dolorosa* of my salvation. Amen.

Forgive me, Lord, I am an unworthy sinner.

SECOND STATION

JESUS RECEIVES THE CROSS

> If any want to become my followers, let them deny themselves
> and take up their cross and follow me.
>
> Mark 8:34

LUKE 23:22-24

²²A third time he said to them, "Why, what evil has he done? I have found in him no ground for the sentence of death; I will therefore have him flogged and then release him." ²³But they kept urgently demanding with loud shouts that he should be crucified; and their voices prevailed. ²⁴So Pilate gave his verdict that their demand should be granted.

Reflection

Lord, what evil did you commit to deserve this vicious human punishment? I cannot imagine the physical torture you had to suffer, the emotional pain you had to bear – all on my behalf.

Prayer

Lord of my salvation, you were denied and deprived of any mercy; please forgive my sins. Lord of my salvation, help my frail dependency on artificial means of salvation. Bind me to your truth with your divine love so that I become worthy of carrying your cross. Amen.

Forgive me, Lord, I am an unworthy sinner.

THIRD STATION

JESUS FALLS FOR THE FIRST TIME

I am the good shepherd. The good shepherd
lays down his life for the sheep.

John 10:11

JOHN 10:25-30

[25]*"I have told you, and you do not believe. The works that I do in my Father's name testify to me;* [26]*but you do not believe, because you do not belong to my sheep.* [27]*My sheep hear my voice. I know them, and they follow me.* [28]*I give them eternal life, and they will never perish. No one will snatch them out of my hand.* [29]*What my Father has given me is greater than all else, and no one can snatch it out of the Father's hand.* [30]*The Father and I are one."*

JOHN 10:16

I have other sheep that do not belong to this fold. I must bring them also, and they will listen to my voice. So there will be one flock, one shepherd.

Reflection

Lord, you carried the heavy weight of my sins on your shoulders, falling over and over again. As long as I keep falling in sin, you will keep falling to forgive me.

Lord, you are the good shepherd. When a shepherd loses a lamb, he leaves his flock to find it. Scared and paralyzed, the lamb cannot walk. Only the warmth of the shepherd's neck on which it rests, restores the lamb and helps it return to the flock.

Lord, beaten and bruised, you fell. You fell because of me, him and her, past, present and future. Your knees could not carry you. Lamb of our salvation that takes away the sins of the world, help us unify your church with values of the good shepherd and follow your example. Amen.

Forgive me Lord, I am an unworthy sinner.

FOURTH STATION

JESUS MEETS HIS MOTHER

Take heart, I am; do not be afraid.

Matthew 14:27

SONG OF SOLOMON 3:1-4

^{1}Upon my bed at night I sought him whom my soul loves; I sought him, but found him not; I called him, but he gave no answer. ^{2}"I will rise now and go about the city, in the streets and in the squares; I will seek him whom my soul loves." I sought him, but found him not. ^{3}The sentinels found me, as they went about in the city. "Have you seen him whom my soul loves?" ^{4}Scarcely had I passed them, when I found him whom my soul loves. I held him, and would not let him go until I brought him into my mother's house, and into the chamber of her that conceived me.

LUKE 2:34-35

^{34}Then Simeon blessed them and said to his mother Mary, "This child is destined for the falling and the rising of many in Israel, and to be a sign that will be opposed ^{35}so that the inner thoughts of many will be revealed – and a sword will pierce your own soul too."

Reflection

She pushed her way through the crowds and stretched out her arm towards her son. Despite a painful shove and a slap on her face by one of the soldiers, Mary was so thankful to reach Jesus' shoulder. The Lord felt her tender touch. As his sorrowful eyes turned to hers, her heart was taken back to that moment when her son spoke, "Dear lady, my Father in heaven has chosen you, and you have consented to his request. You accepted to transform me into flesh. You are a blessing to me."

Mary's eyes welled with tears, "Oh, my beloved son, you suffer so." Jesus spoke to her heart, "Dear mother, you are living the cruelest of days. I can see it in your eyes. Your heart is torn and you doubt you made the right decision. Remember the gift I made for you. Remember that you are a part of God's plan of salvation; who follows his will, has life eternal, and I dwell in him."

As Jesus was dragged away, he heard his mother say, again and again, with a crying but unyielding voice, *"I am the handmaid of the Lord, let it be done to me according to thy word."* [1]

Prayer

Lord Jesus, your mother showed resilience in following you, despite all hardship. You did the same with agony in the garden. Grant me the power and the patience to always endure hardship and proclaim that, *"I am the handmaid of the Lord, let it be done to me according to thy will!"* Amen.

Forgive me, Lord, I am an unworthy sinner.

FIFTH STATION

SIMON THE CYRENE HELPS JESUS CARRY THE CROSS

> I am the bread of life. Whoever comes to me will never be hungry,
> and whoever believes in me will never be thirsty.
>
> John 6:35

MARK 15:21

²¹*They compelled a passer-by, who was coming in from the country, to carry his cross; it was Simon of Cyrene, the father of Alexander and Rufus.*

ISAIAH 53:6-8

⁶*All we like sheep have gone astray; we have all turned to our own way, and the Lord has laid on him the iniquity of us all.* ⁷*He was oppressed, and he was afflicted, yet he did not open his mouth; like a lamb that is led to the slaughter, and like a sheep that before its shearers is silent, so he did not open his mouth.* ⁸*By a perversion of justice he was taken away. Who could have imagined his future? For he was cut off from the land of the living, stricken for the transgression of my people.*

Reflection

Simon must have grumbled to have to carry your cross. He walked ahead of you towards Golgotha, pushed left and right as you fell here and there from the pain of your bruises. Then his heart softened and his grumbling changed to encouragement. "Come on, man," said Simon, "let's keep walking. It will all be over soon."

Around the third hour in the afternoon, after seeing how you died on the cross he helped you carry, he realized how honored he was to have done so.

Prayer

In times of suffering, even strangers can give hope. Lord, teach me how to help others carry their cross and become a good Samaritan, like your servant Simon of Cyrene – all with a loving heart. Amen.

Forgive me, Lord, I am an unworthy sinner.

SIXTH STATION

VERONICA WIPES THE FACE OF JESUS

I am the gate. Whoever enters by me will be saved,
and will come in and go out and find pasture.

John 10:9

ISAIAH 53:2-3

²*For he grew up before him like a young plant, and like a root out of dry ground; he had no form or majesty that we should look at him, nothing in his appearance that we should desire him.* ³*He was despised and rejected by others; a man of suffering and acquainted with infirmity; and as one from whom others hide their faces he was despised, and we held him of no account.*

Reflection

Veronica was another good Samaritan whom God put in your way to relieve some of your suffering. Though her gesture was small, you paid her with such generosity. You gave her an imprint of your face, forever etched in her heart.

Prayer

Lord, you selflessly put down your life for me, knowing that I may not understand. On the way to your death, Veronica showed you compassion and expected nothing in return. I ask you, Lord, to fill my heart with the same selfless compassion towards others. Amen.

Forgive me, Lord, I am an unworthy sinner.

SEVENTH STATION

JESUS FALLS FOR THE SECOND TIME

> For those who want to save their life will lose it,
> and those who lose their life for my sake,
> and for the sake of the gospel, will save it.
>
> Mark 8:35

HEBREWS 5:7-10

7In the days of his flesh, Jesus offered up prayers and supplications, with loud cries and tears, to the one who was able to save him from death, and he was heard because of his reverent submission. 8Although he was a Son, he learned obedience through what he suffered; 9and having been made perfect, he became the source of eternal salvation for all who obey him, 10having been designated by God a high priest according to the order of Melchizedek.

Reflection

The Lord, abandoned himself to the Father, despite the consequences, but the Father did not abandon him. As he fell again, the Cyrene stranger stayed by his side, encouraging him to catch his breath and go the distance towards Calvary. In the face of death, he moved on, making new friends and saving them amidst his suffering.

Prayer

Lord, you had to prove to the whole world that submitting to the will of the Father was more glorious than running away. Grant me the patience and the resolve to go through the tunnel of life with total abandonment to your will. I am fully aware that you are the light I see at the other end. Amen.

Forgive me, Lord, I am an unworthy sinner.

EIGHTH STATION

JESUS ADDRESSES THE WOMEN OF JERUSALEM

Blessed are those who mourn, for they will be comforted.

Matthew 5:4

LUKE 23:27-31

[27]*A great number of the people followed him, and among them were women who were beating their breasts and wailing for him.* [28]*But Jesus turned to them and said, "Daughters of Jerusalem, do not weep for me, but weep for yourselves and for your children.* [29]*For the days are surely coming when they will say, 'Blessed are the barren, and the wombs that never bore, and the breasts that never nursed.'* [30]*Then they will begin to say to the mountains, 'Fall on us'; and to the hills, 'Cover us.'* [31]*For if they do this when the wood is green, what will happen when it is dry?"*

Reflection

The Father knew the burden that you took upon your shoulders. He sent you another sign of consolation. These women of Jerusalem were strangers to you; nevertheless, they wailed for your anguish. Dear Lord, you are truly full of surprises: instead of the women consoling you, you chose to console them.

Prayer

Lord, you said, "*I am the true vine, and my Father is the vine grower.*"[2] I pray that I never be cut off from your true vine. Amen.

Forgive me, Lord, I am an unworthy sinner.

NINTH STATION

JESUS FALLS A THIRD TIME

Blessed are the merciful, for they will receive mercy.

Matthew 5:7

JOHN 10:18

[18]*"No one takes my life from me, but I lay it down of my own accord. I have power to lay it down, and I have power to take it up again. I have received this command from my Father."*

Reflection

Finally, he reached the place of his redemption from earthly sufferings and the place of our salvation. As his weary eyes viewed the site of his execution, his head crowned with thorns, bled with sweat. Pushed and pulled, hearing cries of sympathy from one side and condemning shouts on the other, he collapsed again. "Get up king," yelled a soldier, "on your feet, move or we will drag you there." Suddenly, a man pushed his way through the crowds. From his clothing, he was a member of the Council. The soldiers allowed him to pass. He approached Jesus and helped him up. The Lord said to him, "Joseph of Arimathea, you are a courageous man; I knew you would come."

"Let's go, my son," answered Joseph with a compassionate voice. The Lord continued, "No one takes my life from me, but I lay it down

227

on my own accord."

"I know that, my son," acknowledged the councilman, "I have come to believe that you are the Messiah, the saviour of the world. I know you are the one." Jesus gasped heavily and said as he stood up,

"Wait until the third day has passed, then it will all be revealed, to you and to my disciples."

Prayer

For the sake of your son's sorrowful passion, Father, have mercy on us and on the whole world.[3] Amen.

Forgive us, Lord, we are unworthy sinners.

TENTH STATION

JESUS IS STRIPPED OF HIS GARMENTS

I am the way, and the truth, and the life.
No one comes to the Father except through me.

John 14:6

JOHN 19:23-24

²³When the soldiers had crucified Jesus, they took his clothes and divided them into four parts, one for each soldier. They also took his tunic; now the tunic was seamless, woven in one piece from the top. ²⁴So they said to one another, "Let us not tear it, but cast lots for it to see who will get it." This was to fulfill what the scripture says, "They divided my clothes among themselves, and for my clothing they cast lots."

Reflection

There is no easy way to reach you. During your public ministry you warned that the way to you would be a thorny one. You were stripped of your dignity, and I am unwilling to be stripped of my ego. Blessed are those who allow themselves to be stripped from all unworthy things in the site of God; they will make it to the end.

Prayer

Lord, I want to go to you. Strip me to my bare self so that I focus only on you. Amen.

Forgive me, Lord, I am an unworthy sinner.

ELEVENTH STATION

JESUS IS NAILED TO THE CROSS

I am the light of the world. Whoever follows me will never walk in darkness but will have the light of life.

John 8:12

LUKE 23: 33-43

³³*When they came to the place that is called The Skull, they crucified Jesus there with the criminals, one on his right and one on his left.* ³⁴*Then Jesus said, "Father, forgive them; for they do not know what they are doing." And they cast lots to divide his clothing.* ³⁵*And the people stood by, watching; but the leaders scoffed at him, saying, "He saved others; let him save himself if he is the Messiah of God, his chosen one!"* ³⁶*The soldiers also mocked him, coming up and offering him sour wine,* ³⁷*and saying, "If you are the King of the Jews, save yourself!"* ³⁸*There was also an inscription over him, "This is the King of the Jews."*

³⁹*One of the criminals who were hanged there kept deriding him and saying, "Are you not the Messiah? Save yourself and us!"* ⁴⁰*But the other rebuked him, saying, "Do you not fear God, since you are under the same sentence of condemnation?* ⁴¹*And we indeed have been condemned justly, for we are getting what we deserve for our deeds, but this man has done nothing wrong."* ⁴²*Then he said, "Jesus, remember me when you come into your kingdom."* ⁴³*He replied, "Truly I tell you, today you will be with me in Paradise."*

Reflection[4]

[1]*"For the kingdom of heaven is like a landowner who went out early in the morning to hire laborers for his vineyard.* [2]*After agreeing with the laborers for the usual daily wage, he sent them into his vineyard.* [3]*When he went out about nine o'clock, he saw others standing idle in the marketplace;* [4]*and he said to them, 'You also go into the vineyard, and I will pay you whatever is right.' So they went.* [5]*When he went out again about noon and about three o'clock, he did the same.* [6]*And about five o'clock he went out and found others standing around; and he said to them, 'Why are you standing here idle all day?'* [7]*They said to him, 'Because no one has hired us.' He said to them, 'You also go into the vineyard.'* [8]*When evening came, the owner of the vineyard said to his manager, 'Call the laborers and give them their pay, beginning with the last and then going to the first.'* [9]*When those hired about five o'clock came, each of them received the usual daily wage.* [10]*Now when the first came, they thought they would receive more; but each of them also received the usual daily wage.* [11]*And when they received it, they grumbled against the landowner,* [12]*saying, 'These last worked only one hour, and you have made them equal to us who have borne the burden of the day and the scorching heat.'* [13]*But he replied to one of them, 'Friend, I am doing you no wrong; did you not agree with me for the usual daily wage?* [14]*Take what belongs to you and go; I choose to give to this last the same as I give to you.* [15]*Am I not allowed to do what I choose with what belongs to me? Or are you envious because I am generous?'* [16]*So the last will be first, and the first will be last."*

Prayer

Jesus, remember me when you come into your kingdom. Amen.

Forgive me Lord, I am an unworthy sinner.

TWELFTH STATION

JESUS DIES

I am the good shepherd. The good shepherd
lays down his life for the sheep.

John 10:11

MATTHEW 27:45-54

[45]*From noon on, darkness came over the whole land until three in the afternoon.* [46]*And about three o'clock Jesus cried with a loud voice, "Eli, Eli, lema sabachthani?" that is, "My God, my God, why have you forsaken me?"* [47]*When some of the bystanders heard it, they said, "This man is calling for Elijah."* [48]*At once one of them ran and got a sponge, filled it with sour wine, put it on a stick, and gave it to him to drink.* [49]*But the others said, "Wait, let us see whether Elijah will come to save him."*

[50]*Then Jesus cried again with a loud voice and breathed his last.* [51]*At that moment the curtain of the temple was torn in two, from top to bottom. The earth shook, and the rocks were split.* [52]*The tombs also were opened, and many bodies of the saints who had fallen asleep were raised.* [53]*After his resurrection they came out of the tombs and entered the holy city and appeared to many.* [54]*Now when the centurion and those with him, who were keeping watch over Jesus, saw the earthquake and what took place, they were terrified and said, "Truly this man was God's Son!"*

Reflection

For Jesus: The Lord reached the pinnacle of his mission. He had preached, taught and healed both Jews and Gentiles. Now, to redeem humankind, he needed to release his spirit from his earthly body. Jesus had to die to live in everlasting glory.

For his disciples: It was unbearable for anyone to witness the torture and cruel death of an innocent man, bleeding, barely breathing, and agonizing with every move. His sorrowful mother and a few disciples watched with silent tears. Jesus tried to prepare them over the years for this cruel moment, but nothing could prepare for the reality of seeing a beloved son, master, the very Lord and saviour hanging on a cross. He told them he would rise on the third day, but they did not know what he meant.

For his enemies: The high priest and his entourage oversaw the punishment and execution of Jesus. When he was hanging on the cross, they still demanded for a final sign, proof that he was who he claimed to be, the Son of God.

For us: The good shepherd lays down his life for the sheep. No one has greater love than this, for the saviour to lay down his life for those he loves.

Prayer

Lord, through your life and death, and with the gift you bestowed on me by the institution of the last supper, you made it possible for me, a sinner, to die in sin and to be baptized into a new life and covenant – the covenant of love, the covenant of your resurrection.

Help me understand and live this mystery, Lord, with an open heart. Help me become a living portrait of this mystery. When death knocks on my door, help me understand that it is only one stage on the road to your everlasting kingdom. Amen.

Forgive me, Lord, I am an unworthy sinner.

LUKE 23:34 – *"Father, forgive them, for they know not what they do."* Jesus set the ultimate example of forgiveness and care for others. After being tortured and crucified, Jesus asked the Father to forgive those who harmed him and all other sinners.

JOHN 19:26-27 – *When Jesus saw his mother and the disciple whom he loved standing nearby, he said to his mother, "Woman, behold, your son!" Then he said to the disciple, "Behold, your mother!" And from that hour the disciple took her to his own home.* Here is another example of compassion and care for others. This time, Jesus commissioned the care of his aging mother to a disciple.

MATTHEW 27:46 – *And about the ninth hour Jesus cried out with a loud voice, saying, "Eli, Eli, lema sabachthani?" that is, "My God, my God, why have you forsaken me?"* Jesus' humanity was tested under much suffering. It is probably only here when Jesus addressed the Father as *his* God.

God and sin do not reconcile well. When we are in sin, we separate ourselves from the personal relationship with the Father. Crucified in a human body and carrying the sins of humanity, Jesus temporarily separated from God as a Father. The father-son relationship resumed after his death and resurrection.

JOHN 19:28-30 – *After this, Jesus, knowing that all was now finished, said (to fulfill the Scripture), "I thirst."* When Jesus had received the sour wine, he said, *"It is finished,"* and he bowed his head and gave up his spirit. Jesus' mission of saving humanity was accomplished; he made the ultimate sacrifice for our salvation.

LUKE 23:46 – *Then Jesus, calling out with a loud voice, said, "Father, into your hands I commit my spirit!" And having said this he breathed his last.* Even at Jesus' death, people who knew little about him came to believe in him and the God he represented. Jesus' voice must have echoed deep inside the heart of the centurion overseeing his crucifixion because the moment the soldier heard his cry, he praised God and acknowledged Christ's innocence.

LUKE 23:43 – *He replied (to the thief crucified with him), "Truly I tell you, today you will be with me in Paradise."* Jesus remained thoughtful and forgiving, even at the point of death.

THIRTEENTH STATION

JESUS' BODY IS TAKEN DOWN FROM THE CROSS

> [11]Blessed are you when people revile you and persecute you and utter all kinds of evil against you falsely on my account. [12]Rejoice and be glad, for your reward is great in heaven.
>
> Matthew 5:11-12

MATTHEW 27:55-56

[55]*Many women were also there, looking on from a distance; they had followed Jesus from Galilee and had provided for him.* [56]*Among them were Mary Magdalene, and Mary the mother of James and Joseph, and the mother of the sons of Zebedee.*

JOHN 19:38-40

[38]*After these things, Joseph of Arimathea, who was a disciple of Jesus, though a secret one because of his fear of the Jews, asked Pilate to let him take away the body of Jesus. Pilate gave him permission; so he came and removed his body.* [39]*Nicodemus, who had at first come to Jesus by night, also came, bringing a mixture of myrrh and aloes, weighing about a hundred pounds.* [40]*They took the body of Jesus and wrapped it with the spices in linen cloths, according to the burial custom of the Jews.*

235

Reflection

Lord, you said, "[49]*I came to bring fire to the earth, and how I wish it were already kindled!* [50]*I have a baptism with which to be baptized, and what stress I am under until it is completed!* [51]*Do you think that I have come to bring peace to the earth? No, I tell you, but rather division!* [52]*From now on five in one household will be divided, three against two and two against three.*"[5]

Even before you died, your words were true. Those who chose to follow were baptized in you, and those who rejected you moved further away from you. When you died, the curtain of the temple split top down, exposing not only the empty sanctuary, but also the empty hearts of many.

Your two secret disciples, Joseph the Sadducee and Nicodemus the Pharisee, risked their lives and reputation by claiming your body from Pilate and giving you a proper burial. Their act of generosity towards you would later be condemned by the high priest and his council. But the disciples were unfazed, for they knew wholeheartedly that neither the glories of the temple nor the monies of the whole world were worth more than honoring you.

Prayer

Lord, your servants Joseph and Nicodemus risked much to wash your body for burial. I ask you today to wash away my sins with the baptism of your sacred blood. Amen.

Forgive me Lord, I am an unworthy sinner.

FOURTEENTH STATION

JESUS IS LAID IN A TOMB

> I am the vine, you are the branches. Those who abide in me and
> I in them bear much fruit, because apart from me you can do nothing.
>
> John 15:5

MARK 15:46-47

[46] *Then Joseph bought a linen cloth, and taking down the body, wrapped it in the linen cloth, and laid it in a tomb that had been hewn out of the rock. He then rolled a stone against the door of the tomb.* [47] *Mary Magdalene and Mary the mother of Joses saw where the body was laid.*

JOHN 19:41-42

[41] *Now there was a garden in the place where he was crucified, and in the garden there was a new tomb in which no one had ever been laid.* [42] *And so, because it was the Jewish day of Preparation, and the tomb was nearby, they laid Jesus there.*

Reflection

Lord, your mother Mary, your disciple John, Mary Magdalene and Mary the mother of Joses were there, lending a hand to Joseph and Nicodemus as they washed your body in preparation for a rushed burial.

John must have tried hard to keep your mother from seeing your tortured state, but she kept pushing her way tearfully towards the stone on which your body lay.

Mary Magdalene strived to spread myrrh and spices before the men tied the linen wrappings around your hands and feet then sealed the shroud around your body.

It was a day of deep sorrow and darkness – the day you died.

Lord, the last words you said on that day were, *"It is finished!"* You have accomplished your mission for saving the world and set the gospel to work.

Dear Father, I understand that your son had to face death. And so will I, an unworthy sinner, with the hope to find salvation through the glorious resurrection of your son. Grant me the Holy Spirit, that I may totally abandon myself in life and in death to your loving will. This I pray in the name of the Father, the Son, and the Holy Spirit. Amen.

Forgive me Lord, I am an unworthy sinner.

[17]So if anyone is in Christ, there is a new creation: everything old has passed away; see, everything has become new! [18]All this is from God, who reconciled us to himself through Christ, and has given us the ministry of reconciliation; [19]that is, in Christ, God was reconciling the world to himself, not counting their trespasses against them, and entrusting the message of reconciliation to us. [20]So we are ambassadors for Christ, since God is making his appeal through us; we entreat you on behalf of Christ, be reconciled to God.

II Corinthians 5:17-20

Notes
1. Luke 1:38.
2. John 15:1.
3. From the Chaplet of the Divine Mercy.
4. Matthew 20:1-16.
5. Luke 12:49-52.

> Whoever has God lacks nothing; God alone is enough.
>
> St. Teresa of Avila

CHURCH OF THE HOLY SEPULCHRE

The traditional and historical site for the crucifixion, burial and resurrection of the Lord is found within the compound of the Church of the Holy Sepulchre. Archaeology has proved that the church's location was a disused stone quarry outside the city wall 2,000 years ago. Typical Jewish tombs from the first-century BC to first-century AD were discovered there, authenticating the location beyond the city walls. About 65 years following Titus' leveling of Jerusalem, Emperor Hadrian built on its ruins the city of Aelia Capitolina. The site the disciples venerated as the location of the death and resurrection of Christ was filled to form a base for the emperor's Capitoline Temple, flanked by a shrine honoring Aphrodite.

Constantine had his mother St. Helena demolish Hadrian's temple in AD 326, which led to the building of a church. Bishop Eusebius[1] of Caesarea documented, *"At once the work was carried out, and, as layer after layer of the subsoil came into view, the venerable and most holy memorial of the Saviour's resurrection, beyond all our hopes, came into view."*[2] That first Church of the Resurrection was inaugurated AD 335. It comprised four parts, an atrium, a covered basilica with a main transept, an open courtyard where the rock of Calvary was shown, and the holy tomb in a circular structure. It took years after the dedication of the church to cut away the whole cliff in which the tomb was originally dug. Once all the work was done, a monumental structure was added over the platform where the body of the Lord rested until his resurrection.

The church was burned by Persian conquerors in AD 614, only to be rebuilt soon after by Patriarch Modestus without any significant changes. Muslim Caliph Omar prayed outside the church in AD 638 to prevent it from being turned into a mosque. In 1009, Caliph Al Hakim leveled it mercilessly.

Partial reconstruction began before the conquest of the Crusaders in 1099. At the zenith of their power, they continued the rebuilding until they completed a beautiful Romanesque church and bell tower, much like what stands today. The compound has undergone modifications and renovations by order of the three primary denominations that run it currently – the Roman Catholic, the Eastern Orthodox and the Armenian Apostolic churches. Three other denominations are also represented – the Coptic Orthodox, the Syriac Orthodox and the Ethiopian Orthodox.

239

Church of the Holy Sepulchre, Jerusalem

> I am the resurrection and the life. Those who believe in me, even though they die, will live, and everyone who lives and believes in me will never die.
>
> John 11:25-26

RESURRECTION

JOHN 20:11-18

[11]*But Mary stood weeping outside the tomb. As she wept, she bent over to look into the tomb;* [12]*and she saw two angels in white, sitting where the body of Jesus had been lying, one at the head and the other at the feet.* [13]*They said to her, "Woman, why are you weeping?" She said to them, "They have taken away my Lord, and I do not know where they have laid him."* [14]*When she had said this, she turned around and saw Jesus standing there, but she did not know that it was Jesus.* [15]*Jesus said to her, "Woman, why are you weeping? Whom are you looking for?" Supposing him to be the gardener, she said to him, "Sir, if you have carried him away, tell me where you have laid him, and I will take him away."* [16]*Jesus said to her, "Mary!" She turned and said to him in Hebrew, "Rabbouni!" (which means Teacher).* [17]*Jesus said to her, "Do not hold on to me, because I have not yet ascended to the Father. But go to my brothers and say to them, 'I am ascending to my Father and your Father, to my God and your God.'"* [18]*Mary Magdalene went and announced to the disciples, "I have seen the Lord"; and she told them that he had said these things to her.*

I CORINTHIANS 15:3-7[3]

[3]*For I handed on to you as of first importance what I in turn had received: that Christ died for our sins in accordance with the scriptures,* [4]*and that he was buried, and that he was raised on the third day in accordance with the scriptures,* [5]*and that he appeared to Cephas, then to the twelve.* [6]*Then he appeared to more than five hundred brothers and sisters at one time, most of whom are still alive, though some have died.* [7]*Then he appeared to James, then to all the apostles.*

I CORINTHIANS 15: 12-22

[12]*Now if Christ is proclaimed as raised from the dead, how can some of you say there is no resurrection of the dead?* [13]*If there is no resurrection of the dead, then Christ has not been raised;* [14]*and if Christ has not been raised, then our proclamation has been in vain and your faith has been in vain.* [15]*We are even found to be misrepresenting God, because we testified of God that he raised Christ – whom he did not raise if it is true that the dead are not raised.* [16]*For if the dead are not raised, then Christ has not been raised.* [17]*If Christ has not been raised, your faith is futile and you are still in your sins.* [18]*Then those also who have died in Christ have perished.* [19]*If for this life only we have hoped in Christ, we are of all people most to be pitied.*

[20]*But in fact Christ has been raised from the dead, the first fruits of those who have died.* [21]*For since death came through a human being, the resurrection of the dead has also come through a human being;* [22]*for as all die in Adam, so all will be made alive in Christ.*

Chapel of the Crucifixion (Calvary),
Church of the Holy Sepulchre, Jerusalem

Tomb of Jesus, Church
of the Holy Sepulchre, Jerusalem

Unction stone, Church of the Holy Sepulchre,
Jerusalem

Reflection

The most fundamental belief in Christianity is that Jesus died, was raised from the dead and is now alive. Jesus said, *"Very truly, I tell you, unless a grain of wheat falls into the earth and dies, it remains just a single grain; but if it dies, it bears much fruit."*[4]

Who would have known that the self-sacrifice of a person on a cross, proclaimed by his disciples, could bear much fruit and yield abundant life not only to Jesus himself, but to all human souls?

When Jesus died on the cross, he set free the ultimate truth that God had become man, lived the life of a man and had died at the hands of man. He set free the mystery that had started at the annunciation through the incarnation and unto death for proclamation. He had come to free humanity from the yoke of slavery, from physical and spiritual corruption, but above all, from humanity itself. Through his death on the cross, he gave humanity eternal life.

The death of the grain did not put an end to its life, but gave it eternal life. Our death from Adam's sin will not put an end to our life but will give us eternal life through Christ's resurrection. The moment we believe in that is the beginning of our new birth in eternal life.

Prayer

Strengthen me, Lord, to truly see you. You are the light of the world, and I want to always be in your presence. I acknowledge and repent for my sins, and pledge to live in and through you now, hoping that you will take me into your eternal kingdom. Amen.

Notes
1. Historian of Constantine the Great.
2. Re-quoted in Jerome Murphy O'Conner, *The Holy Land*, Oxford University Press, 1992.
3. Written around AD 32-38, these verses constitute one of the most direct testimonies to the resurrection.
4. John 12:24.

I CORINTHIANS 15:20-22 - [20]*But in fact Christ has been raised from the dead, the first fruits of those who have died.* [21]*For since death came through a human being, the resurrection of the dead has also come through a human being;* [22]*for as all die in Adam, so all will be made alive in Christ.*

ROMANS 6:4 - [4]*Therefore we have been buried with him by baptism into death, so that, just as Christ was raised from the dead by the glory of the Father, so we too might walk in newness of life.*

ROMANS 4:24-25 - [24]*It will be reckoned to us who believe in him who raised Jesus our Lord from the dead,* [25]*who was handed over to death for our trespasses and was raised for our justification.*

I PETER 1:3 - [3]*Blessed be the God and Father of our Lord Jesus Christ! By his great mercy he has given us a new birth into a living hope through the resurrection of Jesus Christ from the dead.*

> We must not grow weary of doing little things for the love of God,
> who looks not on the great size of the work,
> but on the love in it.
>
> Brother Lawrence

FINDING THE HOLY CROSS[1]

There are multiple sources, stories and legends related to the finding of the holy cross.

After the crucifixion of the Lord, the wood of the cross lay hidden underground for over 200 years. Constantine decided to send his mother, St. Helena, to Jerusalem and find the cross. He sent her there because he attributed his father's victory over the Barbarian armies on the banks of the Danube River to a cross that was carried at the head of his father's army.

When St. Helena arrived in Jerusalem, she asked all Jewish scholars where the Lord was crucified, but they were determined to say nothing for fear that the law of Moses would be annulled and the traditions of the fathers wiped out. The queen threatened them with death by fire. Frightened, they handed over one of their own, Judas, to answer her questions.

However, he said nothing, so she had him thrown into a dry well and left to suffer from hunger. After six days, he led them to a temple built by Emperor Hadrian, obliging Christians to worship Venus instead of Christ.

St. Helena had the temple razed and the site plowed. When they had dug down 20 yards, Judas found three crosses and presented them to the queen. Unable to identify the cross of Christ from the crosses of the two thieves, they placed them in the center of the city and waited

Armenian Chapel,
Church of the Holy Sepulchre, Jerusalem

Discovery location of the holy cross,
Church of the Holy Sepulchre, Jerusalem

for the Lord to manifest his glory. During the funeral of a young man, Judas stopped the procession. He held two of the crosses over the body, but nothing happened. He did the same with the third cross, and the dead man came back to life.

Other stories related that a prominent lady of Jerusalem fell sick and was immediately cured when the cross of the Lord touched her body. After the miracle of the young man, Judas was baptized with the name Quiriacus and became the successor to the Bishop of Jerusalem. St. Helena was still seeking the nails from Christ's cross. She sent Quiriacus back to the site of the razed temple where he prayed, and the nails appeared. The queen fell to her knees and paid them much reverence.

St. Helena then brought a piece of the cross to her son, together with the nails. Saint Ambrose narrated, *"She sought the Lord's nails and found them, and had one of them made into a bit and the other worked into the royal crown: it was right that the nail be on the head, the crown at the top, the bridle in the hand, so that the mind should be preeminent, the faith should shine forth, and the royal power should rule."*

Quiriacus was later put to death by Julian the Apostate for finding the holy cross, while the emperor was trying to destroy evidence of it everywhere. And so, the bishop put down his life for the Lord and was made a saint.

Note

1. For more information visit http://blackbiretta.blogspot.co.il/2012/09/the-golden-legend-finding-true-cross.html.

GARDEN TOMB

Outside the Damascus Gate of the old city of Jerusalem, opposite to the old bus station, is a site known as the Garden Tomb. Owned and administered by the Garden Tomb (Jerusalem) Association, it draws attention to two places, a skull looking hill, and an ancient tomb. 'Skull hill' is a sort of an outcropping of rock that was discovered and adopted as Golgotha of the New Testament by General Charles Gordon in 1883. The tomb is venerated as the resting place of Joseph of Arimathea, which served as the tomb for the body of the Lord until his resurrection. It is also recognized by some protestants as an alternative to the Church of the Holy Sepulchre.

Though historical or archaeological evidence supporting the location as the authentic site for the death and resurrection of the Lord is called into question, it gives an idea of a tomb dug in the bedrock and a good visual of a skull-looking hill.

The Garden Tomb is a quiet place away from hustle and bustle. It is reserved for worship and meditation on the most significant miracle of all: the resurrection of the Lord.

Garden Tomb, Jerusalem

> The loving heart will aspire to great things, but God will be pleased
> with smaller accomplishments as well. Little things add up.
>
> St. Francis de Sales

MENSA CHRISTI, GALILEE

CHURCH OF THE PRIMACY OF PETER

Along this shoreline on the Sea of Galilee, Jesus showed himself for the third and last time to his disciples. According to an ancient tradition from the fourth century, the church houses a rock where Jesus lit a charcoal fire and talked with Peter.

JOHN 21:1-25

¹After these things Jesus showed himself again to the disciples by the Sea of Tiberias; and he showed himself in this way. ²Gathered there together were Simon Peter, Thomas called the Twin, Nathanael of Cana in Galilee, the sons of Zebedee, and two others of his disciples. ³Simon Peter said to them, "I am going fishing." They said to him, "We will go with you." They went out and got into the boat, but that night they caught nothing. ⁴Just after daybreak, Jesus stood on the beach; but the disciples did not know that it was Jesus. ⁵Jesus said to them, "Children, you have no fish, have you?" They answered him, "No." ⁶He said to them, "Cast the net to the right side of the boat, and you will find some." So they cast it, and now they were not able to haul it in because there were so many fish. ⁷That disciple whom Jesus loved said to Peter, "It is the Lord!" When Simon Peter heard that it was the Lord, he put on some clothes, for he was naked, and jumped into the sea. ⁸But the other disciples came in the boat, dragging the net full of fish, for they were not far from the land, only about a hundred yards off. ⁹When they had gone ashore, they saw a charcoal fire there, with fish on it, and bread. ¹⁰Jesus said to them, "Bring some of the fish that you have just caught." ¹¹So Simon Peter went aboard and hauled the net ashore, full of large fish, a hundred fifty-three of them; and though there were so many, the net was not torn. ¹²Jesus said to them, "Come and have breakfast." Now none of the disciples dared to ask him, "Who are you?" because they knew it was the Lord. ¹³Jesus came and took the bread and gave it to them, and did the same with the fish. ¹⁴This was now the third time that Jesus appeared to the disciples after he was raised from the dead.

¹⁵When they had finished breakfast, Jesus said to Simon Peter, "Simon son of John, do you love me more than these?" He said to him, "Yes, Lord; you know that I love you." Jesus said to him, "Feed my lambs." ¹⁶A second time he said to him, "Simon son of John, do you love me?" He said to him, "Yes,

Church of the Primacy of Peter, Mensa Christi

Mensa Christi shore, Galilee

Lord; you know that I love you." Jesus said to him, "Tend my sheep." [17]He said to him the third time, "Simon son of John, do you love me?" Peter felt hurt because he said to him the third time, "Do you love me?" And he said to him, "Lord, you know everything; you know that I love you." Jesus said to him, "Feed my sheep. [18]Very truly, I tell you, when you were younger, you used to fasten your own belt and to go wherever you wished. But when you grow old, you will stretch out your hands, and someone else will fasten a belt around you and take you where you do not wish to go." [19](He said this to indicate the kind of death by which he would glorify God.) After this he said to him, "Follow me."

[20]Peter turned and saw the disciple whom Jesus loved following them; he was the one who had reclined next to Jesus at the supper and had said, "Lord, who is it that is going to betray you?" [21]When Peter saw him, he said to Jesus, "Lord, what about him?" [22]Jesus said to him, "If it is my will that he remain until I come, what is that to you? Follow me!" [23]So the rumor spread in the community that this disciple would not die. Yet Jesus did not say to him that he would not die, but, "If it is my will that he remain until I come, what is that to you?" [24]This is the disciple who is testifying to these things and has written them, and we know that his testimony is true. [25]But there are also many other things that Jesus did; if every one of them were written down, I suppose that the world itself could not contain the books that would be written.

Jesus' words provoked many antagonistic feelings to his person among scribes, Pharisees, the elders and others. The way he died on a cross is the ultimate proof of how much his words had caused religious and spiritual turmoil in the hearts of many, especially leaders who thought they had all they needed to be saved; according to him, they barely had the minimum required.

Jesus' words were equally hard to accept by the standards of some of his own disciples. At times, they had difficulty understanding their master's words and intentions. In John 6, following the discourse of the bread of life, many of his disciples *"turned back and no longer went about with him."*[1]

The other side of the coin is that these same words were life changing, and so full of truth to the point of giving eternal life. Peter declared after the same discourse, *"Lord, to whom can we go? You have the words of eternal life. We have come to believe and know that you are the Holy One of God."* [2]

But even with this revealing testimony after years of living with Jesus in his house at Capernaum, Peter, as we learn later in John's gospel, could neither fully grasp the extent of his testimony, nor give unconditional love to Jesus. Peter might have still remembered Jesus' words, which also applied to him, *"The spirit is willing, but the flesh is weak!"*[3] Peter knew that Jesus was the one he needed to follow; he also knew about his own weakness, because being unconditionally committed to Jesus likely had unknown, grim consequences. When Jesus asked him thrice, *"Do you love me?"* Peter struggled to find an answer; he was naked, especially after denying him three times before. The events leading up to this encounter on the shore of Galilee strongly suggest Peter's deep love for Jesus, but his lack of resolve to display it publicly and unconditionally. He loved Jesus as a brother (*filio* in the Greek version of the Bible), but was not ready to face the world (agape or divine love in the Greek version).

Jesus caught Peter off-guard with the question, which weighed heavily on his mind. Knowing how troubled he was, Jesus reached out to him. He offered him a meal as a sign of forgiveness and told him to that in order to prove his agape love, he needed to continue Jesus' work – to feed his sheep.

Do you love Jesus? Why? How?

Interior, Church of the Primacy of Peter, Mensa Christi

Prayer

Lord, I am being tested every day. The apostle Peter was so near to you, yet at times so far. He knew who you were, but did not know your inner depth and strength. He knew you were the Holy One, yet he did not know how to handle your presence in his life. He needed many signs and much encouragement to overcome his fears and troubled thoughts. O Lord, I also know that I need to follow your lead and command, but I am frail and weak. I admit that I need you and honestly love you, but I still do not know how to focus on you.

You have given the prince of the apostles a great gift; a tongue of fire that led his path until the end when he proved his true and unconditional love to you. Bestow on me, O Lord, the same courageous spirit to testify with all my heart that I love you. Amen.

Notes
1. John 6:66.
2. John 6:68-69.
3. Matthew 26:41.

Church of the Primacy of Peter, Mensa Christi

> Our hearts are restless until they rest in you.
>
> St. Augustine

EMMAUS

There are four locations venerated over different periods of the New Testament as the site of Emmaus: Byzantine Emmaus Latrun, Crusader Emmaus Abu Ghosh, Franciscan Emmaus Qubeibeh and a Palestinian village called Emmaus until 1967, today Canada Park. No matter which of these was the real location, the importance lies in the story that happened on the road to the village.

LUKE 24:13-35

[13]*Now on that same day two of them were going to a village called Emmaus, about seven miles from Jerusalem,* [14]*and talking with each other about all these things that had happened.* [15]*While they were talking and discussing, Jesus himself came near and went with them,* [16]*but their eyes were kept from recognizing him.* [17]*And he said to them, "What are you discussing with each other while you walk along?" They stood still, looking sad.* [18]*Then one of them, whose name was Cleopas, answered him, "Are you the only stranger in Jerusalem who does not know the things that have taken place there in these days?"* [19]*He asked them,*

"What things?" They replied, "The things about Jesus of Nazareth, who was a prophet mighty in deed and word before God and all the people, [20]*and how our chief priests and leaders handed him over to be condemned to death and crucified him.* [21]*But we had hoped that he was the one to redeem Israel. Yes, and besides all this, it is now the third day since these things took place.* [22]*Moreover, some women of our group astounded us. They were at the tomb early this morning,* [23]*and when they did not find his body there, they came back and told us that they had indeed seen a vision of angels who said that he was alive.* [24]*Some of those who were with us went to the tomb and found it just as the women had said; but they did not see him."*

[25]*Then he said to them, "Oh, how foolish you are, and how slow of heart to believe all that the prophets have declared!* [26]*Was it not necessary that the Messiah should suffer these things and then enter into his glory?"* [27]*Then beginning with Moses and all the prophets, he interpreted to them the things about himself in all the scriptures.* [28]*As they came near the village to which they were going, he walked ahead as if he were going on.* [29]*But they urged him strongly, saying, "Stay with us, because it is almost evening*

and the day is now nearly over." So he went in to stay with them. ³⁰When he was at the table with them, he took bread, blessed and broke it, and gave it to them. ³¹Then their eyes were opened, and they recognized him; and he vanished from their sight. ³²They said to each other, "Were not our hearts burning within us while he was talking to us on the road, while he was opening the scriptures to us?" ³³That same hour they got up and returned to Jerusalem; and they found the eleven and their companions gathered together. ³⁴They were saying, "The Lord has risen indeed, and he has appeared to Simon!" ³⁵Then they told what had happened on the road, and how he had been made known to them in the breaking of the bread.

Léon Augustin Lhermitte, *Supper at Emmaus,* Museum of Fine Arts, Boston

The two disciples on the road to Emmaus were sad and dismayed at the sorrowful events of that Passover weekend. They had lost their Lord and teacher; a man, whom until that moment, they considered holy and a righteous prophet. They were probably equally disappointed that Jesus was not the warrior Messiah who would liberate Israel from the yoke of Roman rule. They grieved the loss of a great teacher and yet another opportunity for liberation.

Most astounding for the two disciples on the road to Emmaus was hearing from the other disciples that the body of the Lord was not in the tomb – that he was alive! But even Peter, the Lord's prime apostle who witnessed almost all his public ministry, could not believe and understand the things that were happening.

The two incredulous disciples on the road to Emmaus were being challenged over the very meaning and role of God in their life. Hearing of him, being preached about him, and believing in a resurrection at the end of days was one thing, but hearing of their master to be alive after public crucifixion and death was another. In fact, it just was not possible!

The two disciples on the road to Emmaus, over years of discipleship with Jesus, were hearing but not listening, looking not seeing, were so near yet so far. Soaked in their own physical world, they were unable to recognize that they were truly living the most gracious times in their lives; the time of their visitation by the resurrected Christ. On the road to Emmaus, the resurrected Lord appeared, wearing a costume of the glorious resurrection. Their eyes, still focused on their truth failed to see *the* truth of the resurrection walking beside them. Their concern for past events and their lost hope for the future prevented them from living the moment when the one they were grieving for was physically walking with them.

On the road to Emmaus, aware of their dilemmas and frustrations, aware of their lost hopes and moments of doubt, the Lord appeared as a stranger and walked with them. He interpreted all the scriptures concerning the coming of the Messiah. The two disciples listened intently to his words, which brought the scriptures to life and inflamed their hearts. They thought about the striking similarities between the stranger's interpretations and the Lord's life, but they had to be sure.

When they reached Emmaus, they urged him to stay. At supper, he took the bread, blessed and broke it and gave it to them. Suddenly, it was all revealed when they recognized him.

And so the two desciples returned to Jerusalem and announced the gospel of Christ.

Nothing is sweeter than love, nothing stronger, nothing higher,
nothing broader, nothing more pleasant, nothing fuller or better in heaven or on
earth,
because love is born of God and cannot rest finally in anything lower than God.

Thomas A. Kempis

Thoughts for pilgrims in scripture

JOHN 14:15-17

[15]*"If you love me, you will keep my commandments. [16]And I will ask the Father, and he will give you another Advocate, to be with you forever. [17]This is the Spirit of truth, whom the world cannot receive, because it neither sees him nor knows him. You know him, because he abides with you, and he will be in you."*

JOHN 17:25-26

[25]*"Righteous Father, the world does not know you, but I know you; and these know that you have sent me. [26]I made your name known to them, and I will make it known, so that the love with which you have loved me may be in them, and I in them."*

JOHN 15:12

[12]*"This is my commandment, that you love one another as I have loved you."*

GALATIANS 6:2

[2]*Carry each other's burdens and this way you will fulfill the law of Christ.*

JOHN 15:16

[16]*"You did not choose me but I chose you. And I appointed you to go and bear fruit, fruit that will last, so that the Father will give you whatever you ask him in my name."*

EPHESIANS 6:10-17

[10]*Finally, be strong in the Lord and in the strength of his power. [11]Put on the whole armor of God, so that you may be able to stand against the wiles of the devil. [12]For our struggle is not against enemies of blood and flesh, but against the rulers, against the authorities, against the cosmic powers of this present darkness, against the spiritual forces of evil in the heavenly places. [13]Therefore take up the whole armor of God, so that you may be able to withstand on that evil day, and having done everything, to stand firm. [14]Stand therefore, and fasten the belt of truth around your waist, and put on the breastplate of righteousness. [15]As shoes for your feet put on whatever will make you ready to proclaim the gospel of peace. [16]With all of these, take the shield of faith, with which you will be able to quench all the flaming arrows of the evil one. [17]Take the helmet of salvation, and the sword of the Spirit, which is the word of God.*

Prayer

Lord Jesus Christ, I admit that I am foolish and slow of heart
like the two disciples on the road to Emmaus.
In spite of my carrying your name for a long time,
I have taken your presence in my life for granted.
I have allowed my priorities to overshadow my real purpose
of being a true witness to you.

Grant me the gift of the Holy Spirit.
Fill me with the zeal of the apostles
and inflame my heart, as your words did to the two disciples
on the road to Emmaus,
so that I become, like them, a faithful ambassador
of your glorious resurrection.

From today, my life is yours.
I pledge my humble abilities to your service
and resolve to never be indifferent to you again.
I abandon my life to you.

Lead my way, O Lord, lead my way. Amen.

And the Word was made flesh and dwelt among us.

John 1:14

ANNEX 1

A CHRONOLOGY OF THE HOLY LAND

Date		Event
7000	BC	Beginning of urbanization. Jericho is a walled city.
5000-4000	BC	Canaan (Palestine) is occupied by Canaanites, then Amorites and Jebusites.
circa 1850	BC	Time of the patriarch Abraham, Isaac and Jacob.
1500	BC	Abraham's descendants, led by Joseph, move to Egypt.
circa 1250	BC	Period of Exodus from Egypt.
circa 1200	BC	Hebrews under Joshua enter Promised Land. Division of land among 12 tribes.
1000	BC	King David captures Jebus city of the Jebusites, renames it Jerusalem and makes it the capital of his monarchy.
970	BC	King Solomon builds the First Temple.

Schism in the Kingdom

Date		Event
930	BC	The United Kingdom is divided into a northern kingdom of Israel with Samaria as capital and a southern kingdom of Judah with Jerusalem as capital.
722	BC	Northern kingdom is conquered by Assyria and its 10 tribes sent into exile.
701	BC	Assyria conquers much of Judah; Jerusalem is besieged but survives.
586	BC	Nebuchadnezzar destroys Jerusalem and its temple, deporting most of population to Babylon after a failed Israelite revolution

Persian Empire

Date		Event
538	BC	Cyrus the Persian King conquers Babylon and allows Jews to return and resettle on the land.
circa 515	BC	A Second Temple is built in Jerusalem.
circa 444	BC	Nehemiah rebuilds the city walls of Jerusalem.

Hellenistic Greek Empire

333	BC	Alexander the Great conquers the Persian Empire, including all of Palestine.
323	BC	Alexander dies and his kingdom is divided into four parts; Palestine falls under the Ptolemaic Dynasty of Egypt, then under Seleucids of Syria.
175	BC	King Antiochus IV of Seleucid Syria bans traditional Jewish practices and desecrates Temple.
167	BC	Judas Maccabeus leads a successful revolt against the Seleucid Empire, re-dedicates the Temple and restores religious freedom (Feast of Hanukah).

Hasmonean Kingdom

| 63 | BC | Rivalry between Hyrcanus II and Aristobulus II, brings civil war that ends with Roman intervention. General Pompey establishes Roman rule in Palestine. |
| 37 | BC | Caesar and Mark Anthony proclaim Herod the Great as King. Palestine becomes a Roman client state. |

Roman Empire split into East and West

20	BC	Herod rebuilds the temple.
circa 6-4	BC	Jesus Christ is born in Bethlehem.
4	BC	Herod dies and his kingdom is divided among three of his sons, Philip, Antipas and Archelaus.
AD 26		Pontius Pilate becomes procurator of the Roman province of Judea.
27		Jesus is baptized by John the Baptist and begins his public ministry.
circa 30		Jesus is condemned to death and crucified.
circa 34		Paul is converted to Christianity on his way to Damascus.
circa 41-44		King Agrippa I, builds a Third Wall in Jerusalem
circa 50		The first recorded Christian Church Council is held in Jerusalem.
circa 60-100		Books of the New Testament are written.
66		The Great Jewish Revolt against Rome breaks out. Christians in Palestine flee to Pella in Jordan.

70	The Second Temple is destroyed.
73	Masada falls to the Roman Tenth Legion.
130	Emperor Hadrian rebuilds Jerusalem, renaming it Aelia Capitolina, and puts pagan temples over sites of the birth, crucifixion and resurrection of Jesus.
135	Hadrian crushes the Bar Kockba Jewish Revolt and expels Jews from Palestine.
301	Armenia as a nation is baptized unanimously.
AD 313	Emperor Constantine I declares Christianity a tolerated religion.

Byzantine Empire

325	The Council of Nicaea, Bishop Macarius of Jerusalem asks Constantine to reclaim the sites of the Crucifixion and Resurrection and build a church there.
326-7	Constantine's mother, Queen Helena, visits the Holy Land, finds the holy cross and orders churches to be built on sacred sites of the nativity, resurrection and ascension. Pilgrimages to the Holy Land begin.
330	Constantine moves his capital to Byzantium (renamed Constantinople, now Istanbul in Turkey).
335	Church of the Holy Sepulchre is inaugurated.
380	Emperor Theodosius I makes Christianity the official religion of the Roman Empire.
386-420	St. Jerome arrives in Bethlehem and translates the Bible into Latin (Vulgate).
395	The Roman Empire is split into East and West.
570	Birth of Prophet of Islam, Muhammad.
614	Persian conquest of Palestine. An almost total destruction of all churches in the Holy Land.
622	Prophet Muhammad escapes assassination in Mecca and flees to Medina. The Hijra Calendar is inaugurated.

| 629 | Emperor Heraclius I re-captures Jerusalem and the holy cross from the Persians. |

Arab Islamic Empire

638	Islamic armies conquer Jerusalem under Caliph Omar, beginning the rule by succession of Muslim dynasties.
661-1000	Palestine is ruled by a succession of Muslim Caliphs.
691	The Dome of the Rock is built on Temple Mount (Noble Sanctuary).
705	The Al Aqsa (Distant) Mosque is built on the Temple Mount (Noble Sanctuary).
1009	Sultan al-Hakim destroys the Church of the Holy Sepulchre.
1048	The Church of the Holy Sepulchre is rebuilt by Emperor Constantine Monomachus.
1054	Schism splits the Christian Church into Eastern (Greek) and Western (Latin).
1071	Seljuk Turks capture Jerusalem, persecute Christians, desecrate churches and prohibit pilgrimages to the Holy Land.

Crusader Kingdom

| 1099 | The First Crusade under Godfrey de Bouillon captures Jerusalem and establishes the Latin Kingdom. |
| 1149 | The Crusader Church of the Holy Sepulchre is finished and dedicated. |

Ayyubid and Mamluke Islamic Empire

1187	Sultan Saladin defeats the Crusaders at the Horns of Hattin near the Sea of Galilee, then takes Jerusalem.
1219	St Francis of Assisi visits Egypt and addresses Sultan Melek al-Kamil.
1229	During the Sixth Crusade, Roman Emperor Frederick II negotiates the return of Jerusalem and other Christian sites to Crusader rule.
1291	St. John of Acre (Akko) Crusaders' last stronghold falls to the Mamlukes.

1342	Pope Clement VI formally establishes Franciscan custody of the Holy Land.

Ottoman Islamic Empire

1517	The Ottomans capture Palestine from the Mamlukes.
1538	Sultan Suleiman the Magnificent builds city walls of the old city of Jerusalem.
1757	Ottoman Turkish edicts bestow on the Greek Orthodox Church possession of the Church of the Holy Sepulchre and other holy places.
1808	Fire in the Church of the Holy Sepulchre; tomb of Christ severely damaged when dome collapses.
1849	Christ Church in Jerusalem, oldest Protestant church in Middle East is built.
1852	Under pressure from Russia, Ottoman Sultan Abd-ul-Mejid affirms that possession of holy places remains as per the 1757 edict.
1853-56	Possession of holy places escalates to an international conflict and leads to the Crimean War between Russia and major European powers.
1878	The Status Quo defining possession of holy places is incorporated into international law by Berlin Treaty.
1882	European Jewish pioneers settle in Palestine.
1883	General Charles Gordon claims Skull Hill outside the Damascus Gate as Calvary and later the Garden Tomb as Christ's burial site.
1897	The first World Zionist Congress is held in Basel Switzerland. Palestine proclaimed the best location for the establishment of a Jewish state.
1906	Kibbutz Degania at the southern end of the Sea of Galilee is inaugurated as the first in Palestine.
1917	The British government's Balfour Declaration backs a Jewish homeland in Palestine, without prejudice to civil and religious rights of non-Jewish population.

British Mandate

1917	British forces under General Allenby capture Palestine from Ottomans.
1922	The League of Nations approves the British Mandate over Palestine.
1920-47	Jewish immigrants from Europe continue to settle in Palestine.
1936-39	The Great Arab Revolt against Britain demands an end to Jewish immigration and to the transfer of Arab land to them. The revolt fails.
1946	Jordan gains independence from Great Britain.
1947	The United Nations Partition Plan calls for a Jewish state (56%) and an Arab state (43%) in Palestine, with Greater Jerusalem (1%) kept under international control; most Jewish groups accept the plan but Arabs reject it.
1947	The Dead Sea Scrolls are discovered at Qumran.
1948	Civil unrest and violence. Britain ends its Palestinian mandate.

Israel and Palestinian Territories

1948	May 15, Ben Gurion proclaims Israel as an independent state (in Palestine). Arab forces invade the new state.
1949	Israel prevails in the Arab-Israeli War. Israel is established over 78% of Palestine. Egypt controls the Gaza Strip. Jordan controls the West Bank and East Jerusalem. More than 700,000 Palestinians lose their homes and become refugees.
1967	A preemptive strike is launched by Israel. In the Six-Day War against Egypt, Jordan and Syria, Israel occupies the Sinai, Gaza Strip, Golan Heights and West Bank, including East Jerusalem.
1973	The October War is launched by Egypt and Syria. Yom Kippur War (in Israel). Both sides claim victory.
1979	The first Camp David Summit. Israel and Egypt sign a peace treaty; Israel agrees to return Sinai to Egypt in return for full demilitarization of the Sinai.

1981	Israel launches war on Lebanon to wipe out the Palestine Liberation Organization (PLO). Israel occupies southern Lebanon for 18 years.
1987-91	Palestinians first intifada (uprising) against Israeli occupation.
1993	Declaration of Principles. Israel and PLO sign Oslo accords, giving Palestinian National Authority limited autonomy in West Bank and Gaza.
1994	Jordan and Israel sign a peace treaty.
1995	Israel and PNA sign Oslo II interim Agreement. The West Bank is divided into three zones. The main Palestinian cities (zone A) are under full PNA control. Zone B territories are administered by the PNA but Israel controls the security. Zone C territories, Israel controls both administration and security.
2000	Failure of second Camp David Summit between Israel and PLO hosted by USA president Bill Clinton.
2000-2005	A second intifada follows a controversial visit by Israeli opposition leader Ariel Sharon to the Temple Mount.
2002	The Israeli army besieges Palestinian militants and civilians in the Church of the Nativity, in Bethlehem, for 40 days.
2002	Israel begins building 700-km West Bank separation wall.
2005	Israel evacuates its settlers from the Gaza Strip and redeploys its military around it. Israeli control of all facets of life in Gaza continues.
2007	Professor Ehud Netzer discovers Herod the Great's monumental tomb at Herodium.
2008	Israeli siege of Gaza continues. Responding to rocket attacks, Israel launches a 22 day war against Gaza.
2014	Israeli siege of Gaza continues. Responding to rocket fire, Israel launches a seven week war on Gaza.

ANNEX 2

RENEWAL OF BAPTISMAL VOWS[1]

Dear brothers and sisters, through the Paschal Mystery we have been buried with Christ in baptism, that we may walk with him in the newness of life. And so, let us renew the promises of the Holy Baptism, during which we renounce Satan and his works and promise to serve God and share in the dignity of his Divine Son; towards the realization of the Universal Church.

And so I ask you:

V. Do you renounce sin, so as to live in the freedom of the children of God?
R. I do.
V. Do you renounce the lure of evil, so that sin may have no mastery over you?
R. I do.
V. Do you renounce Satan, the author and prince of sin? **R. I do.**
V. Do you believe in God, the Father Almighty, Creator of heaven and earth? **R. I do.**
V. Do you believe in Jesus Christ, his only Son, our Lord, who was born of the Virgin Mary, suffered   death and was buried, rose again from the dead and is seated at the right hand of the Father? **R. I do.**
V. Do you believe in the Holy Spirit, the holy Catholic church, the communion of saints, the forgiveness of sins, the resurrection of the body, and life everlasting?
R. I do.
V. And may almighty God, the Father of our Lord Jesus Christ, who has given us new birth by water and the Holy Spirit and bestowed on us forgiveness of our sins, keep us by his grace, in Christ Jesus our Lord, for eternal life. **R. Amen.**
R. Amen.

WATER BAPTISM CEREMONY[2]
(From the Easter Vigil)

Father, you give us grace through sacramental signs, which tell us of the wonders of your unseen power. In baptism we use your gift of water, which you have made a rich symbol of the grace you give us in this Holy Sacrament. At the very dawn of creation your Holy Spirit breathed on the waters, making them the wellspring of all Holiness.

With the waters of great flood you made a sign of the waters for baptism, that make an end of sin and a new beginning of goodness. Through the waters of the Jordan your Son was baptised by John and anointed with the Holy Spirit. Your Son willed that water and blood should flow from his side as he hung upon the cross. After his resurrection he told his disciples: "Go out and teach all nations, baptising them in the name of the Father, and of the Son, and of the Holy Spirit."

You created man in your likeness. Through this baptism {he/she} is cleansed from sin in a new birth to innocence by water and the Holy Spirit.

[The minister then can touch, sprinkle, pour or immerse and then continue:]

We ask you, Father, with your power to send the Holy Spirit upon the water of this font. May all who are buried with Christ in death of baptism rise also with him to newness of life. We ask this in your name. Amen.

[The minister then asks all to pray]

Sample 2

Minister to the Parents and Congregation:
You have called your child(ren), {child's name} to the cleansing waters and to be birth anew so that by the divine light of the creator. {Parents Name} with your love and compassion and by sharing your faith and by the power of your Faith with {child's name} they might have eternal life. God bless this water in which they will be baptised. As we live in the grace of God. Amen.

Sample 3

Praise to you, almighty God, for you have created water to cleanse and to give life. Praise to you, Lord God the Holy Spirit, for you anointed the children with the waters of life, so that all who are baptised in it may be washed clean of all sin, and be born again to live as your divine children. Amen.

Sample 4

Come to us, Lord God, Father of all, and make Holy this water which you have created, so that all who are baptised in it may be washed clean of all Sin, and be born again to live as your Divine Children. Father God of mercy, through these waters of baptism you have filled us with new life as your very own children. Amen.

Sample 5

From all who are baptised in water and the Holy Spirit, you have formed one people, united in your presence. You have set us free and filled our hearts with the Spirit of your Love, that we may live in your peace. You call those who have been baptised to announce the Good News of Enlightenment to people everywhere. Amen.

Notes
1. http://www.catholicculture.org/culture/liturgicalyear/activities/view.cfm?id=1047.
2. http://www.ulc.co/how-to-perform-a-baptism-a-65.html, n.d.

ANNEX 3

RENEWAL OF WEDDING VOWS[1]

The union of husband and wife is one of the heart, mind, and body and is intended (by the Lord) for their mutual joy, for the help and comfort given to one another in the times of prosperity and adversity. The union grows as the couple become one in more and more ways on a growing basis as their love for one another expands.

Dearly beloved couples, present here today at Cana in Galilee, when you first joined hands and hearts in marriage years ago, you did not know where life would take you!

You promised to love, honor and cherish one another through all things. Life has surely brought you both wonderful blessings and difficult challenges over the years.

As you celebrate here today, at Cana in Galilee, where the Lord blessed with his presence a wedding ceremony, and as you reflect back over all the years as husband and wife, do you now wish to reaffirm the vows you took years ago?

R. We do.

RENEWAL OF VOWS
[The pastor instructs the couples to face each other and join hands.]
[The pastor instructs the husbands to repeat after him.]

I _{husband's name} reaffirm my wedding vow to you _{wife's name} , and will love you, honor and cherish you, in sickness and in health, for richer or poorer, for better for worse, and forsaking all others, be faithful to you for as long as I shall live.

[The pastor instructs the wives to repeat after him.]

I _{wife's name} reaffirm my wedding vow to you _{husband's name} , and will love you, honor and cherish you, in sickness and in health, for richer or poorer, for better for worse, and forsaking all others, be faithful to you for as long as I shall live.

[The pastor instructs the couple to hold his spouse's ring, and both to repeat after him.]

"With this ring I renew my pledge of love and commitment."

[The Pastor now gives a final blessing to the couples, and remembers those whose spouses are not present on the pilgrimage or have passed away.]

[Possible blessings]:

Father, these couples have pledged to love one another in your presence here at Cana in Galilee. Grant them your gifts of eternal love to one another, but above all to you, because only through you can their love truly grow and flourish.

Father, we ask you to bless those couples, whose spouses are not here with us today. They might not be here physically to pledge themselves anew, but you know their hearts and intentions.

Father, we also ask you to remember those, whose loved ones have passed away and are now with you in your Divine Mercy. Grant them, and all of us present here today your gift of eternal life.

This we pray, in the name of the Father, the Son and the Holy Spirit.

You may kiss your wife/husband.

Note
1. Adapted from http://www.themarriageman.com/renewal.htm, n.d.

BIBLIOGRAPHY

- Anon., n.d. *Catholic Encyclopedia online - Bethlehem.* [Online]
  Available at: Catholic Encyclopedia online - Bethlehem
  [Accessed 2014].
- Anon., n.d. *Catholicculture.* [Online]
  Available at: http://www.catholicculture.org/culture/liturgicalyear/activities/view.cfm?id=1047
  [Accessed 2015].
- Anon., n.d. *http://artists.letssingit.com.* [Online]
  Available at: http://artists.letssingit.com/daniel-odonnell-lyrics-here-i-am-lord-t3xtzlf#axzz3OMBP0aVS
- Anon., n.d. *http://blackbiretta.blogspot.co.il/2012/09/the-golden-legend-finding-true-cross.html.* [Online]
  Available at: http://blackbiretta.blogspot.co.il/2012/09/the-golden-legend-finding-true-cross.html
  [Accessed 2015].
- Anon., n.d. *http://blog.cnaughton.com/mediafiles/pdfs/james.pdf chapter 11.* [Online]
  Available at: http://blog.cnaughton.com/mediafiles/pdfs/james.pdf chapter 11
- Anon., n.d. *http://en.wikipedia.org/.* [Online]
  Available at: http://en.wikipedia.org/wiki/Pliny_the_Younger#cite_note-Pliny_10.96-15
  [Accessed 2015].
- Anon., n.d. *http://en.wikipedia.org/.* [Online]
  Available at: http://en.wikipedia.org/wiki/Josephus_on_Jesus
- Anon., n.d. *http://www.ichthus.info/CaseForChrist/03/intro.html.* [Online]
  Available at: http://www.ichthus.info/CaseForChrist/03/intro.html
- Anon., n.d. *http://www.seetheholyland.net/a-pilgrim-is-not-a-tourist/.* [Online].
- Anon., n.d. *http://www.titusinstitute.com/defendingfaith/jesusbornbethlehem.php.* [Online]
  Available at: http://www.titusinstitute.com/defendingfaith/jesusbornbethlehem.php
- Anon., n.d. *https://mdivbound.wordpress.com/concealed-revealed/.* [Online].
- Anon., n.d. *https://mdivbound.wordpress.com/concealed-revealed/.* [Online].
- Anon., n.d. *Wikipedia definition of: The Amarna letters (sometimes Amarna correspondence or Amarna tablets).* [Online]
  Available at: Wikipedia definition of: The Amarna letters (sometimes Amarna correspondence or Amarna tablets)
  [Accessed 2015].
- Bailey, K., 2008. *Jesus through Middle Eastern Eyes.* s.l.: IVP Academic.
- Bailey, K. E., 2003. *Jacob & the Prodigal.* s.l.:IVP Academic.
- Bishop, J., 1977. *The Day Christ Died.* s.l.:HarperSanFrancisco.
- Butler, J., 2012. *Mystic Approaches.* s.l.:Mensa Printers.

- O'Connor Jerome Murphy, 1992. The Holy Land- The Indispensable Archaeological Guide from Travellers: Oxford University Press
- Doyle, F. S., 1985. *The new Pilgrim Guide to the Holy land.* s.l.:The Liturgical Press.
- Miller, J.Maxwell, Hayes, John H., 2006. A History of Ancient Israrel and Judah. In: *2nd Edition.* s.l.:WKJ.
- http://blackbiretta.blogspot.co.il/2012/09/the-golden-legend-finding-true-cross.html, n.d. *blackbiretta.blogspot.co.il.* [Online]
  Available at: http://blackbiretta.blogspot.co.il/2012/09/the-golden-legend-finding-true-cross.html
- http://blog.cnaughton.com/mediafiles/pdfs/james.pdf, n.d. *http://blog.cnaughton.com/mediafiles/pdfs/james.pdf.* [Online]
  Available at: http://blog.cnaughton.com/mediafiles/pdfs/james.pdf
  [Accessed 2014].
- http://individual.utoronto.ca/mfkolarcik/jesuit/IsraelFinkelstein.html & Finkelstein, I., n.d. [Online]
  Available at: http://individual.utoronto.ca/mfkolarcik/jesuit/IsraelFinkelstein.html
- http://wikipedia.org/wiki/Tacitus_on_Christ, n.d. *http://wikipedia.org/.* [Online]
  Available at: http://wikipedia.org/wiki/Tacitus_on_Christ
  [Accessed 2015].
- http://www.catholicculture.org/culture/liturgicalyear/activities/view.cfm?id=1047, n.d. *catholicculture.org.* [Online]
  Available at: http://www.catholicculture.org/culture/liturgicalyear/activities/view.cfm?id=1047
- http://www.christusrex.org/www1/ofm/sites/TSbtjust.html, n.d. *http://www.christusrex.org/www1/ofm/sites/TSbtjust.html.* [Online]
  Available at: http://www.christusrex.org/www1/ofm/sites/TSbtjust.html
- http://www.themarriageman.com/renewal.htm, n.d. *http://www.themarriageman.com/renewal.htm.* [Online]
  Available at: http://www.themarriageman.com/renewal.htm
- http://www.titusinstitute.com/defendingfaith/jesusbornbethlehem.php, n.d. *http://www.titusinstitute.com/defendingfaith/jesusbornbethlehem.php.* [Online]
  Available at: http://www.titusinstitute.com/defendingfaith/jesusbornbethlehem.php
- http://www.ulc.co/how-to-perform-a-baptism-a-65.html, n.d. [Online]
  Available at: http://www.ulc.co/how-to-perform-a-baptism-a-65.html
- Keller, T., 2008. *The Reason for God.* s.l.:Riverhead Books.
- The Paraclete Spiritual Journal, 2012: Paraclete Press
- Martyn, Percy, J. C. J. G. M. G. H.-A. H. G. M. S. W. R. W., n.d. *The Bright Field- Meditations and Reflections for ordinary time.* s.l.:Canterbury Press.
- Merton, T., 1999. The New Man. In: New York: Farrar,Straus & Giroux.
- Miller, J.Maxwell, Hayes, John H., 1986 . *A History of Ancient Israel and Judah.* s.l.:Westminister Press.
- Nouwen, H. J., 2012. *The Inner Voice of Love- A Journey Through Anguish to Freedom.* s.l.:D.L.T.
- Pastor David Robertson, Canada, 2010. The Human Heart Under Renovation: Redifing Hope in a Conflicted World. *Article written for Advent.*

- Sacks, J., 2002,2003. *The Dignity of Difference- How to avoid the clash of civilizations.* s.l.:Continuum.
- Senior, Donald, 1998. *Matthew- Abingdon New Testament Commentaries: Abingdon Press*
- Strobel, L., 1998. The Case for Christ. In: s.l.:Zondervan.
- Tomlinson Dave, 2012. *How to be a bad Christian, And a better human being.* s.l.:Hodder & Stoughton.
- Vamosh, M. F., n.d. Daily life at the times of Jesus. In: s.l.:Palphot.
- Wilkerson, D., 1992. *Hungry for more of Jesus- Experiencing his presence in these troubled times.* s.l.:Chosen Books.
- Word Press, n.d. *A Pilgrim will let oneself go.* [Online] Available at: http://virtualtourof holyland.wordpress.com/

Pilgrim's notes

Pilgrim's notes

Pilgrim's notes